REHABILITATING *LOCHNER*

REHABILITATING *LOCHNER*

Defending Individual Rights against Progressive Reform

DAVID E. BERNSTEIN

THE UNIVERSITY OF CHICAGO PRESS

CHICAGO AND LONDON

A CATO INSTITUTE BOOK

DAVID E. BERNSTEIN is Foundation Professor at the George Mason University School of Law and the author of several books, including, most recently, *You Can't Say That! The Growing Threat to Civil Liberties from Antidiscrimination Laws.*

The University of Chicago Press, Chicago 60637
The University of Chicago Press, Ltd., London
© 2011 by David E. Bernstein
All rights reserved. Published 2011.
Printed in the United States of America

20 19 18 17 16 15 14 13 12 11   1 2 3 4 5

ISBN-13: 978-0-226-04353-1   (cloth)
ISBN-10: 0-226-04353-3   (cloth)

Library of Congress Cataloging-in-Publication Data

Bernstein, David E. author.
    Rehabilitating Lochner : defending individual rights against progressive reform / David E. Bernstein.
        pages ; cm.
    Includes bibliographical references and index.
    ISBN-13: 978-0-226-04353-1 (hardcover : alk. paper)
    ISBN-10: 0-226-04353-3 (hardcover : alk. paper) 1. Lochner, Joseph—Trials, litigation, etc. 2. New York (State)—Trials, litigation, etc. 3. Liberty of contract—United States—History. 4. Judicial review—United States—History. 5. Civil rights—United States. I. Title.
    KF228.L63B47 2011

♾ The paper used in this publication meets the minimum requirements of the American National Standard for Information Sciences—Permanence of Paper for Printed Library Materials, ANSI Z39.48-1992.

CONTENTS

v

ACKNOWLEDGMENTS

M y sincere thanks to Charles Barzun, Les Benedict, Eric Claeys, Barry Cushman, Howard Gillman, Tom Grey, Philip Hamburger, Dan Harper, Michael Klarman, Noga Morag-Levine, Chris Newman, Victoria Nourse, Carol Rose, Stephen Siegel, Mark Tushnet, Ted White, Keith Whittington, John Witt, and Michael Allan Wolf, and to my students Nathaniel Canfield, Katrina Doran, Pasha Majdi, and David Pettit for providing helpful comments on chapters of this book. Special thanks go to Randy Barnett, Jim Ely, Bill Nelson, Julian Sanchez, David Schleicher, Nancy Woloch, and several anonymous referees for reading and commenting on entire draft manuscripts.

I also benefited from feedback on specific chapters at faculty workshops at the University of Arizona, George Mason University, and Washington University law schools; presentations to students and faculty at New York University and the University of Michigan; a presentation at the American Law and Economics Association annual conference; and comments on entire draft manuscripts provided at the Georgetown University Law Center's New Books on Constitutional Law seminar and the NYU Legal History Colloquium.

Portions of this book have been greatly revised from articles and review essays that appeared in the *Georgetown Law Journal, Journal of Supreme Court History, Law and Contemporary Problems, Michigan Law Review, Texas Law Review, Vanderbilt Law Review, Washington University Law Review,* and *Yale Law Journal.* The editors who worked with me on those articles made many helpful comments and suggestions, as did the many colleagues and friends who provided input on my various *Lochner*-related projects over the years.

Dean Daniel Polsby has been extremely supportive of this book project in a variety of ways, large and small. The Law and Economics Center at the George Mason University School of Law provided generous summer research funding for this project. The Searle Foundation paid for an invaluable semester of leave in the spring of 2009, which allowed me to complete an initial draft manuscript.

Finally, thanks go to my wife Sigal for her love and support, and to my daughters Natalie and Eden, for bringing rays of sunshine into my life every day.

Introduction

If you want to raise eyebrows at a gathering of judges or legal scholars, try praising the Supreme Court's 1905 decision in *Lochner v. New York*. *Lochner* invalidated a state maximum-hours law for bakery workers. The Court held that the law violated the right to "liberty of contract," a right implicit in the Fourteenth Amendment's ban on states depriving people of liberty without "due process of law."

Lochner is likely the most disreputable case in modern constitutional discourse. It competes for that dubious distinction with *Scott v. Sandford*, the "*Dred Scott* case."[1] Chief Justice Roger Taney in *Dred Scott* concluded that persons of African descent could not be American citizens because the Constitution's framers believed that blacks "had no rights which the white man was bound to respect." He helped to precipitate the Civil War by adding that Congress may not ban slavery in federal territories.

That's rather ignominious company for *Lochner*, which had the much more modest effect of prohibiting New York state from imprisoning bakery owners whose employees worked more than ten hours in a day or sixty hours in a week. *Lochner*, moreover, was an outlier opinion from a Supreme Court that generally deferred to legislative innovation. The Court quickly limited *Lochner* to its facts in 1908 when it upheld a maximum-hours law for women, and then ignored *Lochner* in 1917 when it approved an hours law that covered all industrial workers. For three decades, the liberty of contract doctrine impeded the growth of the regulatory state to a limited degree, but federal and state government power and authority nevertheless grew apace.[2]

Lochner has since become shorthand for all manner of constitutional evils, and has even had an entire discredited era of Supreme Court jurisprudence named after it. More than one hundred years after their predecessors issued the decision, Supreme Court justices of all ideological stripes use *Lochner* as an epithet to hurl at their colleagues when they disapprove of a decision declaring a law unconstitutional. Even Barack Obama has found occasion to publicly denounce *Lochner*, pairing it with *Dred Scott* as an example of egregious Supreme Court error.[3] And *Lochner*'s infamy has spread internationally, to the point where it plays an important role in debate over the Canadian constitution.[4]

The origin of today's widespread enmity to *Lochner* lies in Progressive-era legal reformers' hostility to liberty of contract. Progressive* critics contended that the Court's occasional invalidation of reformist legislation was a product of unrestrained judicial activism, politicized judicial decision-making, and the Supreme Court's favoring the rich over the poor, corporations over workers, and abstract legal concepts over the practical necessities of a developing industrial economy.

The Supreme Court withdrew constitutional protection for liberty of contract in the 1930s. Since then, a hostile perspective inherited from the Progressives has virtually monopolized scholarly discussion of the Court's liberty of contract decisions. From 1940 until the publication of Bernard Siegan's *Economic Liberties and the Constitution* forty years later, only one law review article expressed even mild support for constitutional protection of liberty of contract.[5]

Lochner has come to exemplify the liberty of contract cases, though the opinion did not always attract such disproportionate attention. Starting in the late 1930s *Lochner* languished in obscurity, cited almost exclusively as just one in a line of discredited cases invalidating legislation for infringing on freedom of contract. Its notoriety increased dramatically when both the majority and dissent in *Griswold v. Connecticut*—a high-profile, controversial case decided in 1965—used it as a foil. *Lochner* has since loomed ever larger in American constitutional debate. By the late 1980s it was perhaps the leading case in the constitutional "anti-canon," the group of wrongly decided cases that help frame the proper principles of constitutional interpretation.

---

* This book refers to the post-*Lochner*, pre–New Deal opponents of liberty of contract, and other pre–New Deal proponents of government activism, as "Progressives," and to their ideology as Progressivism, with a capital *P*. To the extent that "Progressive" is a less-than-precise descriptive term, it hopefully makes up for that lack of precision in consistency and brevity. Confusion sets in, of course, because many on the modern liberal left choose to call themselves progressives, and refer to their preferred policies as progressive. To avoid this confusion, the book refers to those on the post–New Deal liberal left as "liberals," and to their ideology as modern "liberalism." "Liberalism" is also used to describe the values of tolerance, racial and gender egalitarianism, and individual rights protected by law, in whatever era. Opposition to racial segregation, for example, constitutes racial "liberalism" regardless of its source.

Just as *Lochner* phobia was hitting its stride, historians began to discredit some elements of the dominant narrative about liberty of contract inherited from the Progressives. In particular, scholars showed that the Supreme Court justices who adopted the liberty of contract doctrine did not have the cartoonish reactionary motives attributed to them by Progressive and New Deal critics.[6] Rather, the justices, faced with constitutional challenges to novel assertions of government power, sincerely tried to protect liberty as they understood it, consistent with longstanding constitutional doctrines that reflected the notion that governmental authority had inherent limits.[7]

This book takes the revisionist project significantly further. It provides the first comprehensive modern analysis of *Lochner* and its progeny, free from the baggage of the tendentious accounts of Progressives, New Dealers, and their successors on the left and, surprisingly, the right.[8] *Lochner* must be fundamentally reassessed in part because much of our *Lochner*-related mythology is just that, with little if any basis in the actual history of the liberty of contract doctrine. *Lochner* is also due for reconsideration because modern sensibilities diverge significantly from those of the Progressives who created the orthodox understanding of the liberty of contract era.

This book shows that the liberty of contract doctrine was grounded in precedent and the venerable natural rights tradition.[9] The Supreme Court did not use the doctrine to enforce "laissez-faire Social Darwinism," as the traditional narrative asserts. Rather, the Court upheld the vast majority of the laws that had been challenged as infringements on liberty of contract. The Court's decisions that did vindicate the right to liberty of contract often had ambiguous or even clearly "pro-poor" distributive consequences. The bakers' maximum-hours law invalidated in *Lochner*, like much of the other legislation the Court condemned as violations of liberty of contract, favored entrenched special interests at the expense of competitors with less political power.[10]

This book also considers the available contemporary alternative to liberty of contract, the extreme pro-government ideology of liberty of contract's opponents among the Progressive legal elite, including such luminaries as Louis Brandeis, Roscoe Pound, Felix Frankfurter, and Learned Hand.[11] Progressive jurists generally opposed not just *Lochner*'s defense of economic liberty but any robust constitutional protection of individual or minority rights.

In sharp contrast to modern constitutional jurisprudence, neither Progressives nor their opponents typically recognized a fundamental distinction between judicial protection for civil rights and civil liberties, and judicial protection of economic liberties. Rather, both sides thought that Fourteenth

Amendment due process cases raised three primary issues: whether the party challenging government regulatory authority had identified a legitimate right deserving of judicial protection; the extent to which the courts should or should not presume that the government was acting within its inherent "police power"; and, finally, taking the decided-upon presumption into account, whether any infringement on a recognized right protected by the Due Process Clause was within the scope of the states' police power, or whether instead it was an arbitrary, and therefore unconstitutional, infringement on individual rights.

Leading Progressive lawyers believed in strong interventionist government run by experts and responsive to developing social trends, and were hostile to countervailing claims of rights-based limits on government power. Progressive legal elites also were extremely suspicious of the judiciary's competence and integrity in policing the scope of the government's authority to regulate. Progressive legal commentators therefore urged the courts to interpret the police power as sufficiently flexible to permit state-imposed racial segregation, sex-specific labor laws, restrictions on private schooling, and coercive eugenics.[12]

Many Progressives, products of their prejudiced times, actively sympathized with the racism, the paternalistic and often dismissive or condescending attitudes toward women, and the hostility to immigrants and Catholics that motivated these laws. But even unusually liberal Progressive jurists—and elite attorneys tended to be more liberal-minded than other Progressive intellectuals—generally opposed judicial intervention to support any given rights claim brought under the Due Process Clause. Progressive lawyers argued that the benefits of such intervention would likely be substantially outweighed by the damage that additional constitutional limits on the government's police power might ultimately cause to their core agenda of supporting economic—especially labor—regulation.

Meanwhile, advocates of liberty of contract believed that the Fourteenth Amendment set inherent limits on the government's authority to regulate the lives of its constituents. While this belief initially was adopted by the courts in the context of economic regulation, as early as 1897 the Supreme Court announced that the Fourteenth Amendment's Due Process Clause protected an individuals' right to be "free in the enjoyment of all his faculties [and] to be free to use them in all lawful ways."[13] Through the early 1920s, however, with the exception of a few outlier decisions like *Lochner*, the Court's majority was generally cautious about limiting the scope of the states' police power via the Due Process Clause.

But as with their Progressive critics, "conservative" Supreme Court justices' views on the scope of the government's power to infringe on constitutional protections for civil rights and civil liberties were generally consistent with their views on the government's power to interfere with liberty of contract.[14] Once the Court in the 1920s became more aggressive about reviewing government regulations in the economic sphere, the justices naturally began to acknowledge the broader libertarian implications of *Lochner* and other liberty of contract cases and to enforce limits on government authority more generally.

Indeed, the Court's liberty of contract advocates were sufficiently committed to the notion of inherent limits on government power and a limited police power that they voted for liberal results across a wide range of individual and civil rights cases. The *Lochner* line of cases pioneered the protection of the right of women to compete with men for employment free from sex-based regulations, the right of African Americans to exercise liberty and property rights free from Jim Crow legislation, and civil liberties against the states ranging from freedom of expression to the right to choose a private school education for one's children.[15]

Even justices who lacked sympathy for the individuals and groups that were challenging government actions often voted in their favor out of libertarian commitment; the unabashed racist James McReynolds, for example, voted to invalidate a residential segregation law, and wrote an opinion protecting the right of Japanese parents in Hawaii to send their children to private Japanese-language schools. Some of the other justices had equalitarian reasons for their votes. George Sutherland strongly expressed his longstanding support for women's legal equality in a 1923 opinion he wrote invalidating a women-only minimum wage law as a violation of liberty of contract. And sometimes a commitment to limited government seems to have led some jurists to a newfound empathy for groups suffering from what they saw as government overreaching.

With the triumph of the New Deal, the Progressives won the battle over whether the Supreme Court would engage in meaningful review of economic regulation. In that sense, modern Fourteenth Amendment jurisprudence is a product of Progressive ideology. But the New Deal Court and its successors did not fully adopt the Progressives' pro-government, antijudiciary views. The justices instead chose to divide the Old Court's due process opinions into two categories; the Court disavowed precedents that protected economic rights, but elaborated upon, reinterpreted, and most importantly preserved and expanded its civil rights and civil liberties precedents.

Some of the old due process cases were reincarnated during and just after the New Deal as "incorporation" cases applying the Bill of Rights against the states, or as equal protection cases. In later years, the Court revived some of the old cases as pure due process cases. It emphasized these cases' protection of "fundamental" unenumerated rights such as privacy, and ignored their close ties to the liberty of contract cases. Many post–New Deal liberal developments in Fourteenth Amendment jurisprudence can therefore trace their origins to *Lochner* and its progeny.

More generally, modern Fourteenth Amendment jurisprudence owes at least as much to the libertarian values of liberty of contract proponents as to its pro-regulation Progressive opponents.[16] Modern liberal jurists overwhelmingly reject the Progressives' hostility to using the Fourteenth Amendment to protect individual liberty and minority rights from government overreaching. Meanwhile, conservative jurists often favorably cite Progressive heroes like Frankfurter and Justice Oliver Wendell Holmes in support of "judicial restraint," but judicial conservatives like Justices Antonin Scalia and Clarence Thomas have refused to adopt anything approaching the sort of near-absolute judicial deference to the legislature advocated by elite Progressive lawyers. .

While this book is an effort to correct decades of erroneous accounts of the so-called "*Lochner* era," even the soundest history cannot provide a theory of constitutional interpretation, nor can it dictate one's understanding of the proper role of the judiciary in the American constitutional system. History alone cannot tell us, therefore, whether *Lochner* was correctly decided; whether liberty of contract jurisprudence more generally was based on a sound theory of judicial review and constitutional interpretation; and whether *Lochner* or other cases protecting economic rights should be revived.

History is also inherently agnostic on the soundness of such modern outgrowths of *Lochner* and other liberty of contract cases as the incorporation of most of the Bill of Rights against the states via the Due Process Clause, the protection of unenumerated individual rights in cases like *Griswold* and *Lawrence v. Texas*, or other manifestations of what is known today as substantive due process.[17] I do not, therefore, reach any conclusions on these issues, but leave it to interested readers to apply the history presented here to their own understandings of proper constitutional interpretation and construction.

What history can tell us is that the standard account of the rise, fall, and influence of the liberty of contract doctrine is inaccurate, unfair, and anachronistic. *Lochner* has been treated as a unique example of constitutional pathology to serve the felt rhetorical needs of advocates for various theories of constitutional law, not because the decision itself was so extraordinary, its consequences so bad, or its antistatist presumptions so clearly expelled from modern constitutional law. The history of the liberty of contract doctrine should be assessed more objectively and in line with modern sensibilities, and *Lochner* should be removed from the anticanon and treated like a normal, albeit controversial, case. That these rather modest propositions require an entire book in their defense is an indication of *Lochner's* remarkable status in constitutional debate—one that leaves plenty of room for rehabilitation.

CHAPTER ONE

The Rise of Liberty of Contract

Legal scholars across the political spectrum have long agreed that *Loch-ner v. New York* and other cases applying the liberty of contract doctrine to invalidate legislation were serious mistakes. This is hardly unusual. Many constitutional doctrines adopted by the Supreme Court have come and gone over the last two hundred–plus years. But the ferocity and tenacity of the liberty of contract doctrine's detractors is unique. For more than one hundred years, critics have argued that *Lochner* and its progeny did not involve ordinary constitutional errors, but were egregious examples of willful judicial malfeasance.

One common criticism is that the Court's use of the Fourteenth Amendment's Due Process Clause to protect substantive rights, including liberty of contract, was absurd as a matter of textual interpretation.[1] John Hart Ely famously quipped that "substantive due process" is a contradiction in terms, akin to "green pastel redness."[2] This line of attack has persisted even though it is anachronistic; the pre–New Deal Supreme Court's approach to interpreting the Due Process Clause did not recognize the modern categories of "substantive" and "procedural" due process.[3]

The liberty of contract doctrine's academic foes have also asserted that it sprang ex nihilo out of Supreme Court justices' minds in the 1890s with the intent to favor the interests of big business and suppress the working class.[4] The *Lochner* Court's justices are said to have been motivated by pernicious Social Darwinist ideology, and to have believed that "the strong could and *should* exploit the weak so that only the fittest survived."[5]

The true story of the development of a substantive interpretation of the Due Process Clause, and of Supreme Court's subsequent adoption of the liberty of contract doctrine, is a far cry from this traditional morality tale of a malevolent Supreme Court serving as a handmaiden of large-scale capital.[6]

This chapter synthesizes and elaborates on existing revisionist scholarship. I draw two major conclusions. First, the idea that the guarantee of "due process of law" regulates the substance of legislation as well as judicial procedure arose from the long-standing Anglo-American principle that the government has inherently limited powers and the individual citizen has inherent rights. Second, the liberty of contract doctrine, while controversial even in its own heyday, evolved from long-standing American intellectual traditions that held that the government had no authority to enforce arbitrary "class legislation" or to violate the fundamental natural rights of the American people.

THE DEVELOPMENT OF A SUBSTANTIVE INTERPRETATION OF "DUE PROCESS OF LAW"

BEFORE THE CIVIL WAR

In the early nineteenth century, leading American legal theorists recognized that the United States federal government was a government of limited and enumerated powers, restrained by a written Constitution. Some jurists also thought that the exercise of federal power was limited by unenumerated first principles.[7] Unlike the federal government, which could exercise only the powers delegated to it under the United States Constitution, states were thought to have inherent sovereign powers inherited from the British Parliament. State legislatures' power, therefore, could be restrained only by express federal or state constitutional provisions that limited their authority.[8] Litigants opposing exercises of state power naturally turned to these provisions to support their positions.

Many state constitutions banned their governments from taking people's liberty or property without "due process of law," or except according to the "law of the land"—concepts that dated back to the Magna Carta. These concepts became associated with the idea that legislatures acted beyond their inherent powers when they passed laws that amounted to arbitrary deprivations of liberty or property rights.[9]

Starting in the 1830s, a series of state court judicial opinions established that certain types of acts passed by legislatures could not be valid legislation, which naturally led to the conclusion that enforcing them could not be due process *of law*. Courts asserted that inherently invalid acts included legislation that purported to exercise judicial powers, such as by granting new trials; legislation that applied partially or unequally; and legislation that took or taxed private property for private purposes.[10]

By the late 1850s, significant judicial authority held that enforcing the principle of due process of law required judges to carefully scrutinize the purpose of legislation and the means employed to achieve legislative ends.[11] The development of this broad conception of due process of law was uneven, accepted explicitly by only some American jurisdictions, and applied mainly to the protection of vested property rights.[12] Nevertheless, by 1857 numerous state constitutional law decisions held that due process or analogous constitutional provisions forbade legislatures from unjustly interfering with property rights.[13]

Chief Justice Roger Taney's invocation of due process of law to protect substantive property rights in his infamous 1857 Supreme Court opinion in *Scott v. Sandford* thus had a considerable pedigree.[14] Taney argued that the Fifth Amendment's Due Process Clause barred the federal government from banning slavery in the territories, because such a ban amounted to taking without due process of law the property of Southern slaveowners who traveled to those territories.

Robert Bork has claimed that *Scott* marked "the first appearance in American constitutional law of the concept of [what later came to be known as] 'substantive due process.'"[15] As we have seen, however, the role of due process in protecting substantive property rights was widely accepted before *Scott*.[16] In addition to the state court opinions referenced above, five years before *Scott* the Supreme Court had stated, albeit in nonbinding dicta, that Congress would violate the Due Process Clause if it enacted legislation that deprived an individual of lawfully acquired intellectual property.[17]

None of Taney's Supreme Court colleagues disputed the idea that the Due Process Clause protected substantive property rights. This notion was also widely accepted by *Scott*'s Republican critics.[18] Abraham Lincoln, like *Scott* dissenting justice John McLean, argued that the problem with Taney's opinion was not its protection of property rights, but Taney's erroneous belief that for federal constitutional purposes slaves were mere property, like hogs or horses.[19]

More generally, the Republicans and their ideological predecessors consistently relied on a substantive interpretation of "due process of law" to promote antislavery ends.[20] In 1843 the abolitionist Liberty Party adopted a platform resolution at its national convention stating that the Due Process Clause incorporated the Declaration of Independence's statement that all men are created equal and are endowed by their creator with inalienable rights.[21] Future Supreme Court Justice Salmon Chase told an 1845 antislavery convention that the Due Process Clause prohibited the federal government from sanctioning slavery, and from allowing it in any place of exclusive federal jurisdiction.[22]

The 1848 platform of the Free Soil Party—a precursor to the Republican Party that absorbed many Liberty Party members—suggested that any federal recognition of slavery violated the Due Process Clause.[23] The 1856 and 1860 Republican platforms also explicitly argued that permitting slavery in the federal territories violated the Due Process Clause because slavery took slaves' liberty without due process of law.[24]

AFTER THE CIVIL WAR

Before the Civil War, states were thought to have inherent sovereign or "police" powers. With the important exception of a clause prohibiting the impairment of contract, these powers were largely untouched by the federal Constitution. State constitutions' due process or law of the land clauses limited the exercise of the states' police powers only in some jurisdictions, and usually only with regard to vested property rights.

The Civil War, however, undermined the idea of autonomous, sovereign states in favor of the view that states' powers were inherently limited. Thomas Cooley's influential 1868 treatise *Constitutional Limitations* asserted that "there are on all sides definite limitations which circumscribe the legislative authority, independent of the specific restrictions which the people impose by their State constitutions."[25] Courts could set aside a state law as invalid even if the written constitution did not contain "some specific inhibition which has been disregarded, or some express command which has been disobeyed."[26] In 1875, the United States Supreme Court declared that "there are limitations on [government] power which grow out of the essential nature of all free governments."[27]

Even strong advocates of judicial restraint acknowledged the existence of an unwritten American constitution that bound state legislators. For example, prominent attorney Richard McMurtie conceded "that there is an unwritten Constitution here quite as much as there is in England."[28] However, McMurtie claimed that courts had no power to enforce the unwritten American constitution against the legislature, just as English courts had no power to enforce the unwritten English constitution against Parliament.

Other commentators insisted that the American constitutional system's genius, and its improvement over the English system, was precisely that it allowed courts to review the constitutionality of legislation. A. V. Dicey, a leading English commentator on constitutionalism, wrote that judicial review was "the only adequate safeguard which has hitherto been invented against unconstitutional legislation."[29] American legal scholar and treatise author Christopher Tiedeman urged courts to seize upon "general declarations of rights as an authority for them to lay their interdict upon all legislative acts which interfere with the individual's natural rights."[30]

If judges did indeed have the power to enforce the "unwritten constitution" against the states, the source of that power needed to be identified. Soon after the Civil War, the Supreme Court began invalidating state legislation that went beyond what the justices saw as the states' legitimate powers. The Court did this in "diversity" cases, in which the plaintiff and the defendant were citizens of different states.[31] The Court's ruling in *Swift v. Tyson* obligated it to apply general principles of constitutional law in diversity cases involving constitutional claims.[32] Relying on such principles—and not on any specific provisions of the federal or state constitutions—the Court found that taxation must be geared toward public, not private, purposes; that property may not be taken without just compensation; and that rate regulation of public utilities must be reasonable.[33]

Litigants who sought to have the Supreme Court enforce limitations on the states' regulatory authority in non-diversity situations naturally looked to the Fourteenth Amendment. The amendment, enacted in 1868, denied states the power to abridge the "privileges or immunities" of American citizens.[34] The Privileges or Immunities Clause, however, was eviscerated by a 5–4 Supreme Court majority in the *Slaughter-House Cases* in 1873.[35]

Slaughter-House involved a challenge to a state law that dealt with public health hazards attendant to the slaughtering industry by granting a state-chartered monopoly to a single downstream slaughterhouse.[36] Independent butchers could work there if they paid a license fee to the slaughterhouse owner. The butchers, who resented being forced to work in a location dictated by the government and were buoyed by the knowledge of state court decisions that had invalidated similar slaughterhouse monopolies,[37] claimed that the new law violated their Fourteenth Amendment rights. Justice Samuel Miller, writing for the *Slaughter-House* majority, concluded that the Privileges or Immunities Clause protected only an extremely narrow and largely inconsequential category of federal rights. These rights did not include the plaintiffs' asserted right to practice their occupation free from a government-sponsored monopoly.

After *Slaughter-House*, litigants, legal scholars, and judges seeking to limit the scope of state power turned to the Fourteenth Amendment's Due Process Clause. The clause, which parallels the Fifth Amendment's federal Due Process Clause, forbids states from depriving any person of life, liberty, or property without due process of law. In *Slaughter-House*, Justice Miller offhandedly dismissed the suggestion that the Due Process Clause spoke to the issue at hand. Miller declared, "Under no construction of that provision [due process of law] that we have ever seen, or any that we deem admissible," could the law in question be declared void as a deprivation of property without due process of law.[38]

Scholars have often assumed that Miller meant to preclude future reliance on the Due Process Clause to protect substantive rights. But leading jurists, including Justice Stephen Field, contended that the issue of due process and its relationship to the states' inherent police powers had not been properly presented or considered in *Slaughter-House*.[39] Miller may have meant only that the Due Process Clause does not reach *valid* police power measures, like a law regulating slaughterhouses to combat the spread of disease.

The narrower interpretation of Miller's language is supported by his opinion four years later in *Davidson v. New Orleans*.[40] *Davidson* is best known for Miller's complaint that the Due Process Clause "is looked upon as a means of bringing to the test of the decision of this Court the abstract opinions of every unsuccessful litigant in a state court of the justice of the decision against him, and of the merits of the legislation on which such a decision may be founded." But Miller also acknowledged that the Due Process Clause prohibits the invasion of private rights by the states and of vested property rights in particular—a position inconsistent with the notion that the Due Process Clause never protects substantive rights.[41] This and other opinions authored by Miller suggest that he believed courts could invalidate state legislation on due process grounds, at least in exceptional circumstances.[42]

Meanwhile, advocates of an expansive scope for the concept of "due process of law" argued that courts had the power and obligation to enforce all fundamental individual rights deemed essential to American liberty, including economic rights.[43] For example, in 1878 the New York Court of Appeals wrote that the state constitution's due process clause was the "main guaranty of private rights against unjust legislation," including unjust regulations of property, labor, and taxation. This guarantee, the court continued, should not be "construed in any narrow or technical sense."[44]

In 1884, in *Hurtado v. California*,[45] the Supreme Court tied the concept of due process of law to the common law tradition of recognizing inherent limits on government authority. While in England the practical barrier "against legislative tyranny was the power of a free public opinion represented by the commons," in the United States "written constitutions were deemed essential to protect the rights and liberties of the people against the encroachments of power delegated to their governments."[46]

Therefore, while in England the judiciary had no authority to constrain

Parliament, and could only apply due process ("law of the land") provisions of the Magna Carta against "executive usurpation and tyranny," in the United States the due process clauses "have become also bulwarks against arbitrary legislation." They guarantee not just "particular forms of procedure, *but the very substance of individual rights to life, liberty and property.*"[47] "Not every act, legislative in form, is law," the Court continued. In particular, the exercise of "arbitrary power," including by a legislature, "is not law."[48] A few years later, the Court reiterated that some acts of legislation are not a "legitimate exertion" of the police power.[49]

But it was state courts, not the Supreme Court, that were the pioneers in invalidating legislation they deemed to be arbitrary or oppressive as inconsistent with "due process of law." And it was state courts that first enunciated the constitutional doctrine of "liberty of contract."

THE LIBERTY OF CONTRACT DOCTRINE

The liberty of contract doctrine arose from two ideas prominent in late-nineteenth-century jurisprudence. First, courts stated that so-called "class legislation"—legislation that arbitrarily singled out a particular class for unfavorable treatment or regulation—was unconstitutional. Courts used both the Due Process and the Equal Protection clauses as textual hooks for reviewing class legislation claims.[50] Indeed, the opinions were often unclear as to whether the operative constitutional provision was due process, equal protection, both, or neither. Second, courts used the Due Process Clause to enforce natural rights against the states. Judicially enforceable natural rights were not defined by reference to abstract philosophic constructs. Rather, they were the rights that history had shown were crucial to the development of Anglo-American liberty.

CLASS LEGISLATION ANALYSIS AND THE DUE PROCESS CLAUSE

Opposition to class legislation had deep roots in pre–Civil War American thought. After the Civil War and through the end of the Gilded Age, leading jurists believed that the ban on class legislation was the crux of the Fourteenth Amendment, including both the Equal Protection and Due Process clauses.[51] Justice Stephen Field wrote in 1883 that the Fourteenth Amendment was "designed to prevent all discriminating legislation for the benefit of some to the disparagement of others."[52] Each American, Field continued, had the right to "pursue his [or her] happiness unrestrained, except by just, equal, and impartial laws."[53] Justice Joseph Bradley, writing for the Court the same year, declared that "what is called class legislation" is "obnoxious to the prohibitions of the Fourteenth Amendment."[54] In *Dent v. West Virginia*, the Court even declared that no equal protection or due process claim could succeed absent an arbitrary classification.[55] Influential dictum from *Leeper v. Texas* suggested that the Fourteenth Amendment's due process guarantee is secured "by laws operating on all alike."[56]

The Supreme Court, however, interpreted the prohibition on class legislation quite narrowly. In 1884 it unanimously rejected a challenge to a San Francisco ordinance that prohibited night work only in laundries.[57] Justice Field explained that the law seemed like a reasonable fire prevention measure, and that it applied equally to all laundries. The following year, a Chinese plaintiff challenged the same laundry ordinance, alleging that its purpose was to force Chinese-owned laundries out of business. Field, writing again for a unanimous Court, announced that—consistent with centuries of Anglo-American judicial tradition and prior Supreme Court cases—the Court would not "inquire into the motives of the legislators in passing [legislation], except as they may be disclosed on the face of the acts, or inferable from their operation. . . ."[58] The Court's refusal to consider legislative motive severely limited its ability to police class legislation.

In 1888 the Supreme Court again emphasized the narrow reach of the prohibition on class legislation. Justice Field, writing for the Court, explained, "The greater part of all legislation is special, either in the object sought to be attained by it, or in the extent of its application." Special legislation is not illicit class legislation "if all persons brought under its influence are treated alike under the same conditions."[59]

Powell v. Pennsylvania illustrates the laxity of the Supreme Court's interpretation of the class legislation prohibition. Justice John Marshall Harlan wrote the Court's opinion upholding a state ban on margarine.[60] Harlan accepted at face value the state's contention that the law at issue was an antifraud and public health measure and not, as the plaintiff accurately asserted, naked special interest legislation promoted by the dairy industry.[61] Moreover, Harlan explained that the law applied equally to anyone who might sell margarine, "thus recognizing and preserving the principle of equality among those engaged in the same business."[62]

Many state courts, meanwhile, were far more willing than the federal Supreme Court to hold laws challenged as class legislation, especially labor laws, unconstitutional. Several courts, for example, invalidated laws requiring manufacturing and mining concerns to pay their workers in cash, not scrip.[63] These decisions were not subject to Supreme Court review.[64] The many state decisions invalidating class legislation led law professor Ernst

Freund to conclude in his 1904 treatise that the ban on unequal laws was "one of the most effectual limitations upon the exercise of the police power."[65]

By the turn of the century, the Supreme Court occasionally overturned on class legislation grounds legislative classifications that seemed patently arbitrary.[66] While hardly a model of clarity, the opinions relied primarily on the Equal Protection Clause, not due process.[67] These decisions were also relatively rare, as the Court upheld laws that seemed very plausible candidates for condemnation as class legislation.[68]

When *Lochner* reached the Supreme Court in 1905, class legislation challenges had ceased to be a significant threat to labor legislation. *Lochner* itself explicitly focused on the right to liberty of contract, and relegated the more equalitarian concerns raised by the ban on class legislation to an oblique aside. In sharp contrast to the 1880s, when the Due Process Clause's protections were thought to be limited to prohibiting class legislation, after *Lochner* the Supreme Court explicitly questioned whether the guarantee of due process of law applied to class legislation at all.[69] The Court eventually concluded that it did, but that the Due Process Clause only provided a "mere minimum" of protection against unequal legislation.[70]

Nevertheless, judicial hostility to class legislation likely played some role in liberty of contract cases after 1905. Litigants continued to raise class legislation claims, and even the most rhetorically libertarian due process opinions of the post-*Lochner* period usually at least hinted that the legislation in question violated the principle of legislative neutrality among classes.[71] Given a norm among the justices that strongly discouraged concurring opinions, it's impossible to discern what individual justices were thinking in any given case. But in close decisions, like *Lochner* itself, concerns that the law at issue amounted to class legislation may have motivated one or more of the swing voters who joined the narrow majority.[72]

The Supreme Court, meanwhile, repeatedly invoked the anti–class legislation principle in cases involving due process challenges to rate or price regulations. Unlike the *Lochner* line of liberty of contract cases, however, these cases primarily involved claims that property, not liberty, had been taken without due process of law. They therefore descend more directly from the pre–Civil War cases protecting vested rights and prohibiting the government from "taking the property of A to give to B." Other due process cases that involved interference with real property rights, such as challenges to zoning ordinances, were also adjudicated as class legislation cases.[73] Finally, the Equal Protection Clause provided stronger, more specific protection against class legislation than did the Due Process Clause, and it was often invoked in cases challenging unequal state taxes.

Natural Rights Analysis and the Due Process Clause

While class legislation played a very important role in Fourteenth Amendment litigation through the 1930s, the *Lochner* line of liberty of contract cases that is the primary focus of this book arose primarily from natural rights theory. Natural rights theory means, in this context, the idea that individuals possess prepolitical rights that antedate positive law and that can be discovered through human reason. Courts took a historicist rather than purely rationalist approach to discerning the content of natural rights protected by the Due Process Clause. Historicists of the time believed that "societies, social norms, and institutions are the outgrowth of continuous change effected by secular causes," but that they "evolve according to moral ordering principles that are discoverable through historical studies."[74] Courts used natural rights theory not as a source of novel constitutional norms, "but as confirmation of rights they thought were embedded" in the Anglo-American tradition.[75]

Justices Stephen Field and Joseph Bradley's *Slaughter-House* dissents were crucial to the development of the liberty of contract idea, and they were laden with natural rights rhetoric. Bradley's dissent combined natural rights analysis with a historicist perspective; he wrote that "the people of this country brought with them to its shores the rights of Englishmen; the rights which had been wrested from English sovereigns at various periods of the nation's history." He also noted that "the privileges and immunities of Englishmen were established and secured by long usage and by various acts of Parliament."[76] Among those fundamental principles inherited by the American people was the right to be free from government-sponsored monopolies. According to Bradley, the American Constitution incorporated this right through the Fourteenth Amendment, and in any event the right was inherent in American citizenship.[77]

Field's dissent, meanwhile, exhibits the influence of "free labor" ideology—the ideological linchpin of the abolitionist movement and the antebellum Republican Party—on post–Civil War constitutional thought.[78] For example, Field wrote that "it is to me a matter of profound regret that [the statute's] validity is recognized by a majority of this court, for by it the right of free labor, one of the most sacred and imprescriptible rights of man, is violated."[79]

The *Slaughter-House* dissents were extremely influential. Some lower court judges ignored the majority opinion and relied directly on the dissents in arguing that there is a constitutional right to pursue a lawful calling free from unreasonable government interference.[80] In an unusually well-cited concurring opinion in *Butchers' Union Co. v. Crescent City Co.* (1883), Justice Bradley reiterated that the Fourteenth Amendment protects the inalienable right to "follow any of the common occupations of life."[81]

Meanwhile, several state courts explicitly adopted a right to occupational liberty.[82] In *People v. Marx* in 1885, for example, the New York Court of Appeals stated, in language reminiscent of the *Slaughter-House* dissents, that "no proposition is more firmly settled than that it is one of the fundamental rights and privileges of every American citizen to adopt and follow such lawful industrial pursuit, not injurious to the community, as he may see fit."[83]

In that same year the New York Court of Appeals invalidated a law banning the manufacture of cigars in tenements.[84] Liberty, the court wrote, "means the right not only of freedom from actual servitude, imprisonment, or restraint, but the right of one to use his faculties in all lawful ways, to live and work where he will, to earn his livelihood in any lawful calling, and to pursue any lawful trade or avocation." The court concluded that "under the guise of promoting the public health," the legislature had "arbitrarily interfere[d] with personal liberty and private property without due process of law."[85]

The right to pursue an occupation free from government-sponsored monopoly and unequal legislation gradually morphed into a more general constitutional right to "liberty of contract," adopted by the Supreme Court in the 1890s. Despite all the attention the liberty of contract cases have received over the years, no one has adequately described the origins of the liberty of contract doctrine.

The outlines of the story, at least, are as follows. Contractual freedom was a bedrock part of American constitutional consciousness from the beginning of the republic, with roots going back to England.[86] The ideological victory of abolitionism over slavery further elevated the American elite's regard for contractual freedom.[87] Meanwhile, by the 1870s the notion that people have a right to "liberty of contract" became common in contract (not constitutional) law, in both England and the United States. In 1875 Sir George Jessel wrote, in an English opinion much cited on both sides of the Atlantic: "If there is one thing more than another public policy requires, it is that men of full age and competent understanding shall have the utmost liberty of contracting, and their contracts, when entered into freely and voluntarily, shall be held sacred, and shall be enforced by courts of justice. Therefore you have this paramount public policy to consider,—that you are not lightly to interfere with this freedom of contract."[88]

The liberty of contract idea quickly migrated from contract law to constitutional law. In 1886 the Pennsylvania Supreme Court held that virtually any government restrictions on labor contracts were unconstitutional.[89] A worker, the court wrote, "may sell his labor for what he thinks best, whether money or goods, just as his employer may sell his iron or coal, and any and every law that proposes to prevent him from so doing is an infringement of his constitutional privileges, and consequently vicious and void."[90] An editorial in the *Dallas Morning News* applauded this decision and repeatedly referred to the importance of "liberty of contract."[91] The *Morning News* editorial suggests, surprisingly, that educated nonlawyers were aware of the concept of constitutional protection for liberty of contract by this time.

Three years later, New York Court of Appeals judge Rufus Peckham, a future Supreme Court justice and the author of the Supreme Court's *Lochner* opinion, appears to have been the first American judge to use the phrase "liberty of contract" when discussing a constitutional right in a published (albeit dissenting) opinion.[92] By the early 1890s other state courts were holding that liberty of contract was a constitutional right.[93] Legal commentators began writing articles about the scope of this right, and some writers endorsed a strong version of the right—far stronger than the Supreme Court ever adopted—especially in employment cases.[94]

Justice Field's brother, David Dudley Field, published a historicist defense of liberty of contract in 1893.[95] The story of the growth of American liberty, according to Field, was the story of the rise of liberty of contract, including its extension to former slaves and women. An 1894 treatise on contracts stated, "Unless the 'police power' in some way permit [sic], it is unconstitutional [under the Fourteenth Amendment's Due Process Clause] for a State to prevent persons having the general power to contract, from entering into such contracts as they may see fit. Such a proceeding is an unwarrantable interference with the liberty to follow one's business."[96] Professor John F. Dillon explained that the requirement of due process of law protects the fundamental rights of "life, liberty, contracts, and property."[97]

Also in 1894, Supreme Court Justice Henry Brown wrote that government may not "arbitrarily interfere with private business, or impose unusual and unnecessary restrictions upon lawful occupations."[98] The following year, Justice Brewer stated more directly—and without citing any specific constitutional provision—that "generally speaking, among the inalienable rights of the citizen is that of the liberty of contract."[99]

In 1897, in *Allgeyer v. Louisiana*,[100] the Supreme Court invalidated a Louisiana law that discriminated against out-of-state insurance companies. Justice Peckham, writing for the Court, effused that the Fourteenth Amendment's protection of liberty from arbitrary deprivation included "the right of the citizen to be free in the enjoyment of all his faculties; to be free to use

them in all lawful ways; to live and work where he will; to earn his livelihood by any lawful calling; to pursue any livelihood or avocation; and for
that purpose to enter into all contracts which may be proper, necessary and
essential to his carrying out to a successful conclusion the purposes above
mentioned."[101] Several other opinions alluding to the liberty of contract doctrine followed.[102] *Allgeyer* was especially important because, unlike other
opinions that recognized the right to liberty of contract, *Allgeyer* held the
statute in question unconstitutional. But despite Peckham's broad dicta,
Allgeyer's actual holding was narrow: that an individual has the right "to
contract outside the state."[103]

The growing momentum for constitutional protection of liberty of contract in general, and the right to pursue an occupation free from arbitrary
government interference specifically, was likely aided by the labor unrest
and Populist agitation of the period. This fueled fears among conservative
lawyers of imminent socialism or worse.[104]

Yet the once-common notion that Court reacted primarily out of fear of
radical movements is, as historian James Ely concludes, "ultimately over-
drawn and unpersuasive," resting only on "occasional alarmist rhetoric by
judges."[105] Many significant cases limiting the states' regulation power arose
in contexts far removed from debates over socialism. For example, federal
judges in California, including Justice Field sitting as a circuit court judge,
issued a series of influential pro–liberty of contract decisions in California
during the 1880s on behalf of Chinese immigrants faced with laws seeking
to deprive them of their livelihoods.[106] The most libertarian justices on the
Lochner Court, David Brewer and Rufus Peckham, often dissented when
the Court upheld legislation unrelated to the economic controversies of the
day, such as a mandatory vaccination law.[107] Indeed, the justices who most
vigorously supported liberty of contract more generally took libertarian positions in other contexts. Peckham and Brewer, joined by Justices Harlan
(a strong believer in natural rights) and Fuller, consistently argued in the
Insular Cases that the residents of the territories conquered by the United
States in the Spanish-American War were entitled to the protections of the
Constitution.[108]

DID THE PRE–*LOCHNER* SUPREME COURT
ENDORSE LAISSEZ-FAIRE?

Allgeyer v. Louisiana is often seen as a harbinger of the rise of "laissez-faire
jurisprudence" in the Supreme Court, with *Lochner v. New York* the most
significant laissez-faire precedent.[109] However, by the time *Lochner* was

decided in 1905, laissez-faire constitutionalism had already been soundly defeated, in favor of an emphasis on the states' inherent police powers.

Contrasting treatise author Christopher Tiedeman's views with the Supreme Court's holdings demonstrates just how far the Court was from adopting laissez-faire. Tiedeman argued that the states' police power is "confined to the detailed enforcement of the legal maxim, *sic utere tuo, ut alienum non laedas* [use your own (property) in such a manner as not to injure that of another]."[110] Tiedeman, then, would have limited the constitutional scope of American government to something very similar to radical British libertarian Herbert Spencer's "law of equal freedom": "Every man has freedom to do all that he wills, provided he infringes not the equal freedom of any other man."[111]

Tiedeman therefore thought that antimiscegenation laws were obviously unconstitutional: "They deprive the parties, so disposed to marry, of their right to liberty without due process of law."[112] The Supreme Court, by contrast, upheld such laws by unanimous vote.[113] Tiedeman also asserted that the protective tariff, usury laws, antigambling laws, and laws banning narcotic drugs were unconstitutional[114]—all positions either overwhelmingly rejected by the Supreme Court or so far from mainstream jurisprudence that the issues never reached the Court.

Though Brewer and Peckham were not nearly as radical as Tiedeman, they had a sufficiently narrow view of the police power to find themselves frequently dissenting, usually without opinion, from decisions upholding various state and local regulations.[115] The most important of these decisions was *Holden v. Hardy*, in which the Court upheld a state law dictating maximum hours for miners. *Holden* obliterated any chance that the Court would try to enforce a laissez-faire ideal in the context of labor contracts. Through at least the early 1920s, *Holden* (and not *Lochner*) was the most influential precedent on the scope of the states' police power to protect workers. Brewer and Peckham also dissented from decisions upholding other labor laws, as well as laws that did everything from banning futures contracts to requiring smallpox vaccination.[116] But even Brewer and Peckham generally gave "great deference" to state regulations, with Peckham writing several significant opinions upholding regulations as proper exercises of the police power.[117]

By the time the *Lochner* case reached the Supreme Court in 1905, then, the Court clearly was not going to be a champion of limited government along the radical lines advocated by Tiedeman, or even along the more moderate lines promoted by Brewer, Peckham, and some state supreme courts. However, with the exception of Justice Holmes, the Court had reached a consensus that due process of law principles protected fundamental rights that were antecedent to government, including liberty of contract.[118] But the justices disagreed among themselves about how vigorously fundamental rights should be enforced against the states, and more specifically, whether there should be a presumption of constitutionality and how strong such a presumption should be.[119] The question, in other words, was whether the new liberty of contract doctrine was going to put any significant limits on the exercise of the states' claimed police powers, or whether the doctrine, like the prohibition on class legislation before it, would be interpreted so narrowly as to be a mere distracting sideshow to the main event: the growth of the regulatory state.[120]

CHAPTER TWO

The *Lochner* Case

The received wisdom among legal scholars and historians is that *Lochner v. New York* exemplifies the failings of the Supreme Court's liberty of contract jurisprudence. *Lochner* is said to have involved overworked, exploited bakery workers who had managed to win a meager but hard-fought legislative victory limiting their hours of labor to sixty per week. The Supreme Court refused to acquiesce to this minor victory for progress and social justice, and instead protected the interests of large corporations by invalidating the hours legislation under the Fourteenth Amendment's Due Process Clause as a purported violation of "liberty of contract." In doing so, the Court relied on abstract notions of rights divorced from social context and failed to take into account either the gross disparities in bargaining power between workers and their employers, or the obvious health benefits of the legislation. The *Lochner* Court also behaved in a grossly antidemocratic fashion by ignoring popular sentiment favoring hours legislation. In turn, the contemporary media, reflecting public outrage, harshly criticized the *Lochner* opinion.

This conventional account of *Lochner* is tendentious and in some particulars just wrong. As we shall see, the bakers' union conceived of and promoted the hours legislation not simply to address health concerns, but also to drive small bakeshops that employed recent immigrants out of the industry. The union also encouraged selective enforcement of the law against nonunion bakeries. Large corporate bakeries, meanwhile, *supported* and also benefited from the maximum-hours legislation invalidated in *Lochner*. The constitutional challenge to the legislation came from small family-owned bakeries that were usually owned by former bakery workers. The Supreme Court's *Lochner* opinion was not formalistic, but took explicit account of statistical data regarding the health of bakers. Finally, *Lochner* does not seem to have been especially unpopular when it was decided, and indeed it won support from most newspaper editorialists who commented on it.

The dispute before the Supreme Court in *Lochner* had its origins in late-nineteenth century agitation by unionized New York bread bakers for legislation to limit their working hours.[1] Like other workers, the bakers wanted more leisure time. Because they were paid by the day, they expected that their wages would be stable if they won shorter working hours. The bakers' union even claimed that shorter hours would somehow lead to *higher* daily wages.[2] With some support from contemporary medical authorities, the bakers complained that their long working hours and dust-laden working environment left them susceptible to "consumption," an ill-defined catchall for lung diseases.[3]

The union unsuccessfully lobbied in 1887 for state legislation limiting bakers' working hours.[4] Meanwhile, working conditions for many bakers improved as modern commercial bread-baking factories increased their market share at the expense of traditional smaller bakeshops. The larger New York bakeries were staffed mostly by bakers of German descent, along with a smaller group of Anglo-Irish bakers. Most large bakeries were unionized, and Germans came to dominate the Bakery and Confectionery Workers' International Union. The smaller New York bakeries employed a hodgepodge of immigrant groups, with employees generally working for bosses of the same ethnic heritage. Smaller bakeries were generally not unionized, especially those staffed by non-Germans.[5]

By the mid-1890s, unionized bakers employed by large commercial bakeries rarely worked more than ten hours per day and sixty hours per week.[6] However, these bakers believed that their relatively favorable situation was endangered by competition from small, old-fashioned bakeries, especially those that employed Italian, French, and Jewish immigrants. The bakers' union's weekly newspaper, the *Baker's Journal*, condemned these immigrants as "the cheap labor of the green hand from foreign shores."[7] Non-German immigrant bakers were notoriously difficult to organize, and the union expended little effort recruiting them.[8]

The old-fashioned bakeries were often located in the basements of tenement buildings to take advantage of cheap rents and of floors sturdy enough to withstand the weight of heavy baking ovens.[9] More modern factory bakeries operated in shifts with a division of labor among the workers. In contrast, the cellar bakeries often demanded that workers be on call most of the day to be available for all stages of the bread-baking process. The workers slept in or near the bakery during down times, and often worked far more than ten hours per day.[10] As the owner of a large wholesale bakery put it, at the small bakeries it was "necessary to keep men on for sixteen hours to get ten hours of work."[11] A ten-hour-day law would not only aid those unionized bakers who had not successfully demanded that their hours be reduced, but would also drive out of business many old-fashioned bakeries that depended on flexible labor schedules.

The bakers' union's political fortunes grew under the leadership of Henry Weismann, a German immigrant who came to the United States as a young adult. Weismann initially settled in California, where he worked in bakeries, dabbled in anarchism, and was active in the Anti-Coolie League of California.[12] After a jail term for possession of explosives—he later claimed he had been framed by political opponents[13]—Weismann started organizing for the bakers' union, a job for which he was apparently well-suited. Samuel Gompers described Weismann as "splendidly developed physically," with "a stentorian voice which never modulated whether speaking of human freedom or the death of a fly."[14]

Weismann moved to New York in 1890 to become the *Bakers' Journal*'s editor. By 1894, he was the union's unofficial leader and spokesperson and led a new campaign for a ten-hour law in New York.[15] Weismann's clever innovation was to tie hours legislation, of interest mainly to the union, to sanitary reform, which was of interest to a broad range of reformers and also to the general, bread-eating public.[16]

In 1894, a dying Jewish baker was carried from a cellar bakery on the Lower East Side. Weismann publicized the incident and demanded an investigation into the health and sanitary conditions in cellar bakeries in Brooklyn and Manhattan.[17] Weismann persuaded the *New York Press* to send a team of reporters—accompanied by union bakers who were familiar with the worst bakeries—to investigate. The result was an exposé by muckraking reporter Edward Marshall detailing unsanitary conditions in bakeries, as well as poor working conditions, and calling for legislative intervention.[18]

The specifics of Marshall's reporting—or of whether his findings were representative of conditions at many bakeries—are a bit suspect, because he was known for his reformist sympathies, because his article was researched at the urging and with the cooperation of Weismann, and because the piece was timed to coincide with the bakers' union's campaign for a ten-hour law.[19] Moreover, a May 1896 report to the Brooklyn Commissioner of Health found the story to be "greatly exaggerated and most of it absolutely false."[20] On the other hand, the gist of Marshall's article is supported by a state factory inspectors' report issued two years later, based on inspections conducted in 1895, as well as by an 1896 investigation by a *Brooklyn Eagle* reporter.[21] An owner of a small bakery admitted to the *Brooklyn Eagle* in May 1896 that there "are doubtless many dirty shops."[22]

Marshall's article led to the introduction of legislation establishing minimum sanitary conditions in bakeries. Many leading reformers endorsed the bill.[23] Prejudice against certain immigrant groups likely contributed to support for the legislation. A state factory inspector commented, "It is almost impossible to secure or keep in proper cleanly condition the Jewish and Italian bakeshops. Cleanliness and tidiness are entirely foreign to these people, and their bakeshops are like their sweatshops, for like causes produce like effects."[24]

The Bakeshop Act, as it came to be known, was modeled on England's Bakehouse Regulation Act of 1863.[25] The act banned employees from sleeping in bakeries, specified drainage and plumbing requirements, and required various other sanitary measures. The New York proposal added a maximum-hours provision—tacked on at the urging of the bakers' union—that limited biscuit, cake, and bread bakers' hours of labor to ten per day and sixty per week.[26] The hours provision received an important endorsement from state Health Commissioner Cyrus Edson, who wrote, "The provision limiting the hours of worktime of the men is especially good from a sanitary standpoint. There is unmistakable evidence that these men are overworked, and that, in consequence of this, they are sickly and unfit to handle an article of food."[27]

Not surprisingly, the Bakeshop Act received strong support from the bakers' union. The union even published a pamphlet edited by Weismann, drawing on Marshall's work for the *New York Press* and other sources, detailing the poor conditions in many New York bakeshops.[28] The union officially proclaimed that the act was "a sanitary measure solely" and therefore "will stand the closest scruting of constitutional lawyers and the courts."[29] Unofficially, the union also believed that the act, especially its hours provision, would solve the problems faced by (unionized) bakers, including "the lack of work, increased numbers of apprentices, cheap labor, insane competition among employers, [and] the era of 3-cents loaves of bread."[30] Rank and file bakers believed that by dictating shorter hours, work would be spread among more bakers. This would lessen unemployment in the trade and reduce competition among bakers.[31]

Owners of large commercial bakeries also supported the act, albeit less vigorously.[32] These bakeries already met all the act's sanitary rules, and adhered to a ten-hour day or something close to it.[33] The owner of one of the largest bakeries in New York City acknowledged that the "law does not affect the wholesale bakers as I can see." He noted that his employees already worked only ten hours a day.[34]

Contrary to some scholars' speculation,[35] the support the owners of large bakeries displayed for the law was mostly tacit; they did not actively lobby, but were happy to have the new rules and associated costs and inconveniences imposed on their competitors.[36] Owners of smaller but relatively well-established non-cellar bakeshops also foresaw potential gains from the law. Like owners of large bakeries, they hoped that the law's sanitary provisions would improve the reputation and therefore the profitability of the baking industry, which competed with home-baked goods.[37] They also shared an interest in driving the cellar bakeshops owned by recent Jewish, Italian, and French immigrants out of business. Moreover, at the last minute the bill was amended to reduce the burden on small-scale bakers (and reduce doubts about its constitutionality) by exempting bakery owners and their families from the limits on working hours.[38] On the other hand, some bakery owners worried that sanitary and hours rules would be enforced far more strictly against nonunion bakeries than against unionized ones.[39]

The bill thus had the strong support of social reformers and the bakers' union, much less vocal support from the owners of large bakeries, and the tacit support or acquiescence of the owners of smaller, non-cellar bakeries. The Bakeshop Act passed unanimously in both houses of the legislature and was signed into law on May 2, 1895.[40] The union celebrated. An editorial in the *Baker's Journal* noted that the law's supporters had worried about passage of the ten-hour provision, "on account of a possible friction with the constitution."[41]

The law was amended one year later, again unanimously, to effectively close down certain cellar bakeries and limit the opening of new ones by specifying minimum ceiling heights for bakeries, and to create whistleblower protection for employees.[42] By this time, opposition to the hours provision among smaller but well-established bakeries had grown; rumors that the owners of small bakeries would challenge the constitutionality of the ten-hour provision began as early as February 1896.[43] A group of Brooklyn bakers sent a delegation to Albany to unsuccessfully oppose the amended bill.[44] According to Weismann, flour wholesalers, bakers' supply dealers, and wholesale butchers also opposed the legislation but were overcome by the combined forces of the union and "friends of social reform."[45]

Weismann soon rose to international secretary, the bakers' union's highest office. He resigned in 1897 amid allegations of corruption and opened a bakery.[46] He also studied law and graduated as the valedictorian of Brooklyn

Law School's first class in 1903.[47] Weismann became active in Republican politics[48] and in the newly organized New York Association of Master Bakers. The latter represented primarily owners of small, non-basement bakeries, who were mostly immigrants from Germany.[49] The Master Bakers endorsed a bill that would have weakened the Bakeshop Act in some respects. Despite the efforts of Weismann and his remaining allies among Brooklyn bakery workers, the bill failed in the legislature.[50]

Over time, and despite lax enforcement,[51] opposition among bakeshop proprietors to the ten-hour rule grew, mostly because it contained no provision for overtime. The *Bakers Review*, the Association of Master Bakers' publication, opined "that there are occasions when overtime work in a bakery is an absolute necessity."[52] Indeed, the bakers' union itself continued to propose and sign contracts that provided for overtime work for additional pay, in violation of the Bakeshop Act.[53] At least one such agreement was reported in the *Baker's Journal* without negative comment.[54] The union nevertheless continued to support the ten-hour, no-overtime rule because it provided leverage against nonunion bakeries; the union acquiesced when union employers requested overtime, but threatened nonunion shops with prosecution when they sought overtime work from their employees.

Owners of nonunionized bakeries concluded that the ten-hour provision was mainly being used to "blackmail" them.[55] One of the states' four factory inspectors was also a bakers' union official, which lends some plausibility to their claim.[56] Emil Braun, the secretary of the United Master Bakers (a short-lived rival to the National Association of Master Bakers), argued that the ten-hour law gave bakery workers undue leverage which they could use to "harass" their employer or "get him in trouble." The bakers could always "short the yeast, . . . take the water a few degrees colder," or "set the sponge a little stiffer" to ensure that the bread was not quite ready after ten hours of work.[57]

Owners of small New York bakeries began to agitate for a constitutional challenge to the ten-hour provision. They had to overcome the opposition of the ten-hour provision's supporters—owners of large wholesale bakeries where overtime work was relatively rare and unionization common.[58] The National Association of Master Bakers had even endorsed existing "sanitary" laws in 1899, an endorsement that appears to have included New York's ten-hour law.[59] In 1901, the hours law was discussed at the New York Master Bakers Association's annual convention, but the association took no position. It instead resolved to challenge a law banning bakeries from hiring underage apprentices.[60] At its 1902 convention the New York association finally resolved to find an appropriate test case and challenge the ten-hour provision all the way to the Supreme Court.[61] Because the owners of large wholesale bakeries supported New York's Bakeshop Act, the challenge to the hours provision was funded almost entirely with donations from small retail bakers; the large firms "had nothing to do" with the "work and expense" involved.[62]

The New York Association soon found an appropriate case, involving the prosecution of bakery owner Joseph Lochner for violating the ten-hour law. Lochner had emigrated from Bavaria at age twenty in 1882, and worked for eight years in a bakery in Utica, New York. He opened his own bakery in 1894, where he worked alongside his wife and his employees.[63] According to the *Utica Herald*, Lochner's bakery started off as a tiny shop, but expanded because "by neatness and the excellence of its products it soon won an enviable reputation" among local consumers.[64]

Lochner had a tempestuous relationship with the bakers' union that started in 1895, when the union withdrew the union label from his goods and initiated a boycott of his bakery.[65] The union claimed that he had a baker work more than sixty hours a week, and Lochner acknowledged violating union rules by allowing one of his employees, Aman Schmitter, to live above the bakery with his family. (Schmitter responded, "I cannot live with my folks, and do not want to live in a boarding house." He tried to get an exemption from the union, to no avail.)[66]

The union was also involved in an 1899 prosecution of Lochner for violating the ten-hour law.[67] He pleaded guilty and received a twenty dollar fine.[68] When this failed to force Lochner to concede defeat, the union again launched a boycott against him, publishing notices in the local newspapers.[69]

In April 1902 the factory inspector filed a criminal complaint against Lochner for allegedly employing Schmitter for more than sixty hours in one week.[70] Schmitter had sworn out an affidavit stating that he had stayed at work beyond the ten-hour daily limit to learn cake baking.[71] Schmitter traveled with Lochner to New York City in 1899, when he owned his own bakery.[72] His 1941 obituary in the *Utica Daily Press* notes that he worked for Lochner for many years.[73] Given that there could be no successful prosecution unless Schmitter was willing to testify against Lochner, and given the close and longstanding relationship between the two men and Schmitter's own prior bakery ownership, it seems likely that Schmitter's complaint against Lochner was arranged by the Utica Master Bakers Association, of which Lochner was a member, to test the law.

The Utica association invited the state association to take up Lochner's defense and challenge the law, which it agreed to do.[74] The Master Bakers Association had cause to hope for a favorable outcome. By this time there

were many state court precedents invalidating labor regulations as class legislation, or as unduly interfering with the right to pursue an occupation.[75]
The New York Court of Appeals had been among the most aggressive courts
in this regard. Most famously, in 1885 the court invalidated a law banning
cigar manufacturing in tenement apartments as a violation of due process
rights.[76] Even more propitious for the association was a 1901 decision invalidating a requirement that state contractors pay their workers the "prevailing wage."[77] In that case, the Court of Appeals explicitly endorsed state
court decisions from around the country invalidating various types of "paternal" labor regulations. On the other hand, the Court of Appeals had also
issued several opinions upholding labor regulations as being within New
York's police power.[78]

A grand jury indicted Lochner in October. At a pretrial hearing his attorney, William S. Mackie, unsuccessfully requested dismissal on technicali-
ties. At trial in February 1903, Lochner offered no defense, providing further
evidence that Lochner and Schmitter were cooperating in a test case. The
court found Lochner guilty, and he was sentenced to pay a fifty-dollar fine
or spend fifty days in jail.[79]

Lochner appealed to a New York Appellate Division court, which split
3–2 in favor of upholding the hours law.[80] Judge John M. Davy wrote that
the hours law was a valid police power measure intended to improve public
health. He found that the law was not class legislation because it was "directed to all persons engaged in the bakery business" and "neither confers
special privileges, nor makes unjust discrimination."[81] Davy added that the
hours law did not violate the right to pursue an occupation because it only
regulated working hours, and did not prohibit anyone from working as a
baker.[82]

Lochner appealed. He lost once again, this time in a 4–3 decision.[83]
Chief Judge Alton B. Parker wrote the plurality opinion for himself and a
colleague. Parker stated that it was "beyond question" that the public had
an interest in having bread manufactured in clean bakeries, and that the
hours provision would promote this goal by assuring that bakers were well-
rested.[84] Parker added that the law protected the health of bakers and was
therefore within the police power.[85] Parker ran for and received the Democratic nomination for president later that year, making extensive use of his
Lochner opinion in his campaign materials.[86]

Judge John Clinton Gray, concurring, emphasized that the appropriate
rationale for upholding the law was that it protected *public* health and not
just the health of bakers.[87] Judge Irving Vann also concurred. He cited books

and articles, apparently found through his own diligence, discussing the negative effect of flour and sugar particles and excess heat on bakers' health.[88]

Dissenting Judge Denis O'Brien argued that the law had no relation to the production of healthful bread, and that it was class legislation because it applied only to a very small class of bakers and confectioners.[89] O'Brien also rejected the claim that the law protected workers' health. Baking was not known to be unhealthful, O'Brien wrote, and the law allowed self-employed bakers to work as many hours as they wished, providing further evidence that the hours provision was a "labor law," not a health law. O'Brien pointed out that the state legislature codified the hours provision in the New York Code's labor section and not the health section.[90] Dissenting Judge Edward Bartlett echoed O'Brien's contention that there was no evidence that baking was unhealthful. He found the hours provision to be unduly "paternal."[91]

In February 1904, the New York Association of Master Bakers levied an assessment of one dollar on each member to pay for an appeal to the Supreme Court.[92] Attorney Mackie declined to continue to represent the Master Bakers; he informed the organization that its planned Supreme Court appeal was hopeless. The association hired prominent Brooklyn attorney Frank Harvey Field to replace Mackie. Prompted by Adam Kalb, a bakery owner who had been a union activist when the ten-hour law was enacted, the association teamed Field with Henry Weismann.[93] Weismann had the advantage of possessing "absolute knowledge of existing conditions, instead of abstract theories."[94]

As Mackie had concluded, the prospects for Lochner's appeal seemed unpromising. The Supreme Court had acknowledged that illicit class legislation violated the Fourteenth Amendment's Equal Protection Clause, but it had a very narrow conception of what constituted illicit class legislation.[95] Moreover, the Court had consistently upheld laws regulating labor relations, including a maximum-hours law for miners in *Holden v. Hardy*, against class legislation challenges.[96] The dissents in those cases never received more than three votes.

The other possible ground for Lochner's appeal—that the hours provision violated the right of Lochner and his workers to liberty of contract—also seemed like a long shot, at best. Although the Court had recently proclaimed that liberty of contract was a fundamental right protected by the Fourteenth Amendment's Due Process Clause,[97] it had consistently refused to invalidate labor regulations as violations of that liberty.[98]

Moreover, twenty years before *Lochner*, the Supreme Court had unanimously upheld a ban on night work in laundries and rejected the notion that the Fourteenth Amendment protects "the right of a man to work at all times."[99] Justice Stephen Field declared for the Court that the government has the "right to protect all persons from the physical and moral debasement which comes from uninterrupted labor."[100]

Faced with limited and unattractive options, Lochner's attorneys, (Frank) Field and Weismann, relied primarily on the argument that the hours provision was illicit class legislation due to its limited and inconsistent coverage. They noted that the hours provision exempted the many bakers who worked in pie bakeries, hotels, restaurants, clubs, boarding houses, or for private families. The brief alleged that working conditions for those bakers were less sanitary and healthful than those in many bakeries covered by the law. Moreover, the law did not apply to the many family-operated bakeries.[101]

Field and Weismann also tried to show that the hours provision was not within the state's police power because, although it was tacked on to sanitary legislation, it was not itself a health measure. Field and Weismann reiterated Justice O'Brien's arguments in his Court of Appeals dissent, and also noted that the English sanitary law on which the Bakeshop Act was modeled did not regulate adult working hours.[102]

The most interesting (and likely influential) part of the brief was the appendix, which provided statistics about the health of bakers. According to recent mortality figures from England, bakers had a mortality rate somewhat below the average for all occupations. The appendix next cited articles from various medical journals that recommended sanitary and ventilation reforms to aid the health of bakers, but did not advocate shorter hours. Indeed, one article in the British medical journal *The Lancet* mentioned that shorter hours had not alleviated bakers' health problems.[103] The appendix also cited the *Reference Handbook of Medical Sciences*, which showed that out of twenty-one occupations, bakers had the eleventh-highest mortality rate, very similar to the mortality rates of cabinet makers, masons and bricklayers, blacksmiths, clerks, and other mundane occupations. An expert at the British Home Office, meanwhile, found that bakers ranked eighteenth out of twenty-two occupations for mortality, and had the lowest rates of pulmonary disease.[104]

In contrast to Lochner's lengthy and reasonably thorough brief, New York's brief was only nineteen pages long and contained very few citations to precedents. Perhaps New York's attorney general thought *Lochner* was an easy case governed by *Holden* and therefore was not worth wasting resources on. Or perhaps he was distracted by the more pressing—and at the time more controversial—*Franchise Tax Cases*, another Supreme Court appeal he was working on that would determine the constitutionality of New

York's special franchise tax on streetcar lines, gas works, and other public utilities.[105] Regardless, the brief made three arguments: first, that the burden was on Lochner to show that the law was unconstitutional; second, that the Bakeshop Act's purpose was to safeguard both the public health and the health of bakers; and third, that the law was within the police power because it was a health law.[106] The brief also acknowledged that the law targeted immigrant bakers, arguing that the law was justified because "there have come to [New York] great numbers of foreigners with habits which must be changed."[107]

The Supreme Court heard oral arguments on February 23, 1905, and issued its ruling on April 17, 1905. Much to almost everyone's surprise, Lochner won, 5–4.[108] As expected, Justices David Brewer and Rufus Peckham, who had consistently voted to invalidate labor legislation, voted in Lochner's favor. So did Chief Justice Melville Fuller, who had joined Brewer and Peckham in dissent in the Court's most recent major labor regulation case.[109] The majority also managed to attract the votes of two justices who had previously always voted to uphold state labor regulations, Henry Brown (*Holden's* author) and Joseph McKenna.

Lochner's victory was likely a very close call, as several sources suggest that Peckham's majority opinion was originally written to be a dissent, and that John Marshall Harlan's dissenting opinion initially garnered a five-vote majority.[110] As for the surprising votes of Brown and McKenna, they can most plausibly be attributed to the creativity of the statistics-filled appendix to Lochner's brief, combined with the ineffective brief filed by New York.[111] Additionally, McKenna's voting record suggests that he might have been swayed by the argument that the sixty-hours law was class legislation because it applied only to bakers.[112] Or perhaps, as one scholar speculates, his vote was influenced by the fact that his father had owned a bakery.[113] Finally, the swing justices may have been perturbed that the ten-hour law had no provision for emergency or overtime, and provided criminal, not civil, penalties for violation.

Whatever the influence of the class legislation argument on McKenna, overt concern about class legislation is barely evident in Peckham's majority opinion.[114] This is rather surprising, given the focus of Lochner's brief on class legislation, Justice O'Brien's reliance on a class legislation argument in his New York Court of Appeals dissent, a California precedent invalidating a bakers' hours law as class legislation, and Justice Peckham's history of denouncing class legislation.[115]

Peckham instead focused on the right to liberty of contract protected by the Due Process Clause.[116] *Lochner's* emphasis on individual liberty rights rather than hostility to class legislation had the important long-term consequence of establishing the Due Process Clause as a fertile source for the protection of liberty rights against the states. As one historian concludes, *Lochner* "transformed the Fourteenth Amendment['s Due Process Clause] from a bar to arbitrary and unequal state action into a charter identifying fundamental rights."[117]

Peckham began his *Lochner* opinion by finding that the hours provision interfered with liberty of contract.[118] He acknowledged, however, that if the law was needed to redress some deficiency in the bakers' ability to negotiate their contracts, or if the law was a "health law," then it would be constitutionally sound as within the state's police power.

Peckham, however, dismissed the notion that the law was meant to protect public health. He noted that the Bakeshop Act's sanitary provisions were not at issue, and stated that "clean and wholesome bread does not depend upon whether the baker works but ten hours per day or only sixty hours a week." He also concluded that bakers did not need special aid from the state in negotiating their contracts. He argued that unlike women, children, and to some extent "necessitous" male workers such as the miners in *Holden v. Hardy*, bakers are "in no sense wards of the state." Peckham also distinguished *Holden* by noting that the hours laws in question there had an emergency clause allowing deviation from the rule, while the Bakeshop Act allowed for "no circumstances and no emergencies under which the slightest violation of the act would be innocent."

The only remaining potential police power justification for the hours law was that it protected bakers' health.[119] Peckham suggested that either common knowledge or scientific evidence would be sufficient to show that baking, like the underground mining at issue in *Holden*, was an unhealthful profession requiring special hours rules. With regard to common knowledge, Peckham concluded that baking was an ordinary trade, not generally known to be unhealthful. Next, Peckham found that the available scientific evidence suggested that baking was not an especially unhealthful profession. For this conclusion he paraphrased the studies discussed in the appendix to Lochner's brief, showing that bakers had mortality rates similar to those in many ordinary professions that the legislature did not regulate.[120]

Peckham concluded that the hours law was a "mere meddlesome interference [] with the rights of the individual,"[121] and an unconstitutional violation of liberty of contract. Peckham added dicta denouncing various government interferences with the "ordinary trades," including one type of regulation that had previously been upheld by the Supreme Court over his dissent.[122] This illustrates an important, but often overlooked, aspect of

Lochner: Peckham's libertarian rhetoric does not reflect the swing justice's views, even though they joined his opinion. A norm disfavoring concurring opinions, along with the likelihood that Peckham's opinion was hastily transformed from a dissent to the majority opinion, led to a majority opinion that contained dicta accepted in practice only by a minority.

Ironically, then, *Lochner's* rhetoric is not representative of the views of the so-called *Lochner* Court's majority. Nevertheless, *Lochner* caused consternation in Progressive circles because it was the first Supreme Court case to apply the liberty of contract doctrine to invalidate reformist legislation, and the Court applied what appeared to be a strong presumption in favor of that liberty.[123]

Justice John Marshall Harlan, joined by Justices Edward White and William Day, wrote the main *Lochner* dissent.[124] Harlan agreed that the Due Process Clause protects the right to liberty of contract. He added, however, that this right is subordinate to lawful exercises of police power. Harlan contended that the Court should invalidate a purported health or safety law only if that law had "no real or substantial relation to those objects, or is, beyond all question, a plain, palpable invasion of rights secured by the fundamental law." Any doubts, he wrote, should be resolved in favor of the statute.

Harlan then asserted that the hours provision's purpose was at least in part to protect bakers' health. Harlan cited medical treatises and statistics that supported the notion that bakery work was unhealthful. Where he came across this information is unclear. Harlan concluded that it was reasonable for New York to presume that labor in excess of ten hours per day in a bakery "may endanger the health, and shorten the lives of the workmen, thereby diminishing their physical and mental capacity to serve the State, and to provide for those dependent upon them." Because the statute was not "plainly and palpably" inconsistent with the Fourteenth Amendment, it should be upheld.[125]

Peckham and Harlan, then, speaking for a total of eight of the nine justices, agreed that the Constitution protects liberty of contract. They also agreed that the Court could look beyond legal argument to sociological data to determine whether a law that infringed on liberty of contract was nevertheless a proper police power measure. The result in *Lochner* therefore likely came down to a disagreement among the Court's six centrist justices—excluding Brewer, Holmes, and Peckham—regarding whether the bakers' hours law was a legitimate health law, or a law that singled out bakers for no constitutionally legitimate reason.

Justice Oliver Wendell Holmes filed a pithy lone dissent, one of the most celebrated and influential opinions in American history. First, he argued for judicial restraint, vigorously defending what he called "the right of a majority to embody their opinions in law." According to Holmes, the term "liberty" is perverted whenever it is "held to prevent the natural outcome of a dominant opinion." The Court should not interfere with legislation save when everyone could agree that a challenged statute "would infringe fundamental principles as they have been understood by the traditions of our people and our law."[126]

Second, Holmes rejected the idea that the Due Process Clause broadly limits the police power. He attacked what he called the "shibboleth" that a person should have the liberty to do as he likes so long as he does not interfere with the liberty of others to do the same. Holmes famously quipped that the "Fourteenth Amendment does not enact Mr. Herbert Spencer's *Social Statics*"[127]—Spencer's famous 1851 book that defended exactly that "shibboleth," which he called the "Law of Equal Freedom." Holmes noted that the Supreme Court had upheld many government regulations challenged under the Fourteenth Amendment, including usury laws, laws banning lotteries, "blue laws" prohibiting business transaction on Sunday, laws prohibiting options trading, and an eight-hour law for miners.

Holmes was a master of the memorable aphorism, and Spencer's *Social Statics* is a notable alliteration. By citing the "exotic sounding libertarian treatise" written by an Englishman more than fifty years earlier, Holmes tried to make the majority opinion "look esoteric and out of touch."[128] Over the decades, many scholars have incorrectly surmised that Holmes was accusing the Court of following the principles of Social Darwinism,[129] an ideology often, albeit dubiously, associated with Spencer's writings.[130] In context, he was citing Spencer as an example of an advocate of what today we call libertarianism, and was not accusing the majority of Social Darwinism.[131] Finally, Holmes contended that the Court should defer to economic regulations because the Constitution "is not intended to embody a particular economic theory, whether of paternalism and the organic relation of the citizen to the State or of *laissez faire*."[132]

Although Holmes and Harlan both articulated strong presumptions in favor of government regulations, the differences in their opinions are telling. Harlan was a strong believer in natural rights, and was likely appalled by Holmes' commitment to legal positivism and by his hostility to individual rights. Moreover, unlike Harlan, Holmes refused to admit that liberty of contract is a valid constitutional principle.[133] Finally, Holmes put forth the idea that the Constitution is, and was meant to be, neutral between individualist and collectivist economic and social systems. Harlan and the other dissenting justices were not inclined to endorse this radical sentiment.[134] In short, Harlan's dissent was well within the boundaries of both mainstream early-twentieth-century constitutional discourse and long-held American understandings of the proper role of the state; Holmes's dissenting opinion was beyond the pale.[135]

The *Baker's Journal*'s initial reaction to the *Lochner* decision was surprisingly muted.[136] As the decision sank in, however, its editorials grew far harsher. A May 6, 1905, editorial grumbled that "everything that furthers the interests of the employers is constitutional—but everything is unconstitutional which may be undertaken for the welfare of the working people and aims at the emancipation of the proletariat."[137] A May 20, 1905, *Journal* column accused the *Lochner* Court of delivering the "hardest blow ever dealt by the courts of this country to organized labor."[138] A week later, the *Journal*'s editor growled that "the bakery workers die like flies, of consumption, rheumatism and other physical punishments for the breaking of nature's laws. But what do the *learned* justices care for the laws of nature? Capitalist laws are alone sacred to them! What are wage workers for but to be exploited!"[139] The union threatened a massive strike on May 1, but that threat came to naught.[140]

Meanwhile, the New York bakery owners who had financed the challenge to the law were jubilant. On May 16 they held a banquet in honor of Henry Weismann. Weismann called the decision "a warning to the Radicals and Socialists, who would subvert individual liberties to the paternal sway of the State, and an inspiration to those who still believe in the old-time doctrines of Americanism."[141] The *Baker's Journal* retorted that Weismann was a traitor comparable to Judas Iscariot.[142]

The National Baker, one of several national trade journals, concluded that "the baker will have the satisfaction of having no half-worked dough left on his hands on a busy day, as journeymen will have no good reason for refusing to finish a day's work."[143] The journal added that the decision "is a hard blow to scheming politicians who habitually cater to the 'labor vote'; it upholds those who would render exact justice to both masters and bakers."[144]

Ultimately, the practical effect of *Lochner* on bakers' hours was very small. In the ten years since the Bakeshop Act had become law, productivity and working conditions had improved throughout the United States as the nation grew wealthier. Shorter working hours were becoming the norm nationwide, including in the baking industry.[145] By 1909 less than nine percent of bakers nationwide worked more than ten hours a day, and that nine percent was concentrated in basement bakeries that were rapidly becoming obsolete. Even New York's Jewish bakers, considered the worst off of the city's bakers, successfully negotiated for a nine-hour day in 1910. By 1919, eighty-seven percent of bakers nationwide worked nine hours a day or less and only three percent of bakers worked more than ten hours a day.[146] Meanwhile, the Bakeshop Act's sanitary provisions were unaffected by the *Lochner* decision, and indeed new legislation in 1906 strengthened them.[147] A 1909 article in the *New York Sun* proclaimed that thanks to modern technology, New York's bakeries were now sanitary, with their employees working reasonable hours.[148]

Of course, interested observers understood that the *Lochner* decision's ramifications could reach well beyond the issue of bakers' hours, and the decision provoked strong reactions. Historians have asserted that *Lochner* was subject to nearly "unanimous criticism,"[149] but that's far from true. While the decision eventually provoked some famous critiques, of the eight law review articles to comment on *Lochner* shortly after it was released, seven supported it, some vigorously.[150] For example, the *Albany Law Journal* editorialized that the Supreme Court was "unquestionabl[y]" right.[151] The *Central Law Journal*'s editors exclaimed that "the decision gives us personally intense satisfaction."[152]

Also contrary to historical myth, newspaper editorial commentary on *Lochner* was generally supportive.[153] The *New York Times* praised the Supreme Court for refusing to enforce "any contracts which may have been made between the demagogues in the Legislature and the ignoramuses among the labor leaders in bringing to naught their combined machinations."[154] The *New York Sun* defended the Court's decision, noting that the Constitution protects both employers and employees from government interference with their ability to contract to their satisfaction.[155] The *Washington Post* argued that the liberty of contract between employer and employee protected in *Lochner* "is a principle older than the Constitution or the statutes. Its maintenance is indispensable to the preservation of liberty."[156] The *Los Angeles Times* published two editorials praising *Lochner*.[157] The *Nation* opined that the decision's main effect "will be to stop the subterfuge by which, under the pretext of conserving the public health, the unionists have sought to delimit the competition of non-unionists, and so to establish a quasi-monopoly of many important kinds of labor."[158] The *Brooklyn Standard Union* stated that the opinion "places the freedom of the citizen above the power of the states. . . . It saves the minority from a tyrannical majority."[159] *World's Work* magazine suggested that *Lochner* was "a sort of warning, a danger signal, to the labor organizations and all others, that the individual has certain inalienable rights which cannot be legislated away from him."[160] The *Dallas Morning News* editorialized that the "right to contract is one of the most sacred rights of the freeman, and any interference with such privilege by Legislatures or courts is essentially dangerous and vicious."[161] The *Brooklyn Eagle* defended the Court's judgment that "every man be permitted to work out his own destiny with an assurance of freedom from interference."[162] The *Buffalo Commercial, Chicago Tribune, Cleveland World, New York Post, New York Press, New York Tribune, Baltimore Sun, Baltimore News, Philadelphia Inquirer*, and *Philadelphia Record* also praised the decision.[163]

In contrast, the *Lochner* ruling met with immediate condemnation in Progressive and labor union circles,[164] and in a minority of mainstream newspapers including the *Binghamton Press, Brooklyn Times, Brooklyn Citizen, Kansas City Journal, New York Mail and Express, New York World, Philadelphia Press*, and *Sacramento Bee*.[165] The *Milwaukee News* editorialized that the decision "leaves the exploiters of men free to grind the last drop of sweat from their bodies, and to coin the blood of workers into dollars without hindrance."[166]

Unless newspaper editorial opinion radically diverged from public opinion, the editorial reaction suggests that the traditional *Lochner* storyline of a deeply unpopular Supreme Court decision disconnected from public sentiment is exaggerated.[167] Historians, however, have focused on the views of labor union activists and Progressive reformers, to the exclusion of *Lochner* supporters.

Progressive legal scholars were among the most prominent critics of *Lochner* and other judicial decisions applying the liberty of contract doctrine to invalidate legislation. This is hardly surprising because, as we shall see in the next chapter, post-*Lochner* Progressive jurists consistently supported regulation for the purported public good at the expense of judicial protection of constitutional rights, and preferred centralized government control over many aspects of American life to liberal "individualism."

CHAPTER THREE

Progressive Sociological Jurisprudence

Since the early twentieth century, critics have focused on the jurisprudential, ideological, and practical weaknesses of *Lochner* and other liberty
of contract cases. Constitutional protection for liberty of contract, whether
in the relatively radical version advanced by Justices Peckham and Brewer
or the sparer version espoused by Justice Harlan and others, has found few
defenders. To fairly assess the liberty of contract doctrine in historical context, however, one must consider the contemporary practical alternative:
the constitutional ideology of liberty of contract's Progressive opponents.

To do so, it's necessary to avoid the tendency to superimpose modern
ideological divisions on to the debates of past generations, and therefore to
assume that early-twentieth-century Progressives were ideological twins of
modern "liberals," and that liberty of contract proponents shared a constitutional vision with modern "conservatives." Not all jurists with Progressive inclinations were on the political left, and among those who were, few
had sensibilities similar to the liberal Earl Warrens and William Brennans of
a later period. Leading legal Progressives were hostile or indifferent to many
of the priorities of modern liberals, especially regarding what came to be
known as civil liberties and civil rights. Indeed, Progressives typically did
not distinguish among different categories of rights. They instead thought
that the very notion of inherent individual rights against the state was a
regressive notion with roots in reactionary natural rights ideology.

Later chapters of this book will discuss the generally illiberal stance
taken by elite Progressive attorneys and their allies in constitutional battles
over equality for women workers, housing segregation, educational freedom,
and coercive eugenics. This chapter will examine the general constitutional
ideology of leading Progressive jurists, especially a highly influential group

of Progressive judges and law professors associated with Harvard Law School, including Louis Brandeis, Felix Frankfurter, Learned Hand, and Roscoe Pound.[1] This group adopted Justice Oliver Wendell Holmes, and later Brandeis, as its standard-bearers on the Supreme Court. Two themes emerge from this chapter: first, the Progressive legal commentators pioneered a tendentious account of *Lochner* and other liberty of contract cases, and, second, Progressive legal elites' support for "sociological jurisprudence" often masked a political agenda that favored a significant increase in government involvement in American economic and social life.

The rise of the liberty of contract doctrine met with significant resistance among elite lawyers, especially those affiliated with Harvard. Some critics argued for a narrow interpretation of the Fourteenth Amendment. An 1889 *Harvard Law Review* article contended that the amendment was intended to apply only to freed slaves. The author argued that the Due Process Clause therefore permitted just about any regulation of property that did not explicitly discriminate against African Americans.[2]

Charles Shattuck, who later became a judge in Boston, won a prize for the best essay written by a member of the Harvard Law School class of 1890 for an article arguing that the Due Process Clause protects only procedural rights.[3] Shattuck contended that the idea that the Due Process Clause creates a "right to follow any lawful calling," had "little real foundation either in history or principle." Prominent Philadelphia attorney Richard McMurtrie, writing in 1893, deemed a broad constitutional right to liberty of contract "utterly absurd."[4] *Allgeyer v. Lousiana*, the first Supreme Court case to invoke liberty of contract while invalidating a law under the Due Process Clause, provoked a new spate of articles in the *Harvard Law Review* and elsewhere asserting that the clause should be construed very narrowly.[5]

Other critics of the emerging liberty of contract doctrine took issue with the prevailing natural rights/historicist perspective on constitutional law, and argued in favor of judicial deference to legislation. Harvard Law School professor James Bradley Thayer insisted that courts should only invalidate legislation "when those who have the right to make laws have not merely made a mistake, but have made a very clear one,—so clear that it is not open to rational question."[6] Thayer influenced generations of students, including Louis Brandeis and Learned Hand.[7] Thayer's colleague John Chipman Gray argued that law is created by societies to suit their needs, so courts should abandon the notion of immutable natural rights.[8] William D. Lewis emphasized that some powers naturally belong to the legislature and should be considered granted if not expressly withheld.[9]

This opposition to constitutional protection of natural rights and support for judicial deference to legislation never became a full-fledged intellectual movement, but its premises were incorporated into sociological jurisprudence.[10] The rise of sociological jurisprudence was spurred to a significant degree by the *Lochner* decision. Progressives and labor activists had vigorously objected to state court decisions invalidating labor regulations, but they had been relieved that the Supreme Court consistently voted to uphold labor and other reformist legislation.[11] *Lochner* suggested to Progressives that the Supreme Court had joined the forces of reaction.[12]

Roscoe Pound launched the sociological jurisprudence movement with a series of influential attacks on the Supreme Court's nascent liberty of contract jurisprudence. Pound ignored the longstanding free labor and anti-class legislation traditions, and instead took Holmes's polemical dissent in *Lochner* literally.[13] Pound claimed that the Supreme Court began with a "conception" that the Fourteenth Amendment "was intended to incorporate Spencer's *Social Statics* in the fundamental law of the United States." From that premise, Pound claimed, the Court deduced rules "that obstruct the way of social progress."[14]

Even though Justice Peckham's *Lochner* opinion explicitly stated that the Court's view of the relative healthfulness of baking was informed by "looking through statistics regarding all trades and occupations,"[15] Pound and his fellow Progressives lambasted *Lochner* as the product of "mechanical" or "conceptualist" jurisprudence that ignored scientific knowledge about the health effects of long hours on bakers.[16] The doctrine of liberty of contract, according to Pound, was based on "a logical deduction" without regard to the effect "when applied to the actual situation." The Court therefore did not recognize that by enforcing "liberty of contract," it actually destroyed the liberty of workers.[17]

According to Pound and other advocates of sociological jurisprudence, law's purpose is to achieve social aims. Legal rules, including constitutional rights, cannot be deduced from first principles.[18] Judges should therefore consider the public interest and "social facts" when interpreting the Constitution. Because modern industrialized society required increased government regulation, the scope of the states' police power must be interpreted to accommodate this need. Pound added that legislatures relying on expert opinion and taking into account social conditions, not courts limited to legal briefing and oral argument, were in the best position to balance constitutional rights against the needs of the community.[19] Judges should therefore defer to legislation.

Legal Progressives also believed that when deciding constitutional cases with social import, judges should not rely on traditional interpretive tools such as precedent, analysis of the Framers' intent, and concern for protecting individual rights and limiting state power.[20] With the notable exception of Princeton political scientist Edward Corwin, through the mid-1920s Progressive critics of the Supreme Court devoted little effort to arguing that the Court had perverted the intent of the Framers of the Fourteenth Amendment.[21] Progressives instead lambasted the Court for engaging in blind, inflexible originalism and relying on abstract notions of rights.[22] Felix Frankfurter, for example, criticized the courts for relying on "eighteenth-century conceptions of 'liberty and equality.' "[23]

Pound derided inflexible jurisprudential theories like originalism because they fail to respond to changing times. He contended that legal rules should be only a "general guide" to the judge, who should be free "within wide limits to deal with the individual case."[24] One advocate of sociological jurisprudence defined it as "a square recognition by the courts that the constitutionality of social and economic legislation depended in the last analysis upon the actual existence or nonexistence of social or economic conditions justifying such legislation." At the very least, Felix Frankfurter argued, courts must consider the relevant social science data before overruling a legislature that had access to such data. Thomas Reed Powell added that "abstract legal freedom" must give way to considerations of "social policy."[25]

While sociological jurisprudence ultimately came to be associated with legal Progressivism, its underlying rationale did not inherently require judicial deference to legislation. Constitutional law scholar and treatise author Christopher Tiedeman shared many intellectual influences and philosophical positions with adherents of sociological jurisprudence.[26] Perhaps most surprisingly, Tiedeman denied that the Constitution had a fixed meaning. Instead, he shared the sociological view that constitutional law can and should evolve by judicial decision-making based on changes in public opinion and social knowledge. Unlike advocates of sociological jurisprudence, however, Tiedeman thought that the public interest required judicial enforcement of strict limits on the states' police powers. By the first decade of the twentieth century, however, the laissez-faire vision of radical classical liberals like Tiedeman had lost much of its political and intellectual influence. In elite legal circles the Progressive version of sociological jurisprudence emerged dominant, and Tiedeman's influence quickly faded.[27]

Historians disagree on how to interpret Progressivism, and even on whether Progressivism, as such, can be described as a coherent movement.[28] And while the term "progressive" today is often used as a synonym for "left-leaning politically," the Progressivism of the early twentieth century accommodated a significant percentage of prominent individuals who would have blanched at such a description, such as Theodore Roosevelt.[29] But Progressives had at least one thing in common: a commitment to activist government to promote their vision of the common good, and a concomitant impatience, at best, with competing claims of individual right.[30] Opposition to libertarian notions of limited government united trust busters, labor reformers, eugenicists, prohibitionists, and others under the banner of progressive reform.

Many leading Progressive thinkers perceived the primary barrier to their success to be American "individualism"—shorthand for a legal and political system focused on individual rights, especially property and contract rights.[31] Legal Progressives like Pound and Learned Hand shared the general Progressive hostility to individualism. Hand wrote that he "especially deplored" the idea that due process of law "embalms individualistic doctrines of a hundred years ago."[32]

Progressive lawyers believed that judges' legalistic constitutional justifications for invalidating reform legislation masked their underlying individualistic policy preferences.[33] These Progressives thought that these preferences were based on a misunderstanding about the practical realities of markets and regulations. Specifically, they believed that judges who enforced the liberty of contract doctrine wrongly believed that workers could negotiate on reasonably equal terms with their employers, when in fact workers' lack of bargaining power allowed employers to take advantage of them.[34]

Judges' refusal to acknowledge their (incorrect) background assumptions so that they could be corrected by Progressive reformers justified stripping them of their discretion. Hand and Frankfurter both wrote unsigned editorials for *The New Republic* calling for the repeal of the Fifth and Fourteenth Amendments' due process clauses. Privately, Justice Brandeis supported repeal of the entire Fourteenth Amendment.[35]

While in theory sociological jurisprudence constituted a coherent philosophy of law independent of political considerations, in practice it generally served as a jurisprudential justification for its Progressive advocates' political and ideological commitments.[36] Most advocates of sociological jurisprudence were primarily motivated by their desire that reformist legislation, especially legislation regulating the labor market, have a near-absolute presumption of constitutionality.

Progressive lawyers' majoritarianism is evident in their treatment of the dissents in *Lochner*. In criticizing *Lochner*, Pound called for "effective judicial investigation or consideration of the situations of fact behind or bearing upon the statutes," with special attention, and deference, to the legislature's rationale for passing the laws in question.[37] According to this standard, Harlan's *Lochner* dissent was a model sociological opinion. Harlan called for deference to the legislature, and cited highly relevant scientific and medical reports—"social facts"—to show that the statute was within New York's police power. Yet Pound and other leading advocates of sociological jurisprudence largely ignored this opinion, perhaps because of Harlan's controversial 1908 opinion in *Adair v. United States*. In *Adair*, Harlan relied on the liberty of contract doctrine to author an opinion invalidating a federal ban on "yellow dog" contracts that prohibited railroad employees from joining labor unions. Pound's famous attack on liberty of contract in the *Yale Law Journal* began by lambasting this opinion.[38]

Instead of praising Harlan's "sociological" opinion in *Lochner*, Progressive legal scholars reserved their approbation for Justice Holmes's caustic dissent. The dissent made Holmes the intellectual leader of Progressives concerned about constitutional law.[39] Historian Charles Beard, for example, effused that Holmes's opinion was "a flash of lightning [in] the dark heavens of juridicial logic." Benjamin Cardozo asserted that Holmes's dissent was "the beginning of an era. . . . [I]t has become the voice of a new dispensation, which has written itself into law."[40] In 1915, *The New Republic* praised Holmes's "classic" *Lochner* dissent.[41]

While Holmes's dissent is widely regarded even today as extraordinarily well-written and rhetorically powerful, it contained no sociological references, nor any discussion of "social facts." Holmes did not address the health of bakers, and, unlike Harlan, he cited no medical or scientific reports to buttress his opinion. Pound nevertheless proclaimed in 1908 that Holmes's dissent was the best extant example of sociological jurisprudence.[42]

Holmes's *Lochner* dissent marked the beginning of his status as a Progressive idol. He further thrilled Progressives with his 1911 majority opinion in *Noble State Bank v. Haskell*. He wrote that the states' police power may be used "in aid of what is sanctioned by usage, or held by the prevailing morality or strong and preponderant opinion to be greatly and immediately necessary to the public welfare."[43]

The same year as *Haskell*, Holmes wrote a curious and particularly insensitive dissent in *Bailey v. Alabama*.[44] In the decades after slavery ended, southern planters lobbied for a variety of laws that would help them control African American workers. Among these were false pretenses laws, which made it a criminal offense to breach a labor contract.[45] After several false pretenses laws had been invalidated or construed narrowly by federal and state courts, Alabama enacted a law that created a presumption of fraudulent intent whenever a worker breached a labor contract after receiving an advance from his employer. An accused laborer was not permitted to testify "as to his uncommunicated motives, purpose, or intention." The Supreme Court invalidated this law, holding that it effectively criminalized ordinary breach of contract.

Justice Holmes, however, vigorously dissented. He began his decision with the antisociological observation "that this case is to be considered and decided in the same way as if it arose in Idaho or New York. . . . and therefore the fact that in Alabama it mainly concerns the blacks does not matter." He concluded with a strong defense of false pretenses laws that ignored their use to suppress African American workers.[46]

In short, what legal Progressives who showered Holmes with adulation chose to celebrate were not sociological opinions that grappled with the underlying factual questions presented by reform legislation while still exhibiting deference to the legislature. Rather, Progressive jurists embraced majoritarian opinions written by a justice with an obvious and self-proclaimed disdain for facts.[47]

Holmes basked in the favorable attention he received from young Progressive intellectuals after *Lochner*. This attention was undoubtedly gratifying, given Holmes's huge ego and his position as an outlier on the Court. Holmes was a democrat, however, not because he was a Progressive but because he saw democracy as a relatively peaceful way for individuals to engage in the Darwinian struggle for survival.[48] Despite the praise he received from Progressives, Holmes had no interest in being a pioneer of sociological jurisprudence.[49]

Pound nevertheless wrote many years later that sociological jurisprudence "begins with Holmes." Frankfurter wrote in 1916 that Holmes's due process opinions were "the outstanding characteristic of constitutional history in the last decade" and that "to discuss Mr. Justice Holmes's opinions is to string pearls." Learned Hand practically worshipped Holmes. Yale Law School professor Jerome Frank, who was devoted to Freudian theory, deemed Holmes to be "The Completely Adult Jurist," who has "put away childish longings for a father-controlled world" and attained "an adult emotional status, a self-reliant, fearless approach to life." Holmes therefore "can afford not to use his authority as if he, himself, were a strict father."[50]

Holmes's lack of interest in promoting or adhering to sociological jurisprudence suited Progressives so long as he shared their indifference to individual rights and support for deference to legislative majorities.[51] Pound, for example, was clearly exercised by the "individualism" of the majority opinion in *Lochner*. According to Pound, the Court had a warped conception of liberty. Freedom of contract in the hands of "weak and necessitous" bakers, he wrote, "defeats the very end of liberty."[52] And while Pound accused the majority of ignoring relevant facts, his discussion of *Lochner* shows no awareness of the "social facts" in the baking industry in New York that made the battle over the hours law far more complicated than a simplistic "labor versus capital" paradigm would suggest.[53]

Pound and others reconciled their majoritarianism with "sociological" considerations by arguing that only legislatures could fully account for "social facts." Courts, by contrast, either lacked the proper resources to do so, or were not so inclined.[54]

The legacy of the critiques by Pound and others of *Lochner* and its progeny is the familiar association of the *Lochner* line of cases with judicial "formalism" and mechanical deduction.[55] All rules-based systems are "formalist" to some degree, but *Lochner* and other liberty of contract cases fail to betray a reliance on the rigid, mechanical formalism, unconcerned with social consequences, alleged by Pound and others.[56] The battle between advocates of liberty of contract and their Progressive opponents was not primarily one of formalists vs. antiformalists, but of people who thought there were inherent (and judicially enforceable) limits on government power against legal positivists, majoritarians, and opponents of "judicial oligarchy."[57]

Pound also attacked the *Lochner* majority for its purported "Darwinism"—assumedly for adopting what he considered a survival of the fittest, laissez-faire mentality.[58] Yet any Darwinism, "social" or otherwise, in the *Lochner* majority opinion is at best obscure, and Pound's hero Holmes was likely the *Lochner* Court's only true Social Darwinist.[59]

Evolutionary theory directly influenced sociological jurisprudence via two routes besides Holmes. First, Pound's mentors Edward Ross and Lester Ward were Progressive Darwinists who believed in using law as an instrument of social control.[60] Pound had an advanced degree in botany (as did Ward), and was therefore naturally inclined to see the world in evolutionary terms.[61] He defined jurisprudence as a "science of social engineering."[62]

Second, influential Progressives approached constitutional theory from an evolutionist perspective. Woodrow Wilson, for example, wrote that "all that progressives ask or desire is permission—in an era when 'development,' 'evolution,' is the scientific word—to interpret the Constitution according to the Darwinian principle."[63] Wilson wrote that the primary flaw in the Founders' theory of government was that they failed to understand that government "is not a machine, but a living thing. . . . It is accountable to Darwin, not to Newton."[64]

Ironically, the proponents of the *Lochner* line of cases, and not *Lochner's* Progressive enemies, have come to be defamed as "Social Darwinists." In part, this reflects sloppiness by scholars who misconstrued Holmes' *Lochner* dissent. As discussed in chapter 2, when Holmes accused the majority of thinking that the Fourteenth Amendment enacted "Mr. Herbert Spencer's *Social Statics,*" he was referring to Spencer's libertarian political views—not, as generations of commentators have since assumed, Social Darwinism.

Mostly, however, the association of liberty of contract with Social Darwinism is a product of the legal academy's absorption of historians' exaggeration of the connection between Social Darwinism and late-nineteenth-century American "conservative" economic and legal thought, an exaggeration that has been undermined by recent revisionist scholarship.[65] Biologically grounded social thought—which had led many leading Progressives to endorse imperialism, scientific racism, and coercive eugenics—was broadly discredited after Nazi atrocities justified by "science" were revealed.[66] Naturally, post–World War II liberal legal scholars preferred that such social thought be associated with constitutional traditionalists, and not with the Progressives they admired.[67]

As the Progressives' influence grew in the early twentieth century, they increasingly became overtly hostile to the Constitution—which in their eyes represented anachronistic liberal individualism—and to judicial review.[68] Elite Progressive lawyers, not surprisingly, were less hostile to these institutions than were their non-attorney peers. Progressive lawyers instead focused their ire on what they considered the courts' inflexible and doctrinaire enforcement of various constitutional provisions that limited government power. These lawyers had one important standard with which to judge contemporary constitutional law: the extent to which the Constitution was interpreted as a "bar to the adoption of . . . important social reform measures."[69]

The hostility to the Supreme Court that elite Progressive attorneys exhibited after *Lochner*, *Adair*, and several other decisions deemed "anti-labor" soon waned. One year after *Lochner* was decided, Justice Henry Brown, a member of the *Lochner* majority, left the Court. Justice William Moody, Brown's replacement, was strongly inclined to uphold labor legislation.[70] By 1911 Brewer and Peckham, the Court's strongest proponents of liberty of contract, were off the Court, as were the swing voters Fuller and Harlan. Their replacements were overall significantly more in tune with Progressive sensibilities.

Despite Theodore Roosevelt's attacks on *Lochner* in his 1912 Progressive Party presidential campaign,[71] by the middle of the decade elite legal

Progressives were generally satisfied with the Supreme Court, including its due process decisions, which overall were deferential to the police power. In 1913 one Progressive professor deemed *Lochner* an "unfortunate lapse" by a Court that otherwise took a "liberal attitude toward legislation aimed to meet new social and industrial needs."[72] That same year, Charles Warren published two well-cited articles defending the Court's "progressiveness."[73] A year later, the Progressive journal *Outlook* praised the "Great Court."[74] Felix Frankfurter asserted in 1916 that *Lochner* "does not in itself furnish the yardstick" to determine the constitutionality of protective legislation, and "is no longer controlling."[75] *Lochner* seemed to be an "activist island in a sea of judicial restraint."[76]

Congress altered the Supreme Court's jurisdiction in 1914 to allow the Court to review judgments from state courts invalidating state statutes as violations of the federal Constitution.[77] It did so because it saw the Court as a check on state courts that were invalidating reformist legislation, especially labor legislation.[78] Over the next several years, the Court upheld virtually every labor regulation that came before it. What later became known as the *Lochner* era seemed more aptly described as the *Lochner* moment.[79]

In the early 1920s, however, the Supreme Court became much more aggressive about invalidating novel state regulations. Wilson appointee James McReynolds, Taft appointee Willis Van DeVanter, and Harding appointees George Sutherland and Pierce Butler dominated the Court through the early 1930s through alliances with various other justices, especially Harding appointees William Howard Taft and Edward Sanford. New Deal supporters caricatured them as the "Four Horsemen"—as in "of the apocalypse." Contrary to myth, however, they did not always vote as a bloc and did not always vote for recognizably "conservative" outcomes.[80]

In 1923 the Supreme Court froze and formalized various doctrinal exceptions to liberty of contract, such as the government's virtual carte blanche to regulate businesses "affected with a public interest."[81] A majority also announced that "freedom of contract is . . . the general rule and restraint the exception, and the exercise of legislative authority to abridge it can be justified only by the existence of exceptional circumstances."[82] The Court acknowledged that government regulation could be used for traditional police power purposes. Beyond that, it explained that precedent limited legislative interference with liberty of contract primarily to laws (1) "fixing rates and charges to be exacted by businesses impressed with a public interest"; (2) "relating to contracts for the performance of public work"; (3) "prescribing the character, methods, and time for payment of wages"; and (4) "fixing hours of labor" to preserve the health and safety for workers or the public at large.[83] The upshot was that the Court retained the established exceptions to liberty of contract, but limited their scope to prevent further erosion of individual liberty, one of Chief Justice Taft's key goals.[84]

From 1923 through 1934, the Court invalidated what it deemed to be unfair regulation of the use of real property, confiscatory regulation of utility rates, arbitrary regulations of private businesses, and unwarranted interference with private education. But it continued to uphold most laws challenged under the Due Process Clause, including such major regulatory innovations as residential zoning.[85]

The regulatory state at all levels of government continued to grow during the 1920s, much to the chagrin of conservative commentators.[86] Clarence Manion, the dean of Notre Dame's law school, complained that "the American citizen now has practically no rights of person or property that neither Congress nor the State legislature may not impair by legislation."[87] Conservatives were especially alarmed at the growth of the concept of a "living Constitution" that changed with the times.[88]

Meanwhile, Justice Brandeis, initially thought to be something of a clone of Holmes, gradually became the leader of the Court's Progressive wing. Brandeis did not share Holmes's disdain for facts, and his opinions thrilled both old Progressives and the younger scholars who ultimately became legal realists.[89] Brandeis's dissent in *New State Ice v. Liebmann* struck a perfect chord for the early Depression period, and led to his canonization among liberal constitutionalists as a worthy successor to the retired Holmes.[90] In *New State Ice*, Brandeis cited research that supported government monopolization of the ice industry, and condemned free-market competition, which he deemed "ruinous."[91]

Despite Brandeis's sharp interest in relatively mundane regulatory matters, critics of the Supreme Court's due process jurisprudence reserved the bulk of their enmity for the Court's controversial decisions invalidating labor laws[92]—first *Lochner* (which the Court implicitly overruled, or at least severely limited, in *Bunting v. Oregon* twelve years later), then the *Adair v. United States* and *Coppage v. Kansas* cases invalidating bans on antiunion yellow dog contracts (which were implicitly overruled in 1930),[93] and finally the 1923 decision invalidating a minimum wage law for women, *Adkins v. Children's Hospital*, which remained valid precedent until 1937.[94] Legal Progressives also sometimes demonized other, lesser-known labor cases, such as *Wolff Packing Co. v. Court of Industrial Relations*.[95]

While these few cases may seem like thin gruel to attract such vitriolic enmity, Progressive critics thought they were a symptom of a broader problem: the Court's hostility to labor unions and its general unwillingness to countenance "modern" labor laws that would promote industrial de-mocracy.[96] Outside the due process context, the Court upheld lower courts' injunctions against strikes, applied antitrust laws to labor unions, upheld criminal contempt proceedings against union leaders who defied judicial rulings, and interpreted Congress's regulatory authority over interstate commerce to forbid federal regulation of child labor.

Not all Progressives were enamored of labor unions, but support for unions was virtually a defining ideological characteristic of leading legal reformers and constitutional theorists such as Brandeis, Frankfurter, Robert Hale and Thomas Reed Powell. In an era when living standards for industrial workers were low, the welfare state was minimal, and large corporations seemed to wield inordinate power that they could use to abuse individ-ual workers, Progressive jurists were convinced that strong labor unions were needed to counterbalance corporate power. Frankfurter provided a rather stark—and to most modern readers, likely surprisingly insensitive—example of the centrality of prounion labor legislation to many Progressive lawyers' political outlook. In his private journal, he wrote that *Adair* and *Coppage* were as bad as the Court's proslavery decision in *Dred Scott*.[97] Pro-gressive critics accused the justices of dogmatism in their lack of solicitude for labor unions. Roscoe Pound caricatured such judges as believing that industrial workers could bargain over their terms of employment as if they "were farmers haggling over the sale of a horse."[98]

The Supreme Court, however, routinely acknowledged that legislation meant to redress bargaining power disparities between employers and em-ployees was a constitutionally legitimate police power function. In the lead-ing case, *Holden v. Hardy*, Justice Brown wrote for a 7–2 majority that upheld a maximum-hours law for miners that "the proprietors of these establish-ments and their operatives do not stand upon an equality, and that their interests are, to a certain extent, conflicting." The "proprietors lay down the rules, and the laborers are practically constrained to obey them." In such cases, Brown wrote, "the legislature may properly interpose its authority."[99]

Over the next two decades, the Supreme Court upheld many additional ameliorative labor laws.[100] In 1917 it upheld four very controversial labor reforms: workers' compensation laws, a federal law that limited railroad workers to an eight-hour day and fixed wages at the level the workers had received when working longer hours, a minimum-wage law for women (in a 4–4 split with Justice Brandeis recused), and a maximum-hours law for all industrial workers.[101] The only major discontinuity in this pattern of defer-ential decisions, *Lochner*, involved an owner of a small local bakery who had little more economic wherewithal than his employees.[102]

Unlike legal Progressives, however, a majority of the justices were not persuaded that the Progressives' other proposed cure for inequalities in bargaining power—government nurturing of labor unions—was either beneficial to workers or constitutional. The Court therefore refused to defer to laws directly benefiting labor unions. *Adair* and *Coppage* in particular signaled that the Court had a very different view of labor unions than did its Progressive critics.[103]

Progressive lawyers were heavily influenced by the views of Progressive economists, who believed that in the absence of strong unions representing employees, corporations could hold wages and working conditions down to a subsistence level.[104] Progressive legal reformers therefore believed that patchwork regulatory interventions were not sufficient to protect workers; labor unions needed to be nurtured to give "labor" more bargaining power with "capital."[105]

Leading Progressives frequently conflated the interests of workers as a whole with the interest of labor union members, and had little patience for those who didn't share their perspective. Herbert Croly, whose *New Republic* frequently published essays and editorials by Felix Frankfurter, Learned Hand, and other leading Progressive lawyers, wrote that the "nonunion industrial laborer . . . should be rejected as emphatically if not as ruthlessly as the gardener rejects the weeds in his garden for the benefit of fruit and flower-bearing plants."[106]

The fact that the labor movement was dominated by American Federation of Labor craft unions and the Railroad Brotherhoods—which not only represented only a fraction of American workers but typically excluded African Americans, women and sometimes aliens—made no impression on Croly and like-minded Progressives.[107] Support for discriminatory unions did not necessarily reflect hostility to minority groups and women. But it did at least suggest either that the supporters were indifferent to the concerns of the excluded groups, or that they believed the immediate interests of those groups had to be sacrificed to the broader long-term interests of the labor movement.[108]

A stable majority of justices, meanwhile, saw labor unions as potentially self-serving monopolistic organizations that could threaten the freedom of both individual workers and their employers, just as monopolistic corporations threatened small businesses and consumers.[109] While public opinion data does not exist for this time period, such views seem to have been held by a substantial portion of the general public, and were especially prevalent among those who were excluded from most unions, such as African Americans.[110]

In the Court's view, prounion laws like bans on yellow dog contracts did not satisfy the police power because such legislation did not directly ameliorate working conditions. The justices believed that upholding liberty of contract and preventing government-imposed or -endorsed union monopoly was crucial for the long-term prosperity of workers, because the ability of workers to sell their labor in a free marketplace was their primary asset. In *Coppage v. Kansas*, the 1915 yellow dog contract case, Justice Mahlon Pitney wrote for the Court that "the right [to liberty of contract] is as essential to the laborer as to the capitalist, to the poor as to the rich; for the vast majority of persons have no other honest way to begin to acquire property, save by working for money."[111]

The conflict between Progressive jurists and the Supreme Court, then, was not over the question of whether inequality of bargaining power could justify government regulation of labor markets, but over the appropriate remedy. The Court's critics advocated union-led social democracy in place of a regime of general contractual freedom. A majority of justices, by contrast, approved of ameliorative legislation directly addressing what they saw as oppressive corporate labor practices, but believed that preserving a general presumption of liberty of contract not only was constitutionally required but also served workers' interests.

Progressive legal scholars also strongly objected to the Court's use of the due process clauses to invalidate minimum-wage laws, beginning with *Adkins v. Children's Hospital* in 1923.[112] Justices opposed to such laws provided two plausible public policy reasons why minimum-wage laws were problematic. First, they noted that such laws would exclude from the labor market individuals who could not command the government-dictated minimum.[113] Second, they argued that minimum-wage laws would ultimately backfire on workers because if government may establish a minimum, it may establish a maximum—a concern shared by American Federation of Labor president Samuel Gompers.[114]

By contrast, leading Progressive economists supported minimum-wage legislation not *despite* but in part *because* they understood that it would lead to increased unemployment among women, members of minority groups, immigrants, the elderly, the disabled, and other "out" groups that were less likely to be able to command the minimum wage.[115] Many economists believed that some or all of these categories of workers were improperly driving down wages for worthy, native white male (preferably of Anglo-Saxon or Germanic origin) heads of households who needed to earn a "family wage."[116] Society needed to exclude from the labor market "defective" workers who could not command the government-dictated minimum.

Elite Progressive lawyers who defended minimum-wage laws in court tended to be much more sympathetic to the concerns of minority groups than were Progressive economists. Nevertheless, a milder version of the economists' reasoning found its way into Supreme Court briefs in minimum-wage cases. For example, Felix Frankfurter defended a minimum-wage law for women in part by arguing that "the state . . . may use means, like the present statute, of sorting the normal self-supporting workers from the unemployables and then deal with the latter appropriately as a special class, instead of an indiscriminate, unscientific lumping of all workers, with a resulting unscientific confusion of standards."[117] As for concerns about the possibility that the government would use the power it had gained to set minimum wages to also set maximum wages, Progressive reformers pooh-poohed these fears as paranoia at best—what Thomas Reed Powell called in a related context a "parade of imaginary horribles."[118]

The debate between Progressives and their opponents also had an empirical aspect. Progressives were convinced that workers' living standards were falling and in constant danger thanks to unregulated immigration, unregulated labor markets, and a paucity of strong labor unions.[119] Supporters of liberty of contract, by contrast, believed that workers' lot, though often unpleasant, was gradually improving thanks to the American system of contractual freedom.[120]

Also, while most Supreme Court justices displayed at least some skepticism of the honesty and efficacy of state and federal legislators, historian Edward Purcell notes that the Court's Progressive critics "pictured legislatures and their expert administrative agencies relatively abstractly and as they wished them to be, as authentically popular, problem-solving, and even 'scientific' branches of government." Progressives therefore tended to assume that labor reform and other regulations were exclusively public-spirited. By contrast, Progressive legal scholars subjected courts and judges to a "searing realism" leading to withering criticism.[121]

In short, the story we have inherited from Progressive legal scholars is that the Supreme Court was so out of touch with reality that it relied on the "dogma" of liberty of contract and abstract reasoning devoid of social context to deny needed government assistance to workers. The Progressive lawyers failed to recognize that the Court's commitment to constitutional protection for liberty of contract was hardly "dogmatic." They were also largely oblivious of their opponents' coherent, albeit debatable, rationale for their skepticism of certain forms of government intervention into the labor market. This skepticism did not rely on mere ideological abstractions, nor did it neglect to consider the social consequences of judicial decisions.

Nevertheless, as Progressives and their admirers came to dominate the academic world, their understanding of the Court's labor and other due process decisions not only emerged dominant but became more and more exaggerated, until it turned into a morality tale of good-hearted, far-sighted Progressives battling evil Supreme Court reactionaries. Just as the story of *Lochner v. New York* itself has been grossly distorted into a tale of struggling workers versus big business supported by the Supreme Court, the received wisdom regarding the broader battle between Progressive lawyers and their "conservative" opponents amounts to a facile "government regulation good, Supreme Court intervention bad" interpretation of constitutional history.

Ironically, despite the calumny heaped on the due process liberty of contract decisions and the Supreme Court justices who wrote them, modern constitutional jurisprudence implicitly (and sometimes explicitly) draws a great deal from pre–New Deal due process decisions rejecting novel assertions of government power. Indeed, as we shall see in the next several chapters, Lochnerian protection of liberty of contract was invoked to justify some of the most significant early decisions expanding constitutional protections for the rights of African Americans and women and for civil liberties, often over the strong opposition of Justice Holmes and his Progressive allies. Modern "liberal" constitutional jurisprudence, rather than being directly descended solely from the ideas of early-twentieth-century Progressive jurists, is a synthesis of Progressive fondness for government economic regulation, and the classical liberal ("conservative") support for individual rights and skepticism of government power reflected in the liberty of contract cases.

CHAPTER FOUR

Sex Discrimination and Liberty of Contract

As the United States rapidly urbanized at the end of the nineteenth cen-tury, American women increasingly found industrial and other non-traditional employment outside the home. Calls for legislation to protect women from long hours and low wages soon followed. Over the next several decades many states enacted maximum-hours and minimum-wage laws that applied only to women workers. From the 1890s to the 1930s, litigants disputed these laws' constitutionality, with mixed results. Opponents of sex-based labor laws denounced them not only as violations of liberty of contract but as violations of women's right to legal equality. In the process of abandoning meaningful constitutional protection of liberty of contract in the 1930s, the Supreme Court held that women-only labor laws were permissible. This precedent survived for decades.

The fierce battle in the early twentieth century over the constitutional-ity of protective labor laws for women was an outgrowth of the broader bat-tle over the rise of the liberty of contract doctrine. Initially, the Fourteenth Amendment seemed unquestionably to permit sex-based labor legislation. The amendment not only failed to specifically guarantee equal legal rights for women, but also contains the first explicit sex-specific clause in the Constitution, protecting men's right to vote.

In 1873, the Supreme Court upheld Illinois' refusal to license women to practice law.[1] Three of the dissenting justices in the *Slaughter-House Cases*,[2] all of whom had vigorously argued that the Privileges or Immunities Clause protected *men's* right to earn a living free from government-established mo-nopoly, concurred in the ruling. These justices declared that "the natural and proper timidity and delicacy which belongs to the female sex evidently unfits it for many of the occupations of civil life . . . the paramount destiny and mission of woman are to fulfill the noble and benign offices of wife and mother."[3] If Illinois could entirely ban women from becoming lawyers, sex-based protective laws that simply regulated their employment seemed even less vulnerable to constitutional challenge. In 1876, the Massachusetts Supreme Court upheld a law limiting women employed by manufacturing concerns to ten hours of work per day. The court reasoned that the statute was an appropriate means of protecting worker health.[4]

As the liberty of contract doctrine spread in the state courts, however, sex-based protective laws became vulnerable to challenge as a violation of that liberty. *Ritchie v. People* involved a challenge to an Illinois law, supported by a broad coalition of reform groups, limiting women to an eight-hour work day.[5] The case reached the state supreme court in 1895. Illinois argued that women's physical weakness compared to men, combined with women's unique role in childbearing, justified the law as a health measure.[6] The plaintiffs' attorney responded that the law deprived women of their right to make a living, and that "women have equal rights with men to the protection of the Constitution . . . includ[ing] the right to work as they choose." The brief cited the testimony of several of the intended beneficiaries of the law, who complained that their wages had fallen dramatically with their hours and that they could no longer support their families.[7]

The court unanimously invalidated the law. Maximum-hours laws, it asserted, infringed on the right to liberty of contract. Such laws could only be upheld if the state provided a valid police power reason to justify this infringement. States may protect workers who might injure themselves or others, but they could not create a blanket distinction between male and female workers. Women, the court wrote, "are entitled to the same rights under the Constitution to make contracts with reference to their labor as are secured thereby to men. . . . Her right to choice of vocations cannot be said to be denied or abridged on account of sex."[8]

Ritchie outraged reformers such as Florence Kelley, the primary author of, lobbyist for, and ultimately enforcement officer of Illinois' maximum-hours law.[9] She exclaimed that "the measure to guarantee the Negro freedom from oppression [the Fourteenth Amendment] has become an insuperable obstacle to the protection of women and children."[10] Kelley's conflation of women and children, even though child labor was not an issue in the case, is telling; under the common law, women and children were considered wards of the state, inherently subject to police power regulation.

Boston attorney F. J. Stimson, by contrast, wrote that "women are citizens, capable of making their own contracts; particularly in states where they have the right of suffrage, such legislation restricting their hours of labor is unconstitutional." Stimson deemed laws singling out women for

special restrictions to be "class legislation of the worst sort."[11] A representative of the Illinois Manufacturers' Association, which funded the successful
challenge to the law invalidated in *Ritchie*, stated that the decision showed
that "woman is equal to man before the law and that her right to her labor,
which constitutes her property, is as sacred and impregnable as is the similar right of man."[12] The IMA's take on the law was undoubtedly motivated
more by pragmatic self-interest than by egalitarian ideology, but as this and
other examples suggest, opposition to protective laws forced employers and
their lawyers to embrace sexually egalitarian ideals, at least rhetorically.[13]

In 1898, reform organizations formed the National Consumers' League
to lobby for the improvement of industrial standards for workers, especially women workers. Kelley was appointed general secretary and quickly
achieved national prominence in reformist circles.[14] The NCL's efforts were
supported by the newly-formed National Women's Trade Union League.
These groups supported protective legislation for women for contradictory
reasons—both because they thought women workers were easily exploited
and needed special protection, and also as a valuable stepping stone toward
sex-neutral laws that would deny women special protection.[15]

Kelley has sometimes been described as a "social justice feminist,"
which implies that she saw her activist mission in significant part as challenging gender-based hierarchies. In fact, Kelley saw women's labor issues
primarily as a means of promoting socialist goals.[16] She expected that sex-
based protective laws would be an entering wedge for broader legislative
gains for all workers. In turn, the expectation that protective laws for women
would become precedents for broader government interventions into the
labor market encouraged many advocates of liberty of contract for men to
become ardent proponents of such rights for women.

Protective labor legislation for women gained the support of a broad
coalition of Progressive reformers. Advocates of such legislation included
paternalists concerned with women's health; moralists who thought that
low-wage, long-hour jobs tempted women into immorality and prostitu-
tion; "family wage" advocates who sought to protect family men from
"destructive" competition from women workers; "maternalists" who sought
to promote and preserve women's maternal role in the family; and eugenicists who believed that working women "weakened the race."[17] Also, many
Progressives believed that labor unions would ultimately negotiate proper
protection for male workers, but that women were unsuited for unionization.
Women, they noted, were much more likely to take temporary or part-time
jobs that were almost never unionized, to abandon wage employment once

they got married, and to rely on other family members to subsidize their wages. These circumstances made them less inclined than men to fight for better wages and working conditions.[18]

In *Holden v. Hardy* in 1898, the Supreme Court upheld a Utah law mandating a maximum eight-hour day for underground miners.[19] Several state courts subsequently relied on *Holden* in upholding maximum-hours laws for women against constitutional challenges.[20] The Nebraska Supreme Court concluded that women had always been considered "wards of the state," and that therefore their status for constitutional purposes was analogous to that of the "necessitous miners" in *Holden*.[21]

The Supreme Court's *Lochner* ruling invalidating a maximum-hours law for bakers raised new doubts about the constitutionality of laws regulating women's work hours. In *People v. Williams*,[22] the New York Court of Appeals relied on *Lochner* and invalidated a law that prohibited women from working at night. The law attempted not to shorten women's overall hours of labor or improve their working conditions, but simply to ban them from night work based on stereotypical views of women's family obligations. Kelley, for example, opposed women working at night on the grounds that their children were "not mothered, never cherished, they are nagged and buffeted."[23] In fact, however, many women took night work because they desperately needed the money, and working at night was the only way they could work and still take care of their children during the day. The Court of Appeals concluded that "a woman is entitled to enjoy unmolested her liberty of person and her freedom to work for whom she pleases, where she pleases, and as long as she pleases. . . . She is not to be made the special object of the exercise of the paternal power of the state."

The Oregon Supreme Court, in contrast, upheld a ten-hour-day and sixty-hour-week law for women against a challenge from a laundry owner prosecuted under the law, Curt Muller.[24] When Muller appealed to the U.S. Supreme Court with the help of the state Laundry Owners' Association, the fate of all protective laws for women, which had already spread to twenty states, was at stake.[25] Oregon filed a traditional brief focusing on the relevant legal precedents. The brief conceded that the ten-hour law might harm particular workers and employers. Oregon argued, however, that the "welfare of the individual" had to be balanced "against the welfare of the state at large."[26]

Florence Kelley and the National Consumers' League, with the blessing of Oregon's counsel, asked famed Progressive attorney Louis Brandeis to write an additional brief defending the law.[27] Brandeis apparently decided that a frontal attack on *Lochner* was too risky, even though one member of the five-vote majority in that case, Justice Henry Brown, had retired and been replaced by the more Progressive William Moody.[28] Instead, Brandeis resolved to distinguish *Lochner* by showing that women workers were more like the dependent miners of *Holden*, in need of paternalistic state protection, than like the bakers of *Lochner*, who were entitled to liberty of contract.

Lochner, meanwhile, had suggested that maximum-hours laws were permissible if they targeted a health threat recognized either by common knowledge or in the scientific literature.[29] Brandeis, then, needed both to appeal to "common knowledge" about the health effects of long hours on women, and, in case that wasn't persuasive, to present statistical and other evidence in support of restricting women's hours. Brandeis's brief began with an extremely concise legal argument that focused on distinguishing *Lochner*. The rest of the brief attempted to establish and defend "four matters of general knowledge": that (1) women are physically weaker than men, (2) a woman's ill health could damage her reproductive capacity, (3) damage to a woman's health could affect the health of her future offspring, and (4) excess hours of labor for women were harmful to family life.[30] In short, as historian Nancy Woloch concludes, the brief "treats all women as mothers or potential mothers; it either conflates the needs of family and society with those of women or prefers the former to the latter; and it depicts women as weak and defective."[31]

A Brandeis biographer writes that Brandeis's team of researchers, led by his sister-in-law, Josephine Goldmark, transformed "thousands of shards of evidence into a complete, logical statement of the accumulated wisdom on the subject."[32] Other scholars, however, suggest that the brief regurgitated a "hodgepodge" of "junk social science."[33] In any event, the justices did not scrutinize the underlying reliability of Brandeis's evidence, but, as we shall see, found that this evidence simply reinforced conventional wisdom.

Muller's brief, meanwhile, argued that the law at issue was unconstitutional under *Lochner* because like baking, laundry work was not dangerous industrial work and was not considered especially unhealthful.[34] The brief cited *Ritchie* and *Williams* and, like those two opinions, contained a strongly worded appeal for women's equal right to liberty of contract.[35] The brief also challenged the prevailing notion that women didn't need to work, explaining that not all women were "sheltered in happy homes free from the exacting demands" of earning a living. Florence Kelley and her allies argued that to the extent women needed to work, the government was obligated to protect them from exploitation through protective legislation. Muller's lawyers, by contrast, noted that social custom already limited a woman's occupational options, and argued that "her hands" should not "be further tied by statute ostensibly framed in her interests, but intended perhaps to limit and restrict her employment."

Woloch concludes that the *Muller* briefs show that at this point in history, "arguments for freedom of contract and sexual equality were natural allies; they were branches of the same tree, individualism"—or, more precisely, classical liberalism.[36] The briefs reflected the stark conflict between the individualistic, libertarian outlook of *Lochner* and the labor reformers' paternalism and acceptance of women's lack of civic equality. Moreover, protective laws for women were beginning to attract opposition from feminist activists as well as from industrialists and advocates of a limited police power. An Oregon suffragist writing in 1906 in Portland's *Woman's Tribune* objected to the state's hours law because the government "has no right to lay any disability upon woman as an individual."[37]

The Supreme Court upheld the law in an opinion by Justice David Brewer.[38] Brewer was famously libertarian on economic matters.[39] He, along with his colleague Rufus Peckham, consistently dissented from the Court's decisions upholding protective labor legislation. Brewer was also a strong supporter of women's suffrage and contemporary efforts to improve women's status.[40] Nevertheless, like his Progressive counterparts, he believed that paternalism in the employment context was proper. He wrote that "woman's physical structure and the performance of maternal functions place her at a disadvantage in the struggle for subsistence," especially "when the burdens of motherhood are upon her." Prolonged work hours had "injurious effects" on women's bodies and as "healthy mothers are essential to vigorous offspring, the physical well-being of woman becomes an object of public interest and care in order to preserve the strength . . . of the race."[41]

Brewer noted that Brandeis's brief provided additional evidence supporting the "common belief" that long hours of labor were harmful to women and their progeny.[42] While women's legal rights had been extended, "there is that in her disposition and habits of life which will operate against a full assertion of those rights. She will still be where some legislation to protect her seems necessary to secure a real equality of right."[43] Oregon's maximum-hours law was therefore a justified infringement on liberty of contract. Brewer also concluded that the law was not improper class legislation. "Woman," he wrote, is "properly placed in a class by herself, and legislation designed for her protection may be sustained, even when like legislation is not necessary for men and could not be sustained."[44] Later that year, he defended this opinion by arguing that he intended "no disrespect to women," but that "the race needs her, her children need her; her friends need her, in a way that they do not need the other sex."[45]

Brewer's *Muller* opinion won support across the political spectrum, including from sources (such as *The Nation*) that had supported *Lochner*.[46] Brewer's views, today widely seen as regressive in their attitude toward women, were in line with those of Florence Kelley, who wrote: "So long as men cannot be mothers, so long legislation adequate for them can never be adequate for wage-earning women; and the cry Equality, Equality, where Nature has created inequality, is as stupid and as deadly as the cry Peace, Peace where there is no Peace."[47]

The Progressive activists of the National Consumers' League and the National Women's Trade Union League were elated with their victory in *Muller*. The activists believed that protective legislation would empower women to bargain with their employers free from the specter of exploitative hours. The reformers were generally not disturbed by the sexism in the opinion, because it reflected a "maternalist" ideology—emphasizing the importance of women's role as mothers—that the reformers generally shared.[48] For example, the Consumers' League opposed publicly funded day care, government provision of health care to working mothers, and other benefits for working women.[49] Kelley wrote that providing a cash benefit to employed new mothers would amount to "saying to the wage-earning husband: Send your wife in to a mill, factory, or sweatshop, and the public . . . will send you a present for your next baby." Moreover, such a benefit would serve as a "bribe to increased immigration of the kind of men who make their wives and children work."[50] The National Women's Trade Union League's Rose Schneiderman added that "the average working woman" was not concerned about the effects of protective laws on her career because "she is looking forward to getting married and raising a family." Rather than competing with male workers, women workers should cooperate with men "in the struggle for economic justice."[51]

Reformers who did not adopt maternalist ideology, such as many economists associated with the American Association for Labor Legislation, nevertheless supported the outcome in *Muller*.[52] Libertarian or equalitarian qualms over *Muller's* reasoning were considered less important than achieving what the reformers saw as concrete legislative gains for workers.[53] Finally, elite legal reformers were aware that some women workers would likely be harmed by protective legislation. Kurt Muller, for example, apparently fired all his women employees and replaced them with male Chinese.[54] But the reformers thought that such harm was a small price to pay to advance Progressive policies that would benefit women, and eventually all of society.[55] Thomas Reed Powell, for example, wrote that a woman worker threatened with losing her job due to protective legislation must not be regarded "as an isolated individual but as a member of a class . . . the loss to the unemployable is overbalanced by the gain to those whom industry cannot dispense with."[56] Louis Brandeis argued that women who lose their jobs due to legislation were ultimately being done a service. In many cases, he speculated, they would find employment "in occupations where they could be more efficient than the one in which they found themselves," and they also would have an incentive to make themselves "more efficient."[57]

Meanwhile, feminist opposition to protective laws slowly grew. In 1908 Louisa Harding, writing in the Iowa Suffrage Association's journal, condemned *Muller* as an "abominable" decision.[58] Restricting women's work hours, she argued, "practically amounts to confiscation of whatever amount would have been earned during the forbidden hours."[59] Harding wrote in another feminist journal that the true aim of women's labor legislation was not to protect women, but to prevent them from being "enabled in some measure to enjoy the pleasure of an independent life."[60] An editorialist added that "the principle of sex legislation is absolutely wrong and unjust."[61]

Muller settled the constitutionality of maximum-hours laws for women for federal constitutional purposes. The Supreme Court issued several more rulings upholding maximum-hours laws for women, including more draconian eight-hour day laws that threatened to ban women from jobs requiring longer hours, like medical residencies.[62] Opponents of maximum-hours laws also fared badly in state courts after *Muller*. The Illinois Supreme Court reversed *Ritchie* and upheld a new state maximum-hours law.[63] The New York Court of Appeals, meanwhile, reversed *Williams*, while acknowledging that the law "will inflict unnecessary hardships on a great many women who neither ask nor require its provisions."[64]

These and other opinions upholding protective laws for women focused on women's physical differences from men and how those differences affected women's health and the health of their children.[65] The New York Court of Appeals, for example, argued that the government could regulate women's working conditions to ensure "healthy mothers" who could give birth to "vigorous offspring."[66] Many reformers with feminist sympathies would have preferred the courts to instead rely on the perceived need for protection of women workers due to women's inferior socioeconomic position, and the need for government intervention on behalf of workers more generally. Such socioeconomic arguments soon became more prominent, as debate over maximum-hours laws gave way to debate over the constitutionality of women-only minimum-wage laws. The National Consumers' League filed a brief before the Supreme Court on this issue in *Stettler v. O'Hara*.[67] The brief, authored by Brandeis, Goldmark, and Felix Frankfurter, made a sex-neutral argument in favor of minimum-wage laws. It argued that "when no limit exists below which wages may not fall, the laborer's freedom is in effect totally destroyed."[68] True liberty, therefore, was not liberty of contract, but the right to a decent wage.

Other arguments in the brief appealed to contemporary sexism. The brief claimed that women were unable to negotiate effectively with their employers for a variety of biological and socioeconomic reasons. It also asserted a eugenic "mother of the race" argument, contending that "the health of the race is conditioned upon preserving the health of women, the future mothers of the republic." Brandeis, Goldmark, and Frankfurter also appealed to fears that "incompetent and defective" women workers who were unable to command a family wage were "driving down wages."[69]

As in *Muller v. Oregon*, the brief relied on various extralegal sources. Chief Justice (and *Lochner* dissenter) Edward D. White, unimpressed, sardonically remarked that he "could compile a brief twice as thick to prove that the legal profession ought to be abolished."[70] Nevertheless, the *Stettler* Court, in a 4–4 ruling with no opinion, refused to disturb a lower court ruling upholding the law. Brandeis, who had just joined the Court, recused himself. Because Brandeis was a clear fifth vote in favor of upholding the law, the constitutionality of minimum-wage laws for women seemed established, and such laws spread to states around the country.

Meanwhile, opposition to sex-based protective laws from working women and their supporters gradually gained institutional support. Sarah Hagan, an activist in the San Francisco garment workers' union, remarked, "If this minimum wage is so good for women, why isn't it good for men wage-earners? The men say, try it on the women first. We're tired of being tried on."[71] In 1915, women enraged at the displacement of thousands of women workers—especially printers, restaurant employees, and streetcar workers—by New York's prohibition of night work by women founded the Women's League for Equal Opportunity.[72] The League's first president declared that protective legislation "will protect women to the vanishing point."[73] Two years later, another group of women founded the Equal Rights Association to educate the general public about what they saw as the negative effects of protective laws for women.[74] The National Federation of Business and Professional Women also opposed sex-based labor laws.[75] A transportation worker, one of hundreds to lose her job when New York banned night work and adopted a fifty-four-hour maximum work week for women, mocked the claim that New York's law would put woman workers on "Easy Street"; she remarked, "Well, it put us on the street all right!"[76]

The most significant feminist opposition to protective laws for women came from the National Woman's Party. Formerly a suffragist group, the NWP dissolved after the Nineteenth Amendment guaranteed women the right to vote, and reconstituted for the purpose of lobbying for passage of an equal rights amendment (ERA) that would guarantee women full legal equality. Progressive reformers both within and outside the NWP urged the organization to agree to include a provision in the ERA exempting protective laws.[77] After some hesitation the NWP, under the leadership of Alice Paul, refused.[78] Paul and other NWP leaders believed that protective laws prevented women from entering male-dominated professions and set a dangerous precedent for other sex-based legislation.[79]

Critics charged that the NWP's opposition to sex-based protective laws meant that the organization's leaders were tools of big business, or were laissez-faire ideologues.[80] But consistent with the steep decline of classical liberalism in the United States at this time, few NWP members supported laissez-faire economic policies. Indeed, many of them supported protective laws that covered all workers—a position the NWP officially, though somewhat halfheartedly, adopted during the Great Depression.[81] Feminist supporters of free market economic policies, such as Suzanne La Follette, congregated in the small League of Equal Opportunity, which opposed protective labor laws generally, including sex-neutral ones.[82]

The NWP's resolve not to endorse a protective-legislation exception was strengthened by the evolution of Progressive attitudes toward protective laws for women. As we have seen, Progressive reformers had initially sought protective laws for women primarily as an opening wedge to protect all workers. By 1920, however, protecting women from "exploitative" industrial labor, and male workers from female competition, had become an end in itself for many Progressives.

As NWP activists were well aware, in the decade following 1910 the AFL began to endorse and lobby for protective labor legislation that applied only to women, while opposing such legislation for men.[83] Protective laws for women seldom passed without the AFL's active support.[84] As a Department of Labor study concluded, "Ostensibly, the organized workmen supported labor legislation for women on grounds of humanitarianism, but in reality self-protection [from competition by women workers] was the dominant motive."[85] Despite the AFL's self-interested and sexist motives and its fierce opposition to sex-neutral protective labor laws, Florence Kelley and the NCL were happy to ally with the AFL in lobbying for protective laws for women.

Kelley also allied with prounion Progressive economists who supported minimum-wage laws for women because such laws would exclude many women from the workplace.[86] These economists believed that wages tracked the consumption needs of workers, and not marginal productivity as other economists argued (and as is widely accepted today). They also believed that women workers had lower consumption needs then men, either because of their nature or because they often saved on expenses such as rent by living with their parents. Women workers therefore constituted unfair competition with men. Kelley, influenced by these ideas, praised an Australian minimum-wage law for protecting white male workers from the "unbridled competition" of "women, children, and Chinese."[87] Even Progressive economists who accepted marginalist economics argued that industries that paid substandard wages were "parasitic" and should be forced to either invest in technology to improve productivity or go out of business, rather than relying on "sweated labor" and degrading labor standards.[88] Allowing women to work at a "market wage" in these parasitic industries undermined the ability of men to earn sufficient money to provide for their families.

The Progressive economists' understanding of labor markets was reflected in a women-only minimum-wage law Congress enacted for the District of Columbia. The law calibrated the required compensation with results of studies showing the wage a woman needed to earn to be able to afford necessities. The law's supporters also hoped that because the wage rate was set "scientifically," the courts would find that it was not arbitrary, and therefore was not a violation of due process rights.

The D.C. Court of Appeals nevertheless declared the law unconstitutional as a violation of liberty of contract. The District of Columbia hired Felix Frankfurter to defend the law before the Supreme Court. Frankfurter filed a "Brandeis brief" prepared in large part by Molly Dewson, containing more than one thousand pages of documentation supporting the law. Unlike Brandeis's brief in *Muller*, however, Frankfurter also spent substantial energy on legal argument. Also in contrast to the original Brandeis brief, Frankfurter did not focus on women's alleged disabilities. Instead, he "emphasiz[ed] the fictitious nature of freedom of contract when the employee was bargaining for a wage that did not meet her cost of living,"[89] and argued that setting minimum wages would stimulate industrial efficiency.[90] He also argued that "semi-employable" or "unemployable" workers who could not receive an adequate market wage should "accept the status of a defective to be segregated for special treatment as a dependent."[91]

Frankfurter spent only a page contesting the lower court's suggestion that the law unconstitutionally discriminated against women. The brief cited *Muller* for the proposition that the legislature may take differences between men and women into account. The opposing brief, meanwhile, made a strong women's rights argument, relying on information supplied by Alice Paul and the NWP.[92]

To the surprise of most legal observers, who had believed that *Lochner* was defunct after the Supreme Court upheld a maximum-hours law for industrial workers in 1917,[93] and who had observed that several states had upheld minimum-wage laws,[94] the Court revived *Lochner* in *Adkins v. Children's Hospital*, and invalidated the minimum-wage law. Writing for a 5–3 majority—with Justice Brandeis recused—Justice George Sutherland suggested that the law unconstitutionally infringed on liberty of contract in a variety of ways, especially by placing an arbitrary, unfair burden on employers to support employees who lacked the skills to earn a better wage.[95] Moreover, the law imposed the potential burden of unemployment on workers subject to the minimum wage, including Willie Lyons, a plaintiff in the case. Sutherland pointed out that Lyons had testified at trial that she had been fired from her job as an elevator operator because of the minimum-wage law, and had been unable to secure equally desirable employment.[96] Sutherland added that the power "to fix high wages connotes, by like course of reasoning, the power to fix low wages," a power that could be turned against women and other workers.

Sutherland added that despite the claim that the law set minimum wages based on a scientific study of women's consumption, the wage assigned varied by occupation. The government could not explain why the law assumed that women in some fields had lower consumption needs than women in other fields. Sutherland pointed out that the law did not take into account the disparate needs of individual women who shared an occupation.[97] Sutherland described Frankfurter's brief as a "mass of reports" that were "interesting but only mildly persuasive." Faced with the argument that women's disabilities were such that they should not be accorded the same rights as men to make contracts, Sutherland responded that "we cannot accept the doctrine that women of mature age . . . require or may be subjected to restrictions upon their liberty of contract which could not lawfully be imposed in the case of men under similar circumstances." Sutherland noted "the present day trend of legislation," especially the Nineteenth Amendment, "as well as that of common thought and usage," by which women have been "emancipat[ed]" from "the old doctrine that she must be given special protection or be subjected to special restraint in her contractual and civil relationships."

Chief Justice Taft wrote a dissent, as did Justice Oliver Wendell Holmes. Taft criticized the majority for reviving *Lochner*, which he had thought defunct. Holmes mocked the notion that the Nineteenth Amendment signaled that the law should treat women the same as men: "It will need more than the Nineteenth Amendment to convince me that there are no differences between men and women, or that legislation cannot take those differences into account."

Critics outside the Court were even more scathing. Frankfurter attacked Sutherland's opinion as a "triumph for the Alice Paul theory of constitutional law, which is to no little extent a reflex of the thoughtless, unconsidered assumption that in industry it makes no difference whether you are a man or woman."[98] Kelley wrote that the decision gave "the unorganized, the unskilled, the illiterate, the alien, and the industrially sub-normal women wage-earners the constitutional right to starve. This is a new *Dred Scott* decision."[99] Judge Learned Hand anonymously attacked the Court for protecting a "right to starve."[100]

By contrast, a defender of the decision praised the majority for protecting women of below-average ability who could not command the minimum wage from the "severe sentences" of "idleness and pauperism."[101] An article in *The Survey* concluded that it was "distinctly harmful to the best interests of women to limit their opportunities for employment and advancement by artificial distinctions between them and men."[102] The National Woman's Party praised Sutherland's opinion as "women's Magna Charta."[103] Doris Stevens, an NWP activist, wrote that "protection, no matter how benevolent in motive, unless applied alike to both sexes, amounts to actual penalization."[104]

Historians, even those skeptical of sex-based labor laws on feminist grounds, have overwhelmingly sided with Sutherland's critics. William Leuchtenberg captures the tone of this criticism when he suggests that Sutherland's opinion was based on the "dogma" that "a great corporation and its employee—even someone as powerless as a chambermaid—each has an equivalent right to bargain about wages."[105] To the extent that historians have taken note of Sutherland's rhetoric supporting women's rights, they have generally considered it a ploy—at best superfluous and at worst disingenuous—to cover the Court's support of reactionary economic policies.[106] What these critics typically fail to discuss, or even acknowledge, is that despite his reputation as a "conservative," Justice Sutherland was a longstanding and sincere supporter of women's rights. In his pre-Court career as a Republican senator from Utah, he had been a leading supporter of women's suffrage in general,[107] and of the Nineteenth Amendment, which he introduced in the Senate, in particular. (In contrast, Justice Brandeis, Sutherland's nemesis on minimum-wage laws and other issues, was not a feminist and was a belated and somewhat reluctant supporter of women's suffrage.)[108] Sutherland also advised the NWP during the battle to ratify the Nineteenth Amendment, and later in efforts to draft the Equal Rights Amendment.[109]

After *Adkins*, the constitutionality of sex-based protective laws was temporarily settled. Maximum-hours laws remained constitutional under the *Muller* precedent, which the Court declined to overrule after *Adkins*. In *Radice v. New York*, the Court unanimously upheld a state ban on night work by women just a year after *Adkins*.[110] Justice Brandeis told Frankfurter that the initial vote in conference was 5–4 and "was teetering back and forth for some time." Sutherland was the swing voter, and "after a good deal of study" he reaffirmed his vote to uphold the law. The other four justices were not persuaded, and believed that the law arbitrarily banned some types of night work but not others. Rather than attract additional controversy to the Court (which was becoming a major issue in the 1924 presidential elections) by creating a 5–4 decision, those justices chose not to dissent. Brandeis warned Frankfurter that equal protection "looms up even more menacingly than due process."[111]

Some historians have seen inconsistency or hypocrisy in the *Radice* decision. They argue that *Radice* shows that the Court's conservatives were not truly concerned with protecting liberty of contract for women. Rather, combined with *Adkins*, *Radice* suggests that the justices merely wanted to preserve the ability of employers to pay low wages.[112] If the story Brandeis told Frankfurter is correct, this criticism loses force, as four of the five justices in the *Adkins* majority also thought the night-work ban was unconstitutional, even if they didn't bother to express that view in dissent. And there is little doubt that Sutherland supported women's rights, despite his vote in *Radice*.

Moreover, critics typically ignore *Muller's* precedential force. *Muller* held that real physical differences between men and women justified laws limiting women's working hours. Although a clever attorney could find a way to distinguish maximum-hours laws challenged in *Muller* from bans on night work challenged in *Radice*, both kinds of laws were justified as accommodations to women's presumed physical frailty. By contrast, minimum-wage laws were not based on physical differences between men and women and therefore were not controlled by the *Muller* precedent;

Sutherland and the other justices in the *Adkins* majority consistently maintained that women were just as competent to negotiate for wages as were men.[113]

The controversy over the constitutionality of state minimum-wage laws for women revived in the 1930s. In the wake of the Great Depression, some states started to enforce minimum-wage laws that had been dormant since *Adkins*, while other states passed new legislation.[114] A combination of economic hardship and four relatively Progressive appointments to the Supreme Court by Presidents Coolidge and Hoover—Cardozo, Hughes, Roberts, and Stone—suggested that the issue was ripe for reconsideration by the Court. The new justices provided critical votes for the 5–4 majority to *Nebbia v. New York*,[115] a 1934 case that upheld a law regulating the price of milk. The *Nebbia* Court abandoned the notion that government could only regulate prices charged by "businesses affected with a public interest." Because the *Adkins* Court had analogized the government's power over the price of labor to its power over the price of goods, *Nebbia* seemed to signal that the Court would now uphold minimum-wage laws.

Nevertheless, in 1936 the Court invalidated New York's minimum-wage law for women.[116] Justice Owen Roberts, a moderate Hoover appointee, joined the Court's four consistent proponents of a limited state police power in the 5–4 decision. The Court wrote that "the State is without power" to regulate "contracts between employers and adult women workers as to the amount of wages to be paid." It added that "proscribing minimum wages for women alone would unreasonably restrain them in competition with men and tend arbitrarily to deprive them of employment and a fair chance to find work."

Secretary of the Interior Harold Ickes demonstrated that many reformers continued to analogize the appropriate legal status of women to that of minor children. He wrote sarcastically that the Court upheld the "sacred right" of "an immature child or helpless woman to drive a bargain with a great corporation,"[117] even though the issue of child labor had not been before the Court.

After much public outrage over this and other controversial Supreme Court decisions, and the overwhelming reelection of President Franklin Roosevelt, in the following year Roberts switched sides.[118] The Court issued a broad opinion, authored by Chief Justice Charles Evans Hughes, upholding a minimum-wage law for women in *West Coast Hotel v. Parrish*.[119] Its primary argument did not directly challenge the constitutional right to liberty of contract. Instead, the Court narrowed liberty of contract's scope and signaled its acquiescence to protective labor laws, sex-specific or not.

The Court argued that liberty of contract was merely a subset of liberty and could be abrogated in the public interest, as other Supreme Court precedents, such as *Muller*, had shown. Given economic conditions during the Depression, a state legislature could reasonably try to guarantee women workers a living wage, even if this resulted in unemployment among those who could not command the minimum.[120]

Hughes also raised a more direct challenge to the concept of constitutional protection of liberty of contract. He asserted that when an employer pays a worker less than a living wage, the employer is implicitly relying on subsidies from taxpayers in the form of relief payments to sustain the worker.[121] Liberty, according to Hughes, could not be defined as the right of a necessitous worker to make a contract for less than a living wage, nor as the right of the employer to loot the public fisc by relying on government resources to subsidize inadequate wages.

Progressives and New Dealers celebrated their victory in *West Coast Hotel*, and the ruling helped clear the way for extensive federal and state regulation of the labor market, a long-standing reformist goal. The decision, however, was a significant step backwards for women's rights relative to the egalitarian pronouncements in Justice Sutherland's *Adkins* opinion. While *Adkins* emphasized women's civic equality in light of social changes and the passage of the Nineteenth Amendment, *West Coast Hotel* Court adopted a *Muller*-like patriarchical view of women's place in society, even though the opinion's reasoning did not hinge on differentiating between the rights of male and female workers. Hughes quoted *Muller* for the proposition that "though limitations upon personal and contractual rights may be removed by legislation, there is that in [women's] disposition and habits of life which will operate against a full assertion of those rights."[122]

Sutherland, meanwhile, penned another rousing defense of women's rights in his *West Coast Hotel* dissent. He wrote that women should not "be put in different classes in respect of their legal right to make contracts; nor should they be denied, in effect, the right to compete with men for work paying lower wages which men may be willing to accept." Sutherland added that "the ability to make a fair bargain, as everyone knows, does not depend on sex."[123]

For the next three decades, courts relied on Hughes' dicta in *West Coast Hotel* that women had limited rights in the workplace to uphold the constitutionality of laws that excluded women from various occupations. In 1948, for example, the Supreme Court upheld a Michigan law prohibiting women from working as bartenders.[124] The law was purportedly aimed at protecting women's morals, but the law's primary advocates were labor unions representing male bartenders. Moreover, the law allowed women to work as cocktail waitresses, which would seem at least as great a threat to their moral standing.[125] Nevertheless, the Court unanimously upheld the law. Justice Frankfurter, writing for the Court, rejected the plaintiffs' claim that their right to pursue a livelihood was violated. He dismissively responded that this was "one of those rare instances where to state the question is in effect to answer it." By 1960, twenty-six states prohibited women from working as bartenders.[126] Women workers remained subject to special protective legislation until Title VII of the 1964 Civil Rights Act and a series of Supreme Court cases in the early 1970s established that such laws constituted illegal discrimination.

CHAPTER FIVE

Liberty of Contract and Segregation Laws

The relationship between the rise of Jim Crow segregation laws and the police power/due process jurisprudence of the liberty of contract era is often misconstrued. In particular, legal scholars frequently claim that *Lochner* and the notorious 1896 case of *Plessy v. Ferguson*, which upheld a law requiring railroad segregation, were based on similar ideological premises. Bruce Ackerman, for example, argues that the majority opinion in *Plessy* had a "deep intellectual indebtedness to the laissez-faire theories expressed one decade later in cases like *Lochner.*" Cass Sunstein posits an "extremely close link" between *Plessy* and *Lochner* because both cases purportedly relied on the idea that existing resource distributions were neutral. Derrick Bell similarly argues that *Plessy* and *Lochner* each "protected existing property arrangements at the expense of exploited groups."[1]

These scholars neatly tie together modern liberals' hostility to both *Plessy* and *Lochner*, but they ignore or understate some very important differences—indeed, some significant conflicts—between the two cases.[2] In stark contrast to *Lochner*, *Plessy* adopted a broad, deferential understanding of the states' police power. *Lochner* and other cases invoking liberty of contract to invalidate labor regulations were the bête noire of elite Progressive attorneys. *Plessy* and other cases upholding segregation laws, by contrast, met with general Progressive approval. *Plessy*, unlike *Lochner*, reflected a Supreme Court majority influenced by such Progressive ideas as the use of state power to counteract corporate power, the blurring of the line between state and private action, and the importance to constitutional argument of contemporary science and social science, including purportedly scientific understandings of race.[3] As we shall see, the tension between liberty and property rights on one side and segregation laws on the other was resolved in favor of the former in the important but largely neglected case of *Buchanan v. Warley* in 1917.

Plessy involved an 1890 Louisiana statute that required railroads to enforce racial segregation. At the time, segregation in public places was common throughout the South. But segregation was not universal, and it was under increasing pressure from civil rights activism and from the liberalizing influence of urbanization and market interactions between whites and African Americans.[4] To stifle these liberalizing influences and curry favor with white constituents who preferred segregation, politicians began to propose and enact laws requiring separate public accommodations for blacks and whites, including on railroad cars.[5] Railroad companies were often hostile to segregation laws, which they found costly. First, to the extent that states enforced the "equal" part of the "separate but equal" provisions of typical segregation laws, railroads faced dramatically increased expenses. For example, they might be obligated to provide separate first-class cars for whites and blacks, despite limited demand from the latter. Second, train conductors were forced to determine on the spot whether an individual with a medium skin tone was a "light-skinned Negro" relegated to the "colored car" or a "dark-skinned white" required to sit in the "white car." Railroads faced lawsuits both for being insufficiently vigorous in enforcing separate-car laws, and for mistakenly assigning whites to the wrong car.[6]

When the Louisiana legislature was debating a proposed railroad segregation ordinance, a New Orleans-based civil rights group, the American Citizens' Equal Rights Association of Louisiana, led the opposition to it. Like opponents of segregation laws in other parts of the South, the association denounced segregation laws as "class legislation."[7] When the ordinance became law, the association resolved to challenge its constitutionality. With a local train company's cooperation, it arranged Homer Plessy's arrest for violating the law to create a test case.[8] Plessy's attorneys contended that the segregation ordinance violated the Fourteenth Amendment's Equal Protection Clause. The argument was hardly frivolous. A leading treatise author and liberty of contract advocate, Theodore Dwight, argued vigorously that segregation laws were unconstitutional.[9] Nevertheless, the Supreme Court voted 7–1 to uphold the law. In an opinion by Justice Henry Brown, the Court argued that the right to sit in an integrated train was a mere social right, unprotected by the Fourteenth Amendment.[10] Moreover, the Court had already held that laws banning interracial marriage did not infringe the Equal Protection Clause, because they restricted blacks and whites equally.[11] The same principle applied to segregation laws. If African Americans believed segregation to be subordinating, that was no concern of the Court.

Plessy's narrow understanding of the prohibition on class legislation with regard to segregation laws was consistent with the Court's more general equal protection/class legislation jurisprudence, which at this time was extremely deferential to state and local legislation.[12] *Plessy*, however, went much further than necessary to uphold the Louisiana segregation statute. The Court could have limited its reasoning to stating that the Fourteenth Amendment does not protect "social rights" like integration. Instead, it gratuitously endorsed the presumptive constitutionality of segregation laws that infringed on "civil rights." The Court explained that African Americans and whites were both biologically distinct and instinctively hostile to each other; segregation laws were therefore presumptively reasonable exercises of the police power.[13]

Perhaps the most puzzling aspect of *Plessy* is the Court's assertion that allowing the railroad to voluntarily run integrated cars would amount to endorsing an "enforced commingling" of whites and African Americans.[14] The mystery evaporates if one looks at *Plessy* as a railroad case and not just as a segregation case. Railroads were the most unpopular and most regulated industry in late-nineteenth-century America. As common carriers that frequently had monopolies on particular routes, railroads were often treated as quasi-public utilities. Railroad segregation laws were an integral part of a populist/Progressive movement in the South to control perceived corporate abuses via government regulation.[15] To many Southern whites of that era, railroads were abusing their monopoly status and flaunting their disregard for (white) public opinion by running integrated trains, forcing white passengers who wanted to travel on segregated routes to sit in the same cars as African Americans. The *Plessy* majority apparently agreed that Louisiana's segregation law was restoring the natural state of affairs against the *railroads'* "enforced commingling of the races."[16]

Justice John Marshall Harlan, the lone dissenter in *Plessy*, argued that the case was not about social equality, but about the rights of locomotion and association. Harlan argued that "if a white man and a black man choose to occupy the same public conveyance on a public highway, it is their right to do so; and no government, proceeding alone on grounds of race, can prevent it without infringing the personal liberty of each."[17] Harlan explained that the segregation statute was an obvious example of illicit class legislation: "But in view of the constitution, in the eye of the law, there is in this country no superior, dominant, ruling class of citizens. There is no caste here. Our constitution is color-blind, and neither knows nor tolerates classes among citizens. In respect of civil rights, all citizens are equal before the law."[18]

Civil rights advocates were a small and discouraged lot in the early twentieth century, and the Supreme Court's dismissive rejection of the equal protection claim in *Plessy* was disheartening. However, *Lochner*'s defense of liberty of contract, its narrow view of the police power, and its general libertarian presumptions provided hope that the Due Process Clause might aid civil rights activists.[19] *Plessy* itself had suggested that the state may not interfere with truly *voluntary* integration (as opposed to "enforced commingling") of the races, which raised the possibility that some segregation laws could be vulnerable to assertions that they violated liberty of contract.[20]

In *Berea College v. Kentucky* (1908), the Supreme Court confronted the issue of whether *Lochner* could be used as a constitutional weapon to combat legally mandated segregation.[21] Berea College, a private, integrated school, challenged a new Kentucky segregation law. The college argued that the law violated the rights of liberty and property guaranteed by the Fourteenth Amendment. When the case reached the U.S. Supreme Court, Berea argued that as a private school it "stands upon exactly the same footing as any other private business."[22] The college's brief relied on and quoted from what Progressive jurists considered a rogue's gallery of liberty of contract cases, and it included an especially lengthy quote from *Lochner*.[23]

Berea pointed out that the only whites who came into contact with African Americans at the college were those who voluntarily chose to teach or study there. Unlike in *Plessy*, there was no question of an "enforced commingling of the races." The state therefore had no legitimate interest in forcing segregation upon Berea College.[24]

Kentucky's brief, in turn, expressly disputed Berea's contention that the voluntariness or involuntariness of interracial interaction was relevant. Segregation laws were needed not to reinforce social norms, but "to maintain the purity of blood and avoid an amalgamation [i.e., miscegenation]."[25] Kentucky cited studies purportedly demonstrating that African Americans are mentally inferior to whites, and mulattoes even less intelligent. The state argued that these studies showed the dangers of miscegenation; integrated education, it argued, would inevitably lead to miscegenation.[26] Kentucky's brief also reflected Progressive-era hostility to claims that individual rights superseded the government's power to regulate for the common good. "The welfare of the State and community is paramount to any right or privilege of the individual citizen," Kentucky argued. "The rights of the citizen are guaranteed, subject to the welfare of the State."[27]

In short, given the parties' arguments, the Court faced a stark choice between the liberty of contract and narrow scope of the police power it had endorsed in *Lochner*, and the statism and sociological jurisprudence of *Plessy*.

The Court evaded the conflict by ruling on nonconstitutional grounds, upholding the law as a lawful amendment to Berea's corporate charter.[28] Justice Holmes concurred in the judgment but did not join the majority opinion, perhaps because he would have preferred a broader assertion of state authority.

In dissent, Justice Harlan argued that the segregation statute was "an arbitrary invasion of the rights of liberty and property guaranteed by the 14th Amendment against hostile state action."[29] Harlan explained that the right to impart instruction was both a property right and a liberty right under the Fourteenth Amendment. These rights could only lawfully be infringed if the instruction was by nature either harmful to public morals or a threat to public safety. Harlan, citing *Allgeyer v. Louisiana* and the controversial liberty of contract opinion he had authored earlier in 1908 in *Adair v. United States*, noted that the Supreme Court "has more than once said that the liberty guaranteed by the Fourteenth Amendment embraces 'the right of the citizen to be free in the enjoyment of all his faculties,' and 'to be free to use them in all lawful ways.'"[30] Besides the teachers' rights, Harlan asserted that the students themselves had a right to voluntarily sit together in a private institution to receive "instruction which is not in its nature harmful or dangerous to the public."[31] Justice William Day also dissented, but for unknown reasons he did not join Harlan's opinion or write one of his own.

The result in *Berea College* received unanimous support from law review authors who commented on it. Some of the praise for the case reflected overt racism.[32] The Court's opinion also delighted opponents of the liberty of contract doctrine. The *Virginia Law Register* editorialized that the opinion was a "shining star," commendable "not so much for the set back it gives the Negrophile, but for the salutary doctrine laid down as to the right of a State to control its creation, the corporations." *Law Notes* praised the Court for reining in "corporate aggression." Prominent attorney and legal historian Charles Warren praised the Court for its "wise policy" of upholding most of the regulations that came before it, including the segregation law at issue in *Berea College*.[33]

While *Berea College* was a blow to opponents of Jim Crow, the opinion left room for future constitutional attacks on segregation laws that applied to private parties.[34] The Court did not, as it did in *Plessy*, endorse racism or suggest that any "reasonable" segregation statute came within the police power. Moreover, the Court hinted that Kentucky's segregation law would have been unconstitutional as beyond the police power had it been applied to an individual or to an unincorporated business.[35] Most important in hindsight, *Berea College* did not foreclose a challenge to the constitutionality of residential segregation laws. Starting in 1910, many cities in the South, in border states, and in the lower Midwest responded to a wave of African American migration from rural areas by passing laws mandating housing segregation.[36] More cities were prepared to follow suit if the laws survived constitutional challenges.[37]

At this time, vocal opponents of segregation could be found among intellectuals and political activists who agreed on little else, but despite their ideological diversity, they were few and far between.[38] Most Progressive political and intellectual leaders shared the racism of the day and did not support equal rights for African Americans.[39] While segregation was broadly popular in much of the United States, many Progressive reformers found the idea of laws requiring residential segregation especially appealing.

Echoing *Plessy*, some Progressive intellectuals contended that capitalism forced the races to live together.[40] Other Progressives argued that coerced residential segregation was necessary to reduce racial friction, limit the spread of communicable disease, and to protect the value of white-owned property. Meanwhile, leading Progressive social scientists promoted pseudoscientific theories of race differences.[41] The legal world was far from immune from these intellectual trends. Even a generally liberal-minded Progressive scholar like University of Chicago law professor Ernst Freund supported racial zoning.[42] The minority of Progressive jurists who supported racial equality rarely made that support a priority.[43]

Residential segregation laws met with some initial judicial resistance as state courts held that significant restrictions on property rights may not apply retroactively.[44] The Virginia and Georgia supreme courts, meanwhile, upheld residential segregation laws as reasonable exercises of the police power. These courts argued that residential segregation would prevent race friction, disorder, and violence.[45]

The residential segregation case that eventually reached the U.S. Supreme Court, *Buchanan v. Warley*, originated in Louisville, Kentucky.[46] In 1908, wealthy black businessmen and professionals in Louisville began to buy houses in residential neighborhoods dominated by whites. This caused a great deal of alarm and consternation among whites.[47] The result was an ordinance that forbade "any colored person to move into and occupy as a residence . . . any house upon any block upon which a greater number of houses are occupied . . . by white people than are occupied . . . by colored people." The opposite restriction applied to whites.

The Louisville NAACP, backed by the national organization, soon organized a test case. William Warley, an African American, signed an agreement to purchase a lot on a majority-white block from Charles Buchanan, a white real estate agent who opposed the segregation ordinance. The contract between the two parties specified that the transaction would not be consummated unless Warley had "the right under the laws of the state of Kentucky and the city of Louisville to occupy said Property as residence."[48] Buchanan's attorney argued that the law reduced the value of his property by preventing him from selling his property to African Americans. The law therefore violated his client's Fourteenth Amendment right not to be deprived of property without due process of law. The Kentucky courts upheld the law in opinions that combined racist assumptions about African Americans with Progressive notions of the role of modern government.[49] The Kentucky Court of Appeals explained that "the advance of civilization . . . has resulted in a gradual lessening of the dominions of the individual over private property and a corresponding strengthening of the relative power of the state in respect thereof."[50]

The NAACP had little reason to be sanguine about its prospects before the Supreme Court. First, racism was at a post–Civil War peak. The federal government's racial policies exacerbated the deteriorating situation for African Americans. The Wilson administration was unabashedly devoted to white supremacy, and Congress was only marginally better.[51] Second, the Court would somehow have to distinguish *Plessy*, which seemed to hold that segregation was a presumptively proper police-power objective.[52] Third, Progressivism so dominated mainstream legal thought that Charles Warren remarked in 1913 that "any court which recognizes wide and liberal bounds to the State police power is to be deemed in touch with the temper of the times."[53] Fourth, the Supreme Court had consistently upheld land use regulations that had been challenged as violations of the Due Process Clause, and Jim Crow racial segregation was part of a broader pattern of Progressive land use regulation.[54] Fifth, the Court was consistently rejecting challenges to claimed exercises of the police power.[55] Sixth, legal commentators were nearly unanimous in their belief that residential segregation laws were constitutional, just as they had supported the constitutionality of the Kentucky segregation law at issue in *Berea College*.

Law review authors denied that residential segregation laws violated equal protection norms. They argued that the laws restricted both races equally, thus creating a "distinction" but not a "discrimination." Given the *Plessy* precedent, they added, such laws were clearly reasonable exercises of the police power.[56] Legal commentators also disputed the notion that residential segregation laws unconstitutionally interfered with property or contract rights. Segregation was reasonable and necessary, these authors argued, to prevent race conflict. Moreover, they believed that the courts should give the police power a broad scope, in line with the Progressive spirit of the time. A student writing in the *Michigan Law Review* condemned as "ultra-conservative" a state court opinion invalidating a segregation ordinance as a violation of vested property rights.[57]

The one glimmer of hope for the NAACP and other civil rights advocates was that after decades of neglecting African Americans' rights, the Court had recently issued a series of surprisingly liberal race-related opinions. *Bailey v. Alabama* and *United States v. Reynolds* invalidated coercive Southern labor laws that primarily affected African American workers; *McCabe v. Atchison, Topeka & Santa Fe Railway Co.* stated that railroads acting under color of state segregation laws must ensure that African American passengers had the same access as white passengers to first-class accommodations; and *Guinn v. United States* and *Myers v. Anderson* held that "grandfather clauses" that implicitly discriminated against potential black voters violated the Fifteenth Amendment.[58]

When *Buchanan* reached the Supreme Court, the plaintiffs filed two briefs, one written by NAACP president Moorefield Storey and the other by Clayton Blakely, who had argued for the plaintiff on behalf of the Louisville NAACP in the lower courts. The briefs argued that Louisville's segregation law deprived Buchanan of property without due process of law and discriminated against African Americans in violation of the Equal Protection Clause. Storey pleaded with the Court not to let the contemporary wave of racism determine the constitutional status of African Americans. Blakely, meanwhile, distinguished *Plessy* by pointing out that unlike train passengers, property sellers and buyers were engaged in purely voluntary interaction.

Kentucky responded with an extraordinary brief, notable for its length (121 pages) and its blunt racism. The state spent many pages, for example, arguing that segregation was divinely ordained. In response to arguments that the segregation law would restrict African Americans to the poorest and least desirable sections of Louisville, Kentucky responded that if "negroes carry a blight with them wherever they go . . . on what theory do they assert the privilege of spreading that blight to the white sections of the city?"[59] After arguing that *Plessy* and other precedents dictated that the statute be upheld, Kentucky urged the Court to take a sociological approach to its decision, to rely on "social facts" and the wisdom of experts who supported segregation. The state contended that *Buchanan* involved "social and economic imperatives of the most solemn and impressive character" that would lead to violence and lawlessness "if they are not crystallized into law."[60]

Buchanan was initially argued in April 1916. Justice Day missed the argument because of illness. A month later the Court ordered a reargument so that all nine justices could be present.[61] Storey and Blakely filed a new joint brief for the plaintiff. Among other things, they pointed out that the racist statements in Kentucky's brief supported their argument that the ordinance's purpose was to discriminate against African Americans. Storey and Blakely also reiterated that the Louisville ordinance violated the Fourteenth Amendment's Equal Protection and Due Process clauses.

Meanwhile, Kentucky's rehearing brief focused on rebutting Storey's statement at the initial oral argument that trying to prevent miscegenation was not a valid police power concern "because such amalgamation is highly desirable."[62] The state provided a voluminous appendix in the style of a Brandeis brief, consisting of excerpts of books and articles that supported its position. The excerpts can be divided into four categories: apologias for Southern treatment of African Americans; claims that an inherent racial instinct exists; discussion of the purported negative effects of miscegenation; and evidence of purported African American inferiority.

The Court ultimately issued a unanimous opinion holding the segregation law unconstitutional. Justice Day, writing for the Court, essentially ignored the equal protection arguments raised by Storey and Blakely, and instead concluded that the law violated the Due Process Clause by depriving the plaintiffs of liberty and property without a valid police power justification.[63]

Some scholars have incorrectly portrayed *Buchanan* as only vindicating white people's right to alienate property. In fact, Justice Day wrote that "colored persons are citizens of the United States and have the right to purchase property and enjoy and use the same without laws discriminating against them solely on account of color." Day specifically endorsed "the civil right of a white man to dispose of his property if he saw fit to do so to a person of color *and* of a colored person to make such disposition to a white person."[64]

The Court rejected each of Kentucky's asserted police power rationales for upholding the law. Day dismissed the argument that existing "race hostility" was an appropriate rationale for narrowing the scope of citizens' constitutional rights. He added that the legitimate goal of promoting the public peace could not be accomplished "by laws or ordinances which deny rights created or protected by the Federal Constitution."[65] Nor could the law be justified as promoting the "maintenance of the purity of the races." The law did not even prohibit African Americans from working in white households, showing that the law's target was not race mixing per se.

Finally, the Court spurned the claim that the law was necessary to prevent the depreciation in the value of property owned by white people when African Americans became their neighbors. Day noted that property owned by "undesirable white neighbors" or "put to disagreeable though lawful uses" could similarly cause depreciation.[66] In short, *Buchanan* repudiated *Plessy*'s presumption that segregation laws, including those that infringed on civil rights, are reasonable.[67] *Buchanan*, in fact, contains a surprisingly strong assertion of antidiscrimination principles—stronger, in fact, than the rather tepid language of *Brown v. Board of Education*, though in 1917 neither the Court nor the country was ready for a meaningful challenge to public school segregation.[68]

Justice Holmes drafted a dissent in *Buchanan* that he ultimately chose not to deliver for unknown reasons. As we have seen, Holmes had advocated a broad conception of the police power since his dissent in *Lochner*.[69] He had also been especially unsympathetic to African Americans' challenges to hostile state action.[70] For example, he dissented in *Bailey v. Alabama* when the Court invalidated a law that effectively kept African Americans in a state of peonage. Holmes also declined to join the majority's opinion in *McCabe*, which held that the "separate but equal" principle required that African Americans be guaranteed access to the same quality of train accommodations as whites. He wrote a memorandum to Justice Hughes expressing his disagreement with the majority, explaining that he thought that requiring train companies to supply first-class cars to African Americans only when it was economically profitable to do so constituted *"logically exact"* equality. Hughes responded that providing whites but not African Americans with the opportunity to endure a long train journey in first-class accommodations was "a bald, wholly unjustified discrimination against a passenger solely on account of race."[71]

Given Holmes's disregard for the rights of African Americans and his expansive understanding of the police power's scope, his proposed dissent in *Buchanan* is not surprising. Holmes first suggested that the Court had no jurisdiction to hear the case, given that there was no real dispute between the parties. He then asserted that in any event Louisville's segregation statute was well within the police power and therefore did not violate the Due Process Clause.[72]

Buchanan was an extremely significant case. While it did not lead to a rollback of Jim Crow legislation, the decision inhibited state and local governments from passing more pervasive and brutal segregation laws akin to those enacted in South Africa.[73] Moreover, but for *Buchanan*, African Americans' right to own and alienate property may ultimately have come under legal threat, at least in parts of the South. While most African Americans remained poor and essentially assetless during the Jim Crow era, some managed to accumulate sufficient property to give them middle-class status or, far more rarely, wealth. Property ownership not only improved African Americans' economic status, but gave Southern blacks some economic autonomy from local whites, which allowed them to be active in the civil rights movement.[74]

Buchanan did not lead to integration, but it impeded the efforts of urban whites to prevent African Americans from migrating to white neighborhoods and ultimately replacing the white residents. The African American urban population in the United States almost doubled between 1910 and 1929, and continued to grow in later years.[75] Whites tried to use restrictive covenants to prevent the migration of African Americans. The covenants worked in some neighborhoods, but overall they were too difficult and expensive to enforce to prevent an influx of African Americans to American cities.[76] In some cities, whites lobbied for segregation laws precisely because restrictive covenants had proved ineffective in restricting black settlement.[77]

Generations of legal scholars and historians have treated *Buchanan* as a property rights case that rested on laissez-faire ideology, of little if any relevance to the later civil rights revolution. In fact, *Buchanan's* implicit protection of migration to urban areas, north and south, proved a crucial turning point in African American history. Not only did cities provide African Americans with more economic opportunity and personal freedom and security, but African Americans also substantially increased their political power when they moved to areas where they could vote.[78] As for the reasoning of the case, undoubtedly the fact that *Buchanan* involved property rights and liberty of contract played an important role in the decision; it allowed the Court to distinguish *Buchanan* from *Plessy*, which involved what the Court declared were mere social rights.[79] But focusing myopically on the economic rights element of *Buchanan* misses the fact that even property rights and liberty of contract were subject to the police power. The Court's invocation of property rights did not resolve the issue of whether residential segregation laws were a constitutionally proper exercise of the government's regulatory authority.[80]

Plessy had suggested that any "reasonable" segregation law would come within the police power, and the *Plessy* Court applied a lax and racism-infused standard of reasonableness. In contrast, after noting that property rights were subordinate to the police power, the *Buchanan* opinion favorably cited a series of antidiscrimination precedents that no Supreme Court majority had relied upon in almost four decades.[81] The Court specifically invoked the 1866 Civil Rights Act, which stated that African Americans have the same right to make and enforce contracts and own and alienate property as did white persons.

Most significant, the Court for the first time since *Yick Wo v. Hopkins* in 1886 held that discriminatory animus was not a proper police power justification for laws violating individual rights.[82] The Court reached this conclusion in *Buchanan* even though popular and expert opinion, backed by contemporary social science evidence, supported the underlying prejudiced rationale for the residential segregation law, and even though the state justified the law as a response to the risk that integrated housing would lead to miscegenation, racial violence, and other social ills.

The Court's position was hardly a foregone conclusion; indeed, it was grossly unpopular among legal commentators. As we have already seen, pre-*Buchanan* law review commentary had universally argued that residential segregation laws were constitutional. The *Buchanan* opinion changed few if any minds. A student comment in the *Columbia Law Review* praised the Court's ruling,[83] but all other law review commentary was hostile. For example, a student comment in the *Yale Law Journal* attacked the Court for implicitly holding that property rights were more important than the public's interest in segregation.[84] Similarly, a Michigan law student complained that the Supreme Court had declared the Louisville ordinance to be unconstitutional despite "all this direct and emphatic expression of opinion that the ordinance was reasonably necessary and conducive to public welfare."[85] A Harvard Law School student criticized the Court for ignoring the relevant social science evidence regarding the desirability of segregation.[86] The Court should have come to its decision, the student wrote, only "after careful consideration of the *facts*, as to the effect of propinquity and intermingling of the races. Perhaps there is sufficient danger in such contacts as to justify this legislation, perhaps not."[87] A decade later, Columbia professor Howard Lee McBain criticized the Court for destroying whites' right to live in a segregated neighborhood.[88]

Despite this outpouring of criticism, *Buchanan* marked a favorable turning point in the Supreme Court's attitude toward the rights of African Americans. According to one tally, the Court heard twenty-eight cases involving African Americans and the Fourteenth Amendment between 1868 and 1910. Of these, African Americans lost twenty-two. However, between 1920 and 1943, African American Supreme Court litigants won twenty-five of twenty-seven Fourteenth Amendment cases.[89] After the Court confirmed the constitutionality of general residential zoning in 1926 in *Euclid v. Ambler Realty*,[90] various Southern and border-state jurisdictions once again passed residential segregation ordinances. Segregationists hoped that *Euclid* signaled that the Court would be willing to revisit its disapproval of racial zoning.[91] The Court, however, summarily invalidated these laws in 1927 and 1930.[92]

Buchanan could have been used, in combination with cases like *Lochner*, to combat segregation laws regulating private businesses. For example, in 1926 the Georgia Supreme Court relied on liberty of contract reasoning to invalidate a law that prohibited black barbers from cutting white children's hair.[93] However, the NAACP, the only active national organization fighting to vindicate African Americans' constitutional rights, had extremely limited resources and had to devote a substantial portion of them to defeating the residential segregation ordinances that cities enacted in defiance of the Supreme Court. Organizing broader challenges to discriminatory statutes required money, willing plaintiffs, and competent and willing attorneys, all of which were in short supply.[94] Moreover, by the 1920s the NAACP's leadership had an economically "Progressive" outlook, and was therefore hesitant to rely on "conservative" constitutional doctrines like liberty of contract.[95] Northern antidiscrimination activists may also have been uncomfortable relying on liberty of contract arguments to combat state-sponsored discrimination, because such arguments had been used on occasion to challenge Northern states' laws banning discrimination in public accommodations.[96]

Giving *Buchanan* its due does not absolve the Supreme Court of its acquiescence to Jim Crow in other contexts. Nor does it remotely suggest that the pre–New Deal Court's civil rights jurisprudence was superior to that of later Supreme Courts which, like American society more generally, became increasingly egalitarian on race. But, given that advocates of racial equality were a distinct minority among Progressives, the practical alternative to the early twentieth century's liberty of contract jurisprudence was not the Warren Court's liberalism but the indifference or hostility to the rights of African Americans shown by most Progressive legal elites. In the pre–New Deal era, liberty of contract's adversaries among prominent lawyers and scholars adulated not a William Brennan clone but Justice Holmes, the early-twentieth-century justice least willing to vindicate African Americans' constitutional rights, and later (and to a lesser extent) Justice Brandeis, whose judicial record bespeaks a general indifference to African American civil rights.[97]

With notable exceptions, including Justice Harlan, liberty of contract supporters among the legal elite also did not often distinguish themselves as advocates for African American rights. But at least, unlike their Progressives adversaries, their skepticism of statism and their support for constitutional protection for property and contract rights provided one of few counter-weights to overwhelming expert and public opinion that segregation was good social policy.[98] And, as we've seen, by 1920 the tenor of the Court's civil rights decisions had swung dramatically in African Americans' favor.

In short, the conventional story that the Court's pro–liberty of contract decisions are somehow linked to the its tolerance of segregation in *Plessy* and other cases cannot withstand historical scrutiny. Indeed, the opposite is the case. When the Court deferred to "sociological" concerns and gave a broad scope to the police power, as in *Plessy*, it upheld segregation. When, however, the Court adopted more libertarian, *Lochner*-like presumptions, as in *Buchanan*, it placed significant limits on race discrimination.

Arguably, *Buchanan* also shows the potential for a racially egalitarian jurisprudence to have emerged in a political environment far closer to America's classical liberal tradition than what had developed by the 1950s, when the Supreme Court began its war on de jure segregation. At the dawn of the New Deal, the Court had been rapidly moving to a synthesis in which the liberty of contract doctrine protected all Americans from at least some forms of police power regulation. Meanwhile, it was gradually adopting a more vigorous equal protection jurisprudence.[99] Further progress on civil rights matters before the Court, however, required a more favorable political environment and a trained cadre of civil rights attorneys to take advantage of that environment.

The liberalization in American race policy that led to the Court's broad opposition to segregation was not an inevitable result of the New Deal's triumph. President Franklin D. Roosevelt's administration contained several prominent supporters of racial egalitarianism, but Roosevelt himself was largely indifferent to issues of racial justice, and his administration's policies generally reflected that indifference. Several of the justices he appointed turned out to be strong supporters of civil rights, but this was not a criterion that interested the administration's judge-pickers, who focused instead on selecting judges who were strongly inclined to ignore or invalidate any preexisting constitutional limits on economic regulation.[100]

World War II, however, marked the beginning of a new era in American race relations.[101] During this period the social trends that had aided African Americans in the interwar period—rising economic status, migration to the North (where voting rights and greater economic opportunity awaited), and liberalization in white attitudes—rapidly accelerated. African Americans who had served in the military or improved their economic status by working in wartime industries were emboldened to combat violations of their rights, which contributed to a vast expansion in African American legal and political activism. Perhaps most important, the struggle against Nazi racism helped discredit American racism among broad swaths of the public.[102] After the war, the impact of the antifascist struggle was augmented by that of the Cold War, which led influential white elites to view racial oppression as a hindrance to America's efforts to win international support for the struggle against communism, especially among emerging Third World nations.[103]

The Supreme Court seized on the Equal Protection Clause to advance the cause of African American rights, but it could also have relied on pre–New Deal due process cases. The potential for *Lochner*ian due process arguments to be used as a weapon against school segregation was almost realized in 1954 in *Bolling v. Sharpe*, a companion case to *Brown v. Board of Education*. *Bolling* arose in the District of Columbia, so the Court could not rely, as it had in *Brown*, on the Fourteenth Amendment's Equal Protection Clause, which applies only to states. Instead, Chief Justice Warren sought to rely on the Fifth Amendment's Due Process Clause.

Warren apparently did not recognize that the Court needed to draft a separate opinion on public school segregation in the District of Columbia until his clerk pointed it out to him just two weeks before the decision was issued.[104] His hastily drafted *Bolling* opinion relied on the idea that the right to pursue an education, or to educate one's children, was a fundamental liberty. Warren supported this conclusion with citations to a series of liberty-of-contract-era due process cases—*Meyer v. Nebraska*, *Bartels v. Iowa*, *Pierce v. Society of Sisters*, and *Farrington v. Tokushige*.[105] *Meyer* and *Pierce* stated that liberty interests protected by the Fourteenth Amendment's Due Process Clause include the "right to acquire useful knowledge."[106] *Tokushige* relied on those cases in interpreting the Fifth Amendment's Due Process Clause.[107]

Once the right to educational liberty was recognized, it was a short leap to Warren's conclusion that just "as a government may not impose arbitrary restrictions on the parent's right to educate his child, the government must not impose arbitrary restraints on access to the education which the government itself provides."[108] And *Brown* showed that the Court had concluded that segregation based on notions of white supremacy was an arbitrary restraint on public school education.

Warren dropped the initial opinion's citations of the pre–New Deal precedents and its reliance on an explicit liberty interest in educational freedom as a concession to Justice Hugo Black.[109] Black's objections were consistent with his opposition to using the Due Process Clauses to protect unenumerated rights.[110] While Black dissuaded Warren from explicitly relying on pre–New Deal due process opinions, the *Bolling* opinion still concluded that "segregation in public education is not reasonably related to any proper governmental objective, and thus it imposes on Negro children of the District of Columbia a burden that constitutes an arbitrary deprivation of their liberty in violation of the Due Process Clause."[111] The *Bolling* Court, then, relied on a due process argument, but failed to identify precisely what liberty interest was involved. With the exception of *Buchanan v. Warley*, *Bolling* also failed to cite relevant pre–New Deal due process precedents. The due process argument therefore lacks coherence, and seems poorly reasoned.[112]

Indeed, the Court's due process ruling was so watered down and cryptic that Black later claimed, counterfactually, that *Bolling* was actually and solely an equal protection case. Black argued that *Bolling* "merely recognized what had been the understanding from the beginning of the country . . . that the whole Bill of Rights, including the Due Process Clause of the Fifth Amendment, was a guarantee that all persons would receive equal treatment under the law."[113] The Court itself, perhaps unable to decipher Warren's final opinion, later adopted Black's interpretation of *Bolling*.

Warren's original draft, however, makes it clear that *Bolling* was not based on equal protection. Rather, like *Buchanan v. Warley*, it held that a violation of due process rights via racial classification required a legitimate, nondiscriminatory police power justification. Indeed, Warren's draft due process opinion arguably made a stronger case for the unconstitutionality of racial segregation under the Fifth Amendment's Due Process Clause than the Court's opinion in *Brown* made for the unconstitutionality of racial segregation under the Fourteenth Amendment's Equal Protection Clause. If nothing else, the draft *Bolling* opinion logically (if not inevitably) follows from precedents like *Buchanan*, *Meyer*, and *Tokushige*, while *Brown* required the Court to reverse *Plessy*.[114]

Bolling, in short, was a "substantive due process" opinion with roots in several liberty of contract era cases. This belies the oft-heard notion that the *Lochner* line of cases was somehow philosophically at odds with racial equality, and that the overruling of those cases in the 1930s was a necessary prelude to *Brown*.[115] Indeed, the initial draft *Bolling* suggests that existing *Lochner*ian precedents like *Buchanan*, *Meyer*, and *Pierce* were in tension with state-imposed school segregation. And as the first Justice Harlan's career shows, there is no inherent contradiction between support for the liberty of contract doctrine and support for an understanding of the Fourteenth Amendment that undermines the constitutionality of segregation laws.[116] The judicial dismantlement of Jim Crow starting with *Brown* was a result of changes in societal attitudes toward racism, especially among elites—not of the abandonment of the Old Court's due process jurisprudence.

In post–World War II America, liberals generally, and liberal legal elites in particular, embraced legal equality for African Americans as a core element of their political identity. It's worth reiterating, however, that neither racism nor racial egalitarianism was strongly correlated with intellectuals' opinion during the liberty of contract era on the proper role of government in regulating economic and social affairs. Moreover, government regulatory activism was especially dangerous for African Americans in a period when their political influence was at a nadir and their political allies were few.

Civil rights activists ultimately hitched their star to ascendant New Deal liberalism. However, the strong correlation in post–World World II politics between, for example, support for expansive government regulatory authority, support for government nurturing of labor unions, and support for legal equality for African Americans was novel to American history. Once racial liberalism became associated with broad support for government activism on a variety of fronts, the legacy of the pre–New Deal Progressive legal elite's indifference and hostility to the concerns of African Americans was largely forgotten. The Supreme Court's war on Jim Crow, which began in earnest in the late 1940s, happened to coincide with the death of liberty of contract, but it's far too simplistic to conclude that the latter somehow caused the former. The legal establishment's commitment to segregation declined because racism, especially among the intellectual elite, declined precipitously—not because overruling *Lochner* and associated cases somehow made *Brown* inevitable.

Indeed, as we have seen, the rise of a racially egalitarian interpretation of the Fourteenth Amendment began during the liberty of contract era. Nevertheless, in the pre-New Deal period, with racism still dominant, civil rights attorneys in short supply, and negligible support from the political branches for any significant judicial assault on Jim Crow, liberty of contract jurisprudence, with its emphasis on limiting the states' police power, didn't have all that much to offer African Americans who were fighting de jure segregation. But what it offered, and provided in *Buchanan,* was still a lot more than African Americans could expect from contemporary champions of Progressive constitutionalism.

CHAPTER SIX

The Decline of Liberty of Contract, and the Rise of "Civil Liberties"

S tandard narratives of the development of American constitutional law posit that Progressive reformers and their judicial allies were prophetic pioneers in their devotion to civil liberties and individual rights. One historian, for example, writes that "in all the really crucial civil liberties cases, Justices Holmes and Brandeis stood together on the side of the claimed right."[1] The Progressives' pro–liberty of contract adversaries, meanwhile, are said to have been hostile to civil liberties.[2]

This dichotomy anachronistically reads conservative/liberal ideological divisions of the late twentieth century into an earlier era. Unlike their post–New Deal counterparts, late-nineteenth- and early-twentieth-century jurists did not readily distinguish between economic rights and other rights. Elite lawyers who argued that states' power to regulate the economy was strongly limited by constitutional considerations also typically favored analogous limitations on state regulatory power in other areas.[3] Progressive opponents of liberty of contract, meanwhile, typically also opposed judicial intervention to restrain government activism in other spheres, and generally expressed broad contempt for the notion of natural or inherent individual rights.[4] Only toward the end of the liberty of contract era did left-leaning jurists start to distinguish between support for civil liberties, especially freedom of expression, and opposition to judicial enforcement of other, primarily economic, constitutional rights.

Justice Holmes, a hero for elite Progressive lawyers, had little use for individual rights and thought the police power virtually unlimited. Holmes wrote that "a law should be called good if it reflects the will of the dominant forces of the community, even if it takes us all to hell."[5] H. L. Mencken, exaggerating only slightly, wrote that if Holmes's judicial opinions "were accepted literally, there would be scarcely any brake at all upon lawmaking, and the Bill of Rights would have no more significance than the Code of Manu."[6] Like Holmes, Progressive jurists such as Learned Hand and Felix Frankfurter supported broad judicial deference to state regulation, even when civil liberties were trampled.

Legal Progressives' disdain for judicial enforcement of constitutional rights arose in part from their contempt for what they saw as the stubbornly antilabor judiciary, but it also had roots in Progressive hostility to liberal rights-based "individualism."[7] Robert Hale provided additional fodder for this hostility in the early 1920s with his influential attack on the concept of government coercion.[8] Hale believed that the very concept of liberty as freedom from government interference was nonsensical. While he primarily attacked liberty of contract and other economic rights, his ideas were equally applicable to freedom of speech and other noneconomic liberties.[9]

The most significant exception to the pattern of Progressive hostility to constitutional protection for individual rights was that during and after World War I, some Progressives vigorously supported greater constitutional protection of freedom of expression.[10] Brandeis and Holmes took up their cause, though they had significant reservations about using the Fourteenth Amendment to limit states' infringement on freedom of speech.

Federal constitutional protection for civil liberties against the states emerged slowly after the Civil War. Justice John Marshall Harlan argued for decades that the Fourteenth Amendment required the Supreme Court to apply the rights enumerated in the Bill of Rights to the states, but he was always outvoted, sometimes 8–1.[11]

Nevertheless, as the Court became more aggressive about protecting economic rights under the Fourteenth Amendment, hints emerged that other rights might also receive invigorated protection. Justice Peckham's seminal 1897 opinion in *Allgeyer v. Louisiana* announced that the Due Process Clause's protection of liberty from state action included not just liberty of contract, but the right of an individual to be "free in the enjoyment of all his faculties [and] to be free to use them in all lawful ways."[12]

In 1908 the Supreme Court stated that "some of the personal rights safeguarded by the first eight Amendments against national action may also be safeguarded against state action, because a denial of them would be a denial of due process of law."[13] The Court explained that to the extent the Fourteenth Amendment protects such rights, it was "not because those rights are enumerated in the first eight Amendments, but because they are of such a nature that they are included in the conception of due process of law." A year earlier, the Court had reserved for the future the question of whether "there is to be found in the Fourteenth Amendment a prohibition [of restriction of freedom of speech] similar to that in the First."[14]

Meanwhile, influential Progressive constitutional scholars evinced little sympathy for individual rights.[15] Princeton University president (and later U.S. president) Woodrow Wilson, for example, dismissed talk of "the inalienable rights of the individual" as "nonsense." "The object of constitutional government," according to Wilson, was not to protect liberty, but "to bring the active, planning will of each part of the government into accord with the prevailing popular thought and need."[16]

Progressives blamed the "individualist" philosophy of the Constitution, as manifested in its protections for individual rights, for blocking needed Progressive reforms. In his extremely influential book *Progressive Democracy*, Herbert Croly, whose admirers and friends included Frankfurter and Hand, criticized the Bill of Rights for turning the Constitution "into a monarchy of Law superior in right to the monarchy of the people."[17] Morris Cohen, writing in Croly's *New Republic*, questioned the legitimacy of judicial power to invalidate legislation that infringed on individual liberty.[18]

Progressive lawyers' contempt for America's individualist natural rights tradition naturally led to hostility to the Fourteenth Amendment.[19] Felix Frankfurter, writing in the *New Republic*, called for the repeal of the Fourteenth Amendment's Due Process Clause,[20] and Louis Brandeis agreed with him in private conversation.[21] Brandeis even suggested that Frankfurter advise Florence Kelley to advocate repeal of the entire Fourteenth Amendment, but Frankfurter apparently favored retaining the Equal Protection Clause.[22] Brandeis later obliquely warned Frankfurter that equal protection "looms up even more menacingly than due process."[23] Other Progressives called for the repeal of the entire Fourteenth Amendment.[24]

Government control of the economy and suppression of civil liberties during World War I led to a significant backlash against activist government. Warren Harding based his successful 1920 presidential campaign on the promise of "A Return to Normalcy." Harding ended federal "Palmer" raids on radicals and, with the cooperation of Congress, lowered taxes, ended wartime controls of the economy, and cut federal spending. Meanwhile, fear that traditional individualist American values were being eroded by "foreign" ideologies also led to a constitutionalist movement, spearheaded by the American Bar Association, to educate the public about the American system of government.[25] Constitutionalists were especially alarmed at the growth of the Progressive idea of a "living Constitution" that changes with the times.[26] Not surprisingly, Harding's four Supreme Court appointees

were among the leaders of the 1920s revival of liberty of contract jurisprudence. The Court also dramatically expanded the role of the Fourteenth
Amendment's Due Process Clause in protecting civil liberties.

THE EDUCATIONAL LIBERTY CASES

The expansion of due process jurisprudence beyond liberty of contract and
property rights began with cases involving challenges to the autonomy of private education. Historians have emphasized the nativist and anti-Catholic
origins of these laws.[27] Banning or heavily regulating private schools was
also supported by many Progressives who thought public schools essential
in winning the citzenry's loyalty to the increasingly activist state.[28] The
ties of family, religion, and community were a barrier to the realization of
this vision.

The first education case to reach the Supreme Court, *Meyer v. Nebraska*,[29]
prohibited any school or tutor from teaching any subject to any pre–high
school student in any foreign language. Robert Meyer, a Bible teacher in
a Lutheran school who taught in German, challenged the law. When the
case reached the Supreme Court, the state asserted several police power
justifications for the law: to promote civic development and encourage children to acquire American ideals; to ensure that the English was the mother
tongue of all children; and to assimilate a very large foreign-born population that "use[s] foreign words, follow[s] foreign leaders, [and] move[s] in a
foreign atmosphere."[30]

The Court invalidated the law. Justice James McReynolds, writing for
seven justices, acknowledged the importance of ensuring that children at-
tain proficiency in English. But he concluded that the law unconstitutionally "interferes with the calling of modern language teachers, callings
always having been regarded as useful and honorable, essential, indeed to
the public welfare." The law interfered with "the right of the individual to
pursue the coming occupations of life," and was "arbitrary and without
reasonable relation to any end within the competency of the state."[31] Putting aside his own anti-German prejudices,[32] McReynolds wrote that "mere
knowledge of the German language cannot reasonably be regarded as harmful." He added that the Due Process Clause protects the right "to acquire
useful knowledge, to marry, establish a home and bring up children, [and] to
worship God according to the dictates of his own conscience," along with
"other privileges long recognized at common law as essential to the orderly
pursuit of happiness by free men."[33] The opinion's assertion of these broad
liberty rights was supported only by a long string of liberty of contract/due

process decisions, including *Lochner* and *Adkins v. Children's Hospital.*[34] McReynolds's reliance on these precedents, and his seamless transitions between the "economic" right of an individual to pursue a career as a foreign language teacher and such "non-economic rights" as the right "to acquire useful knowledge" demonstrates the lack of demarcation between these categories at the time. *Meyer* also reflects *Lochner*'s shift in the Court's focus in due process cases from class legislation concerns to considerations of individual right: because Nebraska banned *all* foreign languages, a class legislation argument would almost certainly have been unavailing.

Justice Holmes dissented, joined by Justice Sutherland.[35] In a companion case to *Meyer*, *Bartels v. Iowa*, Holmes wrote that "if there are sections in the state where a child would hear only Polish or French or German spoken at home, I am not prepared to say that it is unreasonable to provide that, in his early years, he shall hear and speak only English at school."[36] Holmes concluded that the law "appears to me to present a question upon which men reasonably might differ, and therefore I am unable to say that the Constitution of the United States prevents the experiment's being tried."

Leading Progressive lawyers' response to *Meyer* was skeptical at best. Felix Frankfurter, for example, wrote to Learned Hand that while he regarded "such know-nothing legislation as uncivilized," he would still have voted with Holmes rather than "lodging power in those nine gents in Washington." Hand agreed and added, "I can see no reason why, if a state legislature wishes to make a jackass of itself by that form of Americanization, it should not have the responsibility for doing so rather than the Supreme Court."[37]

Among leading legal Progressives only Justice Brandeis, who joined the majority opinion, publicly supported the outcome in *Meyer*. His background, as a child of German immigrants who had attended a German-language elementary school cofounded by his father, may have colored his perspective.[38] Brandeis told Frankfurter that so long as the Due Process Clause exists, it must be applied to protect fundamental rights including speech and education.[39]

In 1924 Frankfurter, writing in *The New Republic*, repeated his earlier call for the repeal of the Due Process Clause. He wrote that "no nine men are wise enough and good enough to be entrusted with the power which the unlimited provisions of the due process clauses confer."[40] Frankfurter later praised Holmes's dissent in *Bartels* as an example of Holmes's "deference to legislation with which he has no sympathy," though Holmes had in fact evinced some sympathy for the law.[41] More than two decades later, Frankfurter, now serving on the Supreme Court, told one of his colleagues that the *Meyer* dissenters had been correct.[42]

The breadth of the *Meyer* opinion was likely influenced by the justices' awareness that many states were considering banning private elementary schools. Nebraska's legislature had defeated such a measure by one vote, and Oregon voters had already approved a referendum mandating that all children between the ages of eight and sixteen attend public schools.[43] A commentator noted that *Meyer* likely bode ill for the new Oregon law.[44]

A unanimous Supreme Court two years later indeed invalidated the Oregon law, in *Pierce v. Society of Sisters*.[45] The Court reasserted the right of parents to direct their children's education, and completely ignored the state's asserted police power interest in mandating that all children attend the public school "melting pot" that would create a homogenous citizenry.[46]

Frankfurter criticized *Pierce* in *The New Republic*.[47] He argued that Americans were in danger of confusing unwise or unjust legislation with unconstitutional legislation, and he warned his fellow Progressives that a great deal of "highly illiberal" legislation infringing on freedom of thought and freedom of speech was "clearly constitutional."[48] For the Supreme Court to hold otherwise would provide it with even more illegitimate power at the expense of state legislatures. For reasons that he apparently thought self-evident and therefore did not articulate, Frankfurter believed that Court decisions invalidating labor legislation, such as the *Adkins v. Children's Hospital* case invalidating a minimum-wage law for women, were much more damaging than even the worst "repealable" statute invading civil liberties. Two decades later, with the benefit of hindsight, and even though the Fourteenth Amendment no longer posed a threat to labor and other reformist economic legislation, Frankfurter remained hostile to *Pierce*.[49]

The Supreme Court rebuffed another attack on private schooling in 1927 in *Farrington v. Tokushige*, which involved a challenge to a law designed to shut down Japanese-language schools in the federal territory of Hawaii.[50] The government's justification for the law was that Hawaii had "a large Japanese population," and that "the Japanese do not readily assimilate with other races; that they still adhere to their own ideals and customs, and are still loyal to their emperor."[51] The Court, in another opinion by Justice McReynolds, stated that it "appreciated the grave problems incident to the large alien population of the Hawaiian Islands," but "the Japanese parent has the right to direct the education of his own child without unreasonable restrictions; the Constitution protects him as well as those who speak another tongue."[52]

Some historians give the Supreme Court little credit for its decisions in *Meyer*, *Pierce*, and *Tokushige* because, they argue, each case was easy, given the outrageousness of the underlying legislation.[53] This is an anachronistic perspective; at the time these laws had many defenders, including state supreme courts. More plausibly, these opinions reflect the Court's revolt against widespread Progressive notions of state-building and nation-building.[54] The libertarian basis of the opinions is evinced by McReynolds's strong language; McReynolds, notorious for his hostility to African Americans and Jews, likely had little sympathy for the racial and ethnic minorities who were the primary beneficiaries of *Meyer*, *Pierce*, and *Tokushige*.[55] But in a rebuke to statist Progressive notions of educational reform, McReynolds proclaimed that "the child is not the mere creature of the state."[56]

Another civil liberties issue involving government regulation of education arose when Tennessee passed a law banning the teaching of evolution in public schools, which would lead to the famous Scopes "Monkey Trial."[57] Influential journalist Walter Lippmann proposed that liberal attorneys organize a challenge to the law under the Due Process Clause. Thomas Reed Powell, Morris Cohen, Learned Hand, and other leading Progressive jurists responded that the courts should not interfere with the legislatures' prerogatives to determine educational policy.[58]

EUGENICS

Neither the Supreme Court's "Progressives" nor their "conservative" counterparts distinguished themselves as defenders of individual rights when the issue of coercive eugenics reached the Court. Coercive eugenics was a quintessentially Progressive movement in that it reflected ideological commitments to anti-individualism, efficiency, scientific expertise, and technocracy.[59] The inherent statism of government-sponsored eugenics was especially attractive to Progressives. As the British Fabian Sidney Webb wrote, "no consistent eugenicist can be a 'Laisser Faire' individualist unless he throws up the game in despair. He must interfere, interfere, interfere!"[60] Not surprisingly, Progressive-era eugenicists were eager to use the full force of government to promote their agenda.[61]

Eugenics also strongly appealed to Protestant elites who did not share general Progressive enthusiasm for government regulation but feared the growing urban immigrant and African American population. The only organized, consistent opposition to coercive eugenics came from some evangelical Christian denominations; the Catholic Church failed to officially take a stand against it until the 1930s, though many individual Catholics fought against eugenics legislation before that.[62]

By 1927, twenty-three state legislatures had passed sterilization bills. Of those, governors in five states vetoed them, and voters repealed one in a referendum.[63] Many of the laws that survived were challenged in court.

Courts invalidated some of the laws on various constitutional grounds, especially as violations of equal protection (when applied only to individuals committed to state institutions because they suffered from diseases such as epilepsy) or as cruel and unusual punishment (when applied to convicts).[64]

Judges who thought the laws unconstitutional sometimes struck strikingly individualist themes. A Michigan Supreme Court justice, dissenting for himself and two colleagues, accused eugenicists of "invit[ing] atavism to the state of mind evidenced in Sparta, ancient Rome, and the Dark Ages, where individuality counted for naught against the mere animal breeding of human beings for purposes of the state or tribe."[65]

No such sentiments were apparent when the U.S. Supreme Court upheld a sterilization law in 1927 in *Buck v. Bell*.[66] Carrie Buck, a teenager from Virginia, had been committed to a state institution by her foster parents after becoming pregnant. She claimed that her foster parents' nephew had raped her, but the relevant state medical authorities insisted without any real evidence that Buck, her mother, and her daughter were all "feebleminded." After a kangaroo court hearing at which her appointed attorney was apparently in league with the other side, the authorities decreed that she be sterilized.[67]

When the case reached the Supreme Court, Chief Justice Taft assigned the opinion to Justice Holmes, cautioning him that some of their colleagues were "troubled by the case, especially Butler." Taft advised that Holmes emphasize the procedural protections the law provided and the safety of the procedure to "lessen the shock many may feel over such a remedy."[68]

Holmes did indeed explain that "the rights of the patient are most carefully" protected and that "every step . . . was taken in scrupulous compliance with the statute." Holmes went on to dismiss the argument that the law was inherently arbitrary and inhumane and therefore a violation of the state's obligation not to take liberty from an individual without due process of law. Holmes, a thrice-injured Civil War veteran, argued that if the government could draft "the best citizens," it "would be strange if it could not call upon those who already sap the strength of the State for these lesser sacrifices . . . in order to prevent our being swamped with incompetence." He added that instead of waiting to "execute degenerate offspring for crime, or to let them starve for their imbecility," it was best to prevent the "manifestly unfit from continuing their kind." He concluded that "the principle that sustains compulsory vaccination is broad enough to cover cutting the Fallopian tubes." Holmes proclaimed, in language that has since become infamous: "Three generations of imbeciles are enough."

Justice Holmes's opinion is notable for several reasons. First, despite his reputation as a fierce skeptic, he credulously accepted the junk science of early twentieth-century eugenics. Moreover, he evinced no concern for the actual or potential abuse of the government's sterilization power; as researchers have since discovered, Carrie Buck and her daughter had normal intelligence. Meanwhile, Holmes articulated an idea severely at odds with the American constitutional and natural rights traditions: that because the state may force individuals to risk their lives in military service, it may also demand *any* lesser sacrifice from its citizens, including forgoing their ability to bear children. Finally, the analogy between compulsory smallpox vaccination and compulsory sterilization is dubious. In the smallpox case, failure to comply with the vaccination law led to a monetary fine, not to mandatory vaccination. And while vaccination and sterilization involve invasions of bodily integrity, the results are quite different: "no smallpox in the one case and no children in the other."[69]

Only Justice Pierce Butler dissented, but he didn't write an opinion explaining the rationale for his dissent. Whether Butler's dissent was a result of his Catholic faith, his skepticism of government coercion—he was the Court's leading critic of the excesses attendant to the enforcement of alcohol Prohibition—or a combination of both remains unknown.[70]

Felix Frankfurter praised Holmes for voting in *Bell* to uphold legislation he may have thought inefficacious.[71] In fact, while some of Holmes's colleagues had doubts about their decision in *Buck*, Holmes himself reveled in it. He later told a friend, "One decision that I wrote gave me pleasure, establishing the constitutionality of a law permitting the sterilization of imbeciles." He also revealed that his draft opinion had even harsher language than the final version, which is widely considered one of the Supreme Court's cruelest and most intemperate opinions.[72]

At the time, though, Holmes's opinion was considered a Progressive triumph. Justice Brandeis, who joined the opinion, later cited *Bell* as an example of properly allowing the states "to meet modern conditions by regulations which a century ago, or even half a century ago, probably would have been rejected as arbitrary and oppressive."[73] Professor Robert Cushman praised Holmes's reference to "three generations of imbeciles" as a "trenchant" explanation of why the "substance of the law" was "a reasonable social protection, entirely compatible with due process of law."[74] Professor Fowler Harper listed *Bell* as an example of welcome "progressive trends" in law.[75] Of the approximately thirty-six thousand Americans who were forcibly sterilized by 1940, thirty thousand of them were victimized after *Buck v. Bell*.[76]

FREEDOM OF EXPRESSION

Given their hostility to the Supreme Court's educational freedom cases and their support for coercive eugenics, the case that the Progressive opponents of liberty of contract favored constitutional protection of civil liberties must rest on their support for freedom of speech. Before the United States entered World War I, most leading Progressive lawyers—Learned Hand was a notable exception—evinced little interest in freedom of expression in general, and even less in judicial intervention on behalf of expressive rights.[77] Herbert Goodrich's views reflected the dominant Progressive attitude: "The same kind of argument and the same line of thought which upholds a law which restricts a man in the contracts he may make upholds a law limiting the exercise of his tongue when the majority wills it."[78]

At least among Progressives allied with the political left, wariness of individualistic speech rights was tempered by the trauma of wartime repression of pacifists and other dissenters, and the postwar "Red Scare."[79] With labor radicals, pacifists, socialists, and other left-wingers being jailed or deported, constitutional protection of freedom of speech became an important item on the left's agenda, especially among its more radical elements. The American Civil Liberties Union, for example, was founded as a response to the growth of government repression during the war.[80] Moreover, as ideological insurgents challenging a dying classical antistatist American liberalism, the Progressive left had every incentive to advocate a free marketplace of ideas.

Consistent with their contempt for constitutional individualism, leading Progressive defenses of freedom of expression relied on utilitarian considerations, and not on freedom of expression as a fundamental individual right. The Progressive identification of freedom of speech as a *civil* liberty was intended to differentiate it from what they thought of as the obsolete, individualist, natural-rights based liberties of the American past.[81] Zachariah Chafee's enormously influential 1920 book, *Freedom of Speech*, suggested that freedom of speech should receive constitutional protection not because it was an inherent individual right, but because of the importance of political speech to the functioning of a democracy.[82] By contrast, an earlier, less influential group of radical speech libertarians had fought obscenity prosecutions as vigorously as they had fought restrictions on political speech.[83]

Justice Holmes initially expressed no sympathy for judicial protection for freedom of expression. As late as June 1918, he told Learned Hand that free speech "stands no differently than freedom from vaccination."[84] Yet

Holmes, under pressure from his Progressive acolytes, and disturbed by the inanities of wartime speech prosecutions, soon began to enunciate a newly speech-protective interpretation of the First Amendment in cases involving federal criminal prosecutions.[85] Justice Brandeis, who in his pre-Court career had evinced little interest in freedom of expression,[86] joined him. Brandeis's defense of free speech resulted from his conviction that the more his favored Progressive causes were publicly discussed and debated, the more popular support they would garner.[87]

Many "conservative" scholars gave short shrift to freedom of expression, not because they thought it was an unimportant right, but because they believed that the right was limited by the traditional broad police power to protect public morals and prevent disorder. The political right, however, also had its own libertarian elements that supported relatively broad speech rights. This perspective filtered into public debate and public policy, especially in the Harding administration.[88]

By 1920, most prominent conservative jurists had concluded that state governments were constitutionally obliged by the Fourteenth Amendment's Due Process Clause to respect freedom of expression.[89] The Supreme Court, however, remained agnostic on the question of whether the Fourteenth Amendment protected freedom of speech against the states. In 1920, in *Gilbert v. Minnesota*, a state law penalizing interference with or discouragement of enlistment in the military or naval service of the United States was challenged as obnoxious to "the inherent right of free speech."[90] Justice McKenna, writing for the Court, concluded that the law in question was within the police power, and therefore would be upheld even if the right to freedom of speech was properly in play. Justice Brandeis, dissenting, argued that the Fourteenth Amendment protected freedom "to teach, either in the privacy of the home or publicly, the doctrine of pacifism." He added, "I cannot believe that the liberty guaranteed by the Fourteenth Amendment includes only liberty to acquire and to enjoy property."[91]

In 1925 in *Gitlow v. New York*, the Supreme Court finally announced that "freedom of speech and of the press . . . are among the fundamental personal rights and 'liberties' protected by the due process clause of the Fourteenth Amendment from impairment by the States."[92] The Court nevertheless upheld Benjamin Gitlow's conviction for disseminating pamphlets that advocated the violent overthrow of the government. The majority saw legislation banning efforts to overthrow the government and to inhibit breaches of the peace as legitimate police power limitations on freedom of expression.[93] Justice Holmes, joined by Justice Brandeis, argued in dissent for broader constitutional protections for freedom of speech.[94] Holmes's dissent is often celebrated for its expansive vision of freedom of expression. Far less often noted is the grudging nature of his assertion that the "principle of free speech must be taken to be included in the Fourteenth Amendment, in view of the scope that has been given to the word 'liberty' as there used."[95] In other words, Holmes would have preferred that neither liberty of contract nor freedom of speech receive Fourteenth Amendment protection, but if the former was to be protected, the latter deserved protection as well.

Some Progressives, especially those who did not identify with the political left, were unhappy with the Supreme Court's application of the Due Process Clause to protect freedom of speech. Charles Warren, the leading legal historian of his day, complained that "if the doctrine of the *Gitlow* case is to be carried to its logical and inevitable conclusion, every one of the rights contained in the Bill of Rights ought to be and must be included within the definition of 'liberty,' and must be held to be guaranteed by the Fourteenth Amendment against deprivation by a State 'without due process of law.'" Warren contended that like the liberty of contract line of cases, Supreme Court decisions protecting freedom of expression would inhibit "legislation enacted by each state to meet local conditions and to regulate local relations."[96]

Two years after *Gitlow*, the Court unanimously invalidated a state conviction for "criminal syndicalism" as a violation of the right to freedom of speech.[97] Also in 1927, Justice Brandeis penned a concurrence in *Whitney v. California* in which he asserted that the Fourteenth Amendment's Due Process Clause, correctly interpreted, applies only to matters of procedure.[98] He favored protecting freedom of speech against the states only because settled precedent held that the clause protects substantive rights. Brandeis's *Whitney* opinion defended freedom of speech primarily on the instrumental ground that it promoted free and rational public discussion, which was essential for the American people to govern themselves. By asserting that freedom of speech was in essence a matter of the social interest in democratic self-government rather than a libertarian matter of fundamental individual rights, Brandeis tried to cleanse freedom of speech from any association with liberty of contract.[99] In doing so, he helped decouple judicial protection of "civil liberties" and "economic liberties" in the minds of left-leaning jurists, which in turn helped ensure that constitutional protection for freedom of speech would survive the Supreme Court's eventual abandonment of liberty of contract.

In 1931, the Supreme Court used the Fourteenth Amendment's Due Process Clause to invalidate a California law banning the display of the Communist flag.[100] Justices McReynolds and Butler dissented on technical grounds, but all nine justices agreed that the Clause protects freedom of expression. Two weeks later, the Court held that the states were obligated to respect freedom of the press, and not just speech or expression more generally. Chief Justice Hughes wrote that it was "impossible to conclude that this essential personal liberty of the citizen was left unprotected by the general guaranty of fundamental rights of person and property."[101]

By 1932, the idea that the Due Process Clause protects freedom of speech was sufficiently accepted across the Court's ideological spectrum that Justice Sutherland invoked freedom of expression in *New State Ice v. Liebmann* to criticize Brandeis's dissent.[102] Just as no "theory of experimentation in censorship" could justify interference with freedom of the press, Brandeis's states-as-laboratories-of-democracy approach could not justify interference with "the opportunity to apply one's labor and skill in an ordinary occupation."

In 1936, a unanimous Court cited *Allgeyer v. Louisiana* for the principle that the word "liberty" in the Fourteenth Amendment "embraces not only the right of a person to be free from physical restraint, but the right to be free in the enjoyment of all his faculties as well." The Court concluded that freedom of speech and of the press are fundamental rights, "safeguarded by the due process of law clause of the Fourteenth Amendment."[103]

In short, the Supreme Court started treating freedom of expression as an important constitutional right in the 1920s and early 1930s. The New Deal and its aftermath, therefore, were not responsible for the emergence of constitutional protection of free speech.[104] However, while the Court's majority treated freedom of expression as a traditional individual right subject to the states' police power, Holmes and Brandeis thought free speech should receive special protection because it served the interests of majoritarian democracy.[105] Both sides, however, agreed that the Fourteenth Amendment's Due Process Clause protected freedom of expression because it was fundamental to American liberty, not because the Bill of Rights singled out freedom of expression for protection.[106]

THE SALVATION OF THE "CIVIL LIBERTIES" PRECEDENTS

While protection for freedom of expression by the Supreme Court gradually grew, the scope of the liberty of contract doctrine began to shrink. By the 1920s libertarian views, especially on economics, had been marginalized among American intellectuals.[107] These views retained a tenuous foothold in elite legal circles despite the onslaught of sociological jurisprudence and legal realism.[108] But the Court's position that liberty of contract was fundamental to Anglo-American liberty became untenable as the Depression wore on. With almost no support among leading intellectuals, with the unemployed and underemployed clamoring for government intervention, and with statism ascendant across the globe in the forms of fascism, communism, and social democracy—each of which had its share of admirers in the United States—the Court's commitment to limited government and liberty of contract seemed outlandishly reactionary to much of the public.

Given the lack of intellectual and public support for liberty of contract, its demise was inevitable, but it required a change of personnel on the Court. President Herbert Hoover, a Progressive Republican, put the first nails into liberty of contract's coffin by appointing to the Court Justices Charles Evan Hughes, Owen Roberts, and Benjamin Cardozo, each of whom had views well to the left of the justices who had dominated the Court in the 1920s. They joined Coolidge appointee Harlan Fiske Stone and Wilson holdover Louis Brandeis—Holmes retired in 1932—to form a bloc far more open to economic experimentation and regulation than were their four more traditionalist counterparts.

In 1934 the Court expanded the "affected with a public interest" doctrine to the point where just about any regulation of prices passed muster under the Due Process Clause.[109] This holding suggested that wage regulations were also constitutional. After a short period of resistance to the New Deal's more extreme elements, the Court capitulated on a broad range of constitutional issues.

In 1937 it reversed *Adkins v. Children's Hospital* and upheld a minimum-wage law for women in *West Coast Hotel v. Parrish*.[110] Debate has raged among historians as to whether *West Coast Hotel* marked an abrupt break with the past, or whether the Court simply chose to follow the more liberal precedents regarding the police power's scope from cases such as *Holden v. Hardy*.[111] Regardless, it seems reasonably clear that as of 1937 there were not yet five votes to completely abandon liberty of contract.[112] None of this mattered in the long term, because President Franklin Roosevelt was poised to appoint eight new justices to the Court over the next several years, and the Roosevelt administration had one key criterion for its Court nominees: they had to believe that the Constitution permitted virtually any legislation regulating economic activity.[113]

Roosevelt tried to rush the process of constitutional change through his "court-packing" initiative of early 1937. This approach failed, but the Court soon declared that economic legislation was subject only to the most minimal constitutional scrutiny.[114] By 1941, with all the "conservatives" gone, the Court unanimously upheld the Fair Labor Standards Act's wage and hour provisions.[115]

With Roosevelt appointees joining a growing Progressive/liberal majority on the Court, the New Dealers had the opportunity to fulfill the old Progressive dream of emasculating the Due Process Clause and limiting its scope to purely procedural rights.[116] But the Court did not abandon what soon came to be known as "substantive due process." Instead, it continued to protect freedom of expression rights against the states via the Due Process Clause, and later "incorporated" other rights from the Bill of Rights into that clause. The Court also continued to review state and local legislation under the Equal Protection Clause, and eventually used the clause aggressively to protect African Americans from state-sponsored segregation.

The post-*Lochner* reincarnation of the Supreme Court's fundamental rights jurisprudence began in 1937 in *Palko v. Connecticut*. All of the Progressive and liberal justices joined a Cardozo opinion stating that the Fourteenth Amendment protects rights mentioned in the Bill of Rights that are "implicit in the concept of ordered liberty."[117]

The famous Footnote Four of the 1938 *Carolene Products* case also reflected the new liberal majority's reluctance to entirely abandon judicial review of purported police power regulations.[118] Justice Stone, writing for the Court, stated that economic regulations would have a very strong presumption of constitutionality, but that a weaker presumption applied when plaintiffs asserted rights under the Fourteenth Amendment that were enumerated in the Bill of Rights.[119] Stone also asserted that laws directed at particular religious, or national, or racial minorities "may call for a correspondingly more searching judicial inquiry." The Court creatively reinterpreted—that is, intentionally misinterpreted—*Meyer* and *Pierce* as decisions invalidating laws because the laws discriminated against minorities.[120] This was the Court's first of several attempts to preserve to preserve these precedents by disentangling them from their roots in the now-obsolete liberty of contract line of cases.[121] The result was that the Court, following Brandeis's lead, created a distinction in American constitutional law between economic rights on the one hand and civil rights and liberties on the other. This distinction allowed liberals to preserve the Court's role in protecting individual rights from overreaching by the government, while distinguishing their jurisprudence from that of the dreaded liberty of contract era.

The Court refused to completely refrain from using the Due Process Clause to protect individual liberties for several reasons. First, judicial regard for civil liberties allowed New Dealers, within and outside the Court to plausibly claim that they were committed to preserving individual rights even while vastly expanding the size and scope of the federal government. And while by the 1930s the Court's liberty of contract decisions were very unpopular, its tentative forays into civil libertarianism, ranging from *Pierce* and *Meyer* to its free speech cases to protecting the "Scottsboro Boys" from grossly unfair criminal prosecutions, had received general public approbation.[122] These decisions were especially popular among the ethnic and religious groups that formed the core of the New Deal coalition.[123]

Second, judicial restraint always looks better when your side doesn't control the courts. Once the "left" took over the Supreme Court, the idea that the justices should always defer to state legislatures became far less attractive.[124] This was especially true because state legislatures were often dominated by rural, conservative interests with agendas that broadly conflicted with ascendant urban liberalism.

Third, the New Deal coalition included many intellectuals with a decidedly modern liberal, as opposed to old-fashioned Progressive, ideological bent. While these individuals supported increased government activism in the economic sphere, they were also concerned with civil rights and civil liberties. Some of these New Deal liberals were apostate classical liberals, such as Oswald Garrison Villard, whose *Nation* had praised the *Lochner* decision. Others were Catholics, Jews of Eastern European descent, and African Americans who had previously been relatively marginal players in Progressive intellectual and political circles, and who tended to be much more sensitive than were most Progressives to minority rights and freedom of expression.[125]

Fourth, the enthusiasm for government activism that the New Dealers inherited from the Progressives was tempered by the rise of fascism in Europe. Given the fall of liberal democracy in Germany and elsewhere to popular acclaim or at least acquiescence, the confidence the Progressives had expressed in majoritarianism seemed grossly misplaced.[126] German legal positivism, which had strongly influenced Progressives, also lost its attraction under the weight of Naziism.

Fifth, the elite bar received part of its prestige from the prominent role the Supreme Court played in American life. Once it became clear that the old constitutional order based on property rights and limited government was dead, elite attorneys quickly became advocates of an expanded role for the Supreme Court in protecting freedom of expression and minority rights. The justices' self-interest, meanwhile, required maintaining the Court's significance.[127]

Finally, and for many of the reasons noted above, the Roosevelt administration encouraged the Supreme Court's emerging civil liberties jurisprudence. After losing the court-packing fight, the administration focused on
changing the public's understanding of the Constitution's essence. The
Constitution, the New Dealers argued, was not about protecting property
and establishing limited government, but guaranteeing individual civil liberties. Not only was a large and active federal government not a constitutional problem, but Americans needed such a government to protect them
from abuses of state and corporate power.

President Roosevelt ordered federal employees working on ceremonies
related to the Constitution's 150th anniversary in 1937 to emphasize the
Bill of Rights instead of the original Constitution.[128] The government's 1941
celebration of the 150th anniversary of the Bill of Rights, in turn, emphasized the First Amendment, as did the Court's emerging civil liberties jurisprudence.[129] The justices preserved and built upon the pre-1937 freedom of
expression/due process cases by reinterpreting them as decisions "incorporating" the text of the First Amendment against the states.

The Court was unwilling at this point to revive constitutional protections
for unenumerated rights, as evidenced by its next encounter with eugenics.
The credibility of eugenics declined dramatically from the late 1920s on-
ward. New scientific research called into question the genetic theory used to
support it, and its reputation suffered as it increasingly came to be identified
with Nazi atrocities—not unfairly, given the close intellectual ties between
American and German eugenicists in the early years of the Nazi regime.

When a case challenging mandatory sterilization of certain classes of
"habitual criminals" reached the Supreme Court in 1942, in *Skinner v. Oklahoma*,[130] no justice argued that coerced sterilization presumptively took an
individual's liberty without due process of law. Instead, the Court, in an
opinion by Justice William O. Douglas, held that the law violated the Equal
Protection Clause. The Court reasoned that the law arbitrarily and irratio-
nally classified certain criminal acts as a product of hereditary factors neces-
sitating sterilization, while ignoring others. Chief Justice Stone concurred,
arguing that the law afforded inadequate procedural protections and therefore deprived its targets of liberty without due process of law. Justice Robert
Jackson also concurred, to note his agreement with both Stone and Douglas.
Skinner, as Douglas acknowledged to an interviewer years later, did not
overrule *Buck v. Bell*.[131] Douglas's private notes show that he thought the
cases were distinguishable; he contrasted the issue of sterilizing "moronic
minds" (as in *Buck*) with the sterilization of criminals (as in *Skinner*), on
which there were "no statistics."[132]

Though coercive eugenics was discredited among the general public after the revelation of Nazi crimes, it remained popular much longer among certain intellectual heirs to Progressivism, such as the anti-Catholic author Paul Blanshard.[133] Because the *Skinner* Court had refused to find an unenumerated right to procreate and to declare coerced sterilization presumptively unconstitutional, coerced sterilizations continued in some states through the 1970s.

In sum, the controversies discussed in this chapter refute the conventional wisdom that liberty of contract jurisprudence was in conflict with judicial protection for other individual rights, and that critics of that jurisprudence farsightedly sought to replace liberty of contract with protection for civil liberties against the states. The justice most often credited with such farsightedness, Brandeis, preferred that the Fourteenth Amendment's Due Process Clause be interpreted to provide *no* substantive protections against states and their subsidiaries. Indeed, and as discussed in the next chapter, modern Fourteenth Amendment civil liberties jurisprudence owes more to liberty of contract advocates and their suspicion of government power than to the Progressives and their cramped understandings of individual rights. As we shall see, post–New Deal Supreme Court justices pretended to utterly reject the due process opinions of the "conservative" justices of the pre–New Deal era while in fact absorbing many of these opinions, modifying them, reclassifying them, and ultimately using them to promote liberal ends.

CHAPTER SEVEN

Lochner in Modern Times

*L*ochner's star fell long before it was overruled. Between 1925 and 1935, only one Supreme Court case cited it. After the Court's abandonment of the liberty of contract doctrine beginning in the mid-1930s, courts and legal scholars referenced *Lochner* primarily for Justice Holmes's dissenting opinion. Holmes anticipated the post–New Deal consensus that the courts should not invoke the Fourteenth Amendment's Due Process Clause to invalidate economic legislation. The Court adopted Holmes's accusation that *Lochner* and other liberty of contract cases were products of the justices' economic ideology, and that liberty of contract was foreign to the Constitution's text.

After World War II, the Supreme Court rejected challenges to even overtly protectionist economic regulations.[1] In an admirable display of nonpartisan consistency, the justices even upheld laws that directly contradicted the interests of the Democratic coalition that had put their political allies into power, such as a state law that banned closed union shops.[2] Justice William Douglas proclaimed in 1955 that the "day is gone when this Court uses the Due Process Clause of the Fourteenth Amendment to strike down state laws, regulatory of business and industrial conditions, because they may be unwise, improvident, or out of harmony with a particular school of thought."[3]

Lochner, however, was destined to play a crucial role in constitutional debate starting in the mid-1960s. *Lochner*'s modern notoriety arose largely because the post–New Deal Supreme Court, though abandoning liberty of contract, continued to rely on the authority of two opinions in the *Lochner* line of cases, *Meyer v. Nebraska* and *Pierce v. Society of Sisters*.[4] *Meyer*, in particular, became an important basis for the Warren and Burger Courts' protection of unenumerated rights under the Due Process Clause in the land-mark cases of *Griswold v. Connecticut* and *Roe v. Wade.*

While the Supreme Court beat the dead horse of liberty of contract for decades after the New Deal, civil liberties fared far better. The Court not only continued to protect freedom of expression against the states, but even-tually expanded the protections of the Fourteenth Amendment's Due Pro-cess Clause to include most of the other rights found in the Bill of Rights. In contrast to the liberty of contract era, when Progressive luminaries sought to restrict the Due Process Clause to issues of judicial procedure, the liberal New Dealers on the Supreme Court unanimously agreed that the Court had some obligation to use the clause to protect individual rights against state legislation.

In the 1940s, Justice Hugo Black developed his theory of "total incor-poration." Black believed that the Supreme Court should protect individ-ual liberty against the states, but that the liberty of contract era showed that courts must be restrained from reading their own policy preferences into the Constitution. To accomplish these twin goals, he argued that the Court should hold that the first eight amendments of the federal Bill of Rights were applicable to the states via "incorporation" into the Fourteenth Amendment's Due Process Clause, but that the clause did not protect any unenumerated rights.

Justice Felix Frankfurter, meanwhile, though no longer committed to limiting the Due Process Clause to procedural matters, opposed Black's incorporation doctrine.[5] He argued that the Court should continue to look to natural law and the heritage of the past to determine the scope of the rights protected by the clause. He wanted to retain the pre–New Deal Court's pro-tection of rights foundational to Anglo-American liberty, but thought the Court should exhibit great restraint in identifying those rights.[6]

The Court ultimately adopted neither justice's position. It gradually applied most, but not all, of the Bill of Rights to the states on a case-by-case basis.[7] To blunt criticism that they were emulating their discredited pre–New Deal predecessors, the justices and their defenders asserted that the liberty of contract cases involved illegitimate "substantive due process," while cases "incorporating" the Bill of Rights against the states did not.

Applying the concept of substantive due process to the liberty of con-tract cases was anachronistic, because no justice on the pre–New Deal Court adopted the view that substance and procedure were distinct categories under the clause.[8] But even if the liberty of contract cases could accurately be de-scribed as examples of substantive due process, exempting the incorporation cases from that moniker was more a matter of rhetoric than logic. For example, enforcing the First Amendment right of freedom of speech against the states via the Due Process Clause is literally an exercise in protecting a substantive right through that clause, and therefore is "substantive due process."

The post–New Deal Justices did try mightily to differentiate their due process jurisprudence from that of their predecessors. Black, for example, insisted that incorporation of the Bill of Rights, unlike liberty of contract, was dictated by the original intent of the Fourteenth Amendment. And the justices generally distinguished economic *interests,* which they thought could be adequately protected by the political process, from individual and civil *rights,* which were subject to majoritarian suppression. In the end, though, it's hard to escape the conclusion that in the most fundamental sense the liberal justices of the post–New Deal period were emulating their pre–New Deal predecessors: identifying rights they deemed fundamental to American liberty, and decreeing that the Due Process Clause protects those rights against the states.

Adoption of the incorporation doctrine did not prevent the justices from exercising discretion based on their ideological proclivities. First, the Court engaged only in "selective incorporation." The rights not incorporated, such as the right to a grand jury hearing and the right to bear arms, were the rights that the justices either disapproved of or thought unimportant.[9] Second, the Court interpreted some incorporated rights, such as the Fifth Amendment's ban on taking private property without just compensation, and some other rights found explicitly in the Constitution's text, such as the Article I, Section 10 ban on states impairing contractual obligations, far more narrowly than it interpreted rights favored by liberal intellectuals, such as freedom of expression. In short, if *Lochner* and other liberty of contract cases were examples of dubious "substantive due process" based on the justices' ideological proclivities, then so, a fortiori, were the incorporation cases.

In a sense, in fact, the Court eventually out-Lochnered *Lochner.*[10] Before the New Deal, the scope of liberty of contract and other Fourteenth Amendment due process rights recognized by the Supreme Court, including freedom of expression, was constrained by the states' police powers. After the New Deal, police power considerations were eventually replaced with the test of whether government infringement on freedom of speech served a "compelling interest," a significantly stricter test.[11] The right to freedom of expression under the Due Process Clause, which the Court deemed a "preferred freedom," quickly became far broader than the right to liberty of contract ever had been.[12]

The Supreme Court also began to aggressively deploy the Equal Protection Clause to protect African Americans from state-sponsored discrimination, most famously in *Brown v. Board of Education*.[13] *Brown* and like-minded cases were a modern version of the Court's old class legislation jurisprudence.[14] The Old Court had interpreted the ban on class legislation narrowly, because it had no reliable or consistent way to differentiate between legitimate classifications with a proper legislative purpose and illegitimate classifications intended to annoy or oppress legislative losers. The Warren Court's answer was to defer to almost all legislative classifications and not meaningfully police economic regulations through the Equal Protection Clause. Classifications based on race and other immutable characteristics would, however, be treated as inherently suspect and therefore subject to strict scrutiny. The Court would only uphold such classifications if they were "narrowly tailored" and served a "compelling government interest." And in contrast to the pre–New Deal Court, the Warren and Burger Courts considered legislative motivation when deciding whether a law violated the Equal Protection Clause.

The Court's increasingly aggressive Fourteenth Amendment jurisprudence attracted relatively little backlash from legal elites. The legal academy, in particular, was thoroughly dominated by New Deal liberals who supported the Court's trajectory. Most liberals happily abandoned the left's pre–New Deal opposition to "government by judiciary" in favor of what came to be known as the rights revolution. Some old-school Progressives, however, objected.[15] As the Supreme Court grew increasingly bold about enforcing rights against the states via the Fourteenth Amendment, first Justice Frankfurter (with regard to incorporation) and later Justice Black (with regard to the protection of unenumerated rights) came to be seen as "conservatives" for their reluctance to join in. This purported conservatism, however, largely consisted of continued adherence to their longstanding skepticism of giving the Supreme Court the discretion to invoke—or, according to critics, invent—rights via the Due Process Clause.

In 1958, an eighty-six-year-old Learned Hand shocked liberal academia by delivering a series of lectures at Harvard Law School in which he denounced the Supreme Court's recent civil rights and civil liberties jurisprudence.[16] Hand criticized the Court's protection of freedom of expression via incorporation of the First Amendment into the Fourteenth Amendment's Due Process Clause. He alleged that there is "no constitutional basis" for the Court to exercise any more supervision over state and local regulation of freedom of expression than it did over regulation of economic activity.[17] He went on to decry the notion that the Bill of Rights can or should be applied to the states.[18] Hand then criticized the Court's emerging civil rights jurisprudence, as reflected in *Brown v. Board of Education*. He analogized *Brown's* invalidation of public school segregation to the "old [liberty of contract] doctrine," through which, he said, the Court had protected economic interests. Hand concluded by accusing the Court of acting as a "third legislative chamber" and exercising such power only through a continuing *"coup de main."*[19]

Columbia Law School professor Herbert Wechsler also caused a stir by criticizing the Court's ruling in *Brown*.[20] As a Progressive law student at Columbia in the late 1920s, Wechsler had developed an "unqualified disdain" for the Supreme Court's pre–New Deal jurisprudence.[21] Though he was sympathetic to the civil rights movement, he believed that like the liberty of contract cases, *Brown* involved illegitimate judicial policymaking. According to Wechsler, the only plausible justification for *Brown* was that segregation violated African Americans' right to freedom of association. Integration, however, "forces an association upon those for whom it is unpleasant or repugnant." Wechsler concluded that no "neutral principle" justified favoring blacks' desire to associate with whites over whites' desire not to associate with blacks.

Scholars have puzzled over Wechsler's remarks ever since, but he seems to have adopted the view propounded by Robert Hale that there is no such thing as a coherent "negative" liberty right.[22] Rather, there is a fixed amount of coercion in society. In the context of segregation laws, this meant that the government could either coerce whites to associate with blacks, or coerce blacks to segregate themselves from whites. Wechsler's views on the constitutionality of state-imposed segregation also echoed the understanding of segregation laws that he likely encountered as a Columbia student. Progressive Columbia professor Howard Lee McBain, writing in 1927, reacted to the Supreme Court's refusal to countenance residential segregation ordinances by accusing the Court of destroying the right of whites to live in a segregated neighborhood.[23]

The diminishing group of old-school Progressives found allies among a new generation of conservatives. The few influential conservative commentators on constitutional law abandoned traditional conservative limited-government and natural-rights constitutionalism, and instead focused on containing the Warren Court's emerging judicial liberalism. In the process of doing so, they adopted the Progressives' majoritarian critique of the Supreme Court's pre–New Deal liberty of contract jurisprudence.[24]

A telling example is a short 1952 memo written by a young conservative Supreme Court clerk (and future chief justice of the United States), William

Rehnquist, to Justice Robert Jackson.[25] Rehnquist argued that the Court should rule against the plaintiffs in the pending school segregation cases, lest it write its own views into the Constitution. He accused the pre–New Deal Court of ignoring Justice Holmes's wise admonition "that the Fourteenth Amendment did not enact Herbert Spence's [sic] Social Statics" and instead allowing "business interests" to "dominate the Court." Rehnquist wrote that if the Court invalidated public school segregation laws, "it differs from the McReynolds court only in the kinds of litigants it favors and the kinds of special claims it protects."

As Rehnquist's memo suggests, in the post–New Deal period Holmes's dissenting opinion was quoted regularly for its skepticism of aggressive judicial review. But the *Lochner* majority opinion did not yet have the symbolic resonance that it later acquired. Legal scholars and commentators generally treated it as one of several notorious cases invalidating economic regulations. When the Supreme Court cited *Lochner*, it was almost always as part of a laundry list of discredited "substantive due process" cases.[26] Perhaps the most dramatic evidence of *Lochner*'s relative obscurity is a 1962 article by prominent political scientist Robert McCloskey in the *Supreme Court Review* examining pre–New Deal "economic due process" jurisprudence. *Lochner* makes only an extremely brief cameo in one footnote, quoting Justice Black's denunciation of "the *Allgeyer-Lochner-Adair-Coppage*" doctrine.[27]

Meanwhile, the long-standing controversy over judicial protection of unenumerated rights through the Due Process Clause seemed to be over. The Supreme Court had not invalidated a law based on an unenumerated right since 1936. Putting what seemed to be a final nail in the coffin of "substantive due process," in 1963 the Court, overruling a 1917 precedent, unanimously upheld a state law banning the profession of debt adjustment.[28] Justice Black wrote for the Court that "a state legislature can do whatever it sees fit to do unless it is restrained by some express prohibition in the Constitution."

In a dramatic reversal, however, judicial enforcement of unenumerated rights via the Due Process Clause returned just two years later in *Griswold v. Connecticut*.[29] *Griswold* involved a challenge to a Connecticut law that prohibited doctors from prescribing contraceptives, even to married couples. Yale Law School professor Thomas Emerson represented the plaintiffs. Emerson's brief asked the Supreme Court to rely on the broad understanding of due process articulated by Justice McReynolds in *Meyer v. Nebraska*, and he also favorably cited *Pierce v. Society of Sisters*. He distinguished these cases, which he argued involved "the freedom of the individual to live a fruitful life or to sustain his position as citizen," from the discredited cases involving purely economic regulation.[30] "In short," he concluded, he was not asking "for reinstatement of the line of due process decisions exemplified by *Lochner v. New York*."[31] This was the only mention of *Lochner* in any of the briefs.

At oral argument, the justices questioned Emerson about his due process argument. Emerson took great pains to argue that *Meyer* and *Pierce* were unrelated to the liberty of contract cases:

> THE COURT: But you expect us to determine whether, it's sufficiently shocking to our sense of what ought to be the law, because this applies to married people only?
>
> MR. EMERSON: Yes, Your Honor. But it is not broad due process in the sense in which the issue was raised in the 1930's. In the first place, this is not a regulation which deals with economic or commercial matters. It is a regulation that touches upon individual rights: the right to protect life and health, the right of advancing scientific knowledge, the right to have children voluntarily. And therefore, we say we are not asking this Court to revive *Lochner against New York*, or to overrule *Nebbia* or *West Coast Hotel*.
>
> THE COURT: It sounds to me like you're asking us to follow the constitutional philosophy of that case.
>
> MR. EMERSON: No, Your Honor. We are asking you to follow the philosophy of *Meyer against Nebraska* and *Pierce against the Society of Sisters*, which dealt with—*Meyer against Nebraska*—
>
> THE COURT: Was the one that held it was unconstitutional, as I recall it, for a state to try to regulate the size of loaves of bread—
>
> MR. EMERSON: No, no, no.
>
> THE COURT: —because people were being defrauded; was that it?
>
> MR. EMERSON: That was the *Lochner* case [sic; it was actually *Jay Burns Baking Co. v. Bryan*, 264 U.S. 504], Your Honor. *Meyer against Nebraska* held that it was unconstitutional for a state to enact a law prohibiting the teaching of the German language to children who had not passed the eighth grade. And *Pierce against the Society of Sisters* held that it was unconstitutional for a state to prevent the operation of private schools in a state. And those were both due process cases, were decided as due process cases. . . . and we distinguish those from the cases which involved commercial operations like *Lochner against New York* and *West Coast Hotel against Parrish*. We make that very definite distinction.[32]

The Supreme Court invalidated the law, and Justice Douglas's plurality opinion relied in part on *Meyer* and *Pierce* for the proposition that the Due Process Clause protects a right to privacy sufficiently broad to encompass the decision of a married couple to use contraceptives. Douglas denied, however, that he was relying on a *Lochner*-like understanding of the Due Process Clause. He wrote: "Overtones of some arguments suggest that *Lochner v. State of New York* should be our guide. But we decline that invitation. . . . We do not sit as a super-legislature to determine the wisdom, need, and propriety of laws that touch economic problems, business affairs, or social conditions."[33]

Douglas rejected Emerson's suggestion that the Court create a categorical distinction between due process cases raising economic or commercial claims and those raising claims of personal liberty. He instead argued, in language that has been widely mocked ever since, that the "penumbras, formed by emanations" of the First, Third, Fourth, Fifth and Ninth amendments created a right to privacy.[34] Douglas justified relying on *Meyer* and *Pierce* by treating them as First Amendment cases, even though neither case mentioned the First Amendment specifically, nor freedom of expression more generally.

Justice Arthur Goldberg's concurring opinion for three justices cited *Meyer* for the proposition that the Fourteenth Amendment's Due Process Clause protects rights not enumerated in the Bill of Rights.[35] Goldberg cited the Ninth Amendment's protection of unenumerated rights ("the rights retained by the People") to support his conclusion that when interpreting the Fourteenth Amendment's Due Process Clause, the Court may, as in *Meyer*, go outside the Bill of Rights to determine which rights should be deemed "fundamental" and therefore worthy of constitutional protection.

Justice John Marshall Harlan II's lone concurrence, meanwhile, referred readers to his dissent in *Poe v. Ullman*.[36] In *Poe*, Harlan directly relied on *Meyer* and *Pierce* to support his view that the right of a married couple to use contraceptives was protected by the Fourteenth Amendment. *Poe* also cited several liberty-of-contract-era cases for the broad proposition that the Due Process Clause protects individual "freedom from all substantial and arbitrary impositions and purposeless restraints." Justice Byron White's *Griswold* concurrence added that "this is not the first time this Court has had occasion to articulate that the liberty entitled to protection under the Fourteenth Amendment includes the right 'to marry, establish a home and bring up children,' *Meyer v. State of Nebraska* and 'the liberty * * * to direct the upbringing and education of children,' *Pierce v. Society of Sisters.* . . ."[37]

In short, all the justices in the *Griswold* majority relied on *Meyer* and *Pierce*, which in turn were firmly in the *Lochner* line of cases.[38] *Meyer* and *Pierce*, and therefore to some extent *Lochner* and other liberty of contract cases, are the true progenitors of *Griswold* and the Court's subsequent rulings protecting the right to terminate pregnancy and to engage in private consensual sex.[39]

Justice Black, dissenting on behalf of himself and Justice Potter Stewart, accused his colleagues of resurrecting the early twentieth century's discredited due process jurisprudence. Black contended that cases like *Lochner* would support the majority's decision in *Griswold*, but the majority chose not to cite them and to pretend that its decision was not consistent with them.[40] Black added, "The two they do cite and quote from, *Meyer v. Nebraska*, and *Pierce v. Society of Sisters*, . . . elaborated the same natural law due process philosophy found in *Lochner v. New York*." Black noted that *Meyer* specifically relied on *Lochner* "along with such other long-discredited decisions" such as *Adkins v. Children's Hospital.*[41] His opinion, however, turned out to be "the last gasp of the argument that only textually-based rights could be judicially enforced."[42]

Douglas and Black's debate over *Lochner* in *Griswold* led scholars to devote significantly greater attention to *Lochner*. For example, Robert McCloskey, who had previously ignored *Lochner* in his 1962 article on "economic due process," after *Griswold* identified the doctrine of "constitutional supervision in the economic field" as the "*Lochner* doctrine."[43] More generally, legal scholars increasingly cited *Lochner* as the paradigmatic pre-New-Deal-era due process/police powers case.[44] Critics often charged the Warren Court with *Lochner*ian judicial activism.[45] For example, Alfred Kelly, writing in the *Supreme Court Review*, argued that *Griswold's* reasoning was "little more than a way of returning to an open-ended concept of substantive due process after *Lochner*."[46]

Despite the increased attention paid to *Lochner*, it did not become a ubiquitous negative touchstone until at least the early 1970s. Indeed, the now-standard use of the phrase "*Lochner* era" to denote the Court's pre–New Deal constitutional jurisprudence was virtually unknown until 1970, when the phrase appeared several times in Gerald Gunther's popular constitutional law casebook.[47] By contrast, no other constitutional law textbook published between 1965 and 1973 used the phrase "*Lochner* era," and some ignored *Lochner* completely. After Gunther popularized the phrase "*Lochner* era," it began to appear sporadically in the law review literature, including in important *Harvard Law Review* forewords by Gunther and Laurence Tribe.[48]

Lochner's notoriety increased further after the Supreme Court's 1973 decision in *Roe v. Wade*.[49] In *Roe*, a 7–2 majority relied on the Due Process Clause to invalidate state restrictions on abortion. Justice Harry Blackmun, writing for the Court, rejected both a Ninth Amendment argument and reliance on penumbras and emanations. He instead located the right to terminate pregnancy "in the Fourteenth Amendment's concept of personal liberty and restrictions upon state action."[50] Blackmun cited *Meyer v. Nebraska* to support *Roe's* interpretation of the Fourteenth Amendment.

Blackmun denied that the Court was engaging in illegitimate judicial activism, and he favorably cited Holmes's *Lochner* dissent.[51] Justice William Rehnquist retorted in dissent that "while the Court's opinion quotes from the dissent of Mr. Justice Holmes in *Lochner v. New York*, the result it reaches is more closely attuned to the majority opinion of Mr. Justice Peckham in that case."[52] Blackmun's opinion also inspired a famous critique by Professor John Hart Ely in the *Yale Law Journal*. Ely spent a significant portion of the article analogizing *Roe* to *Lochner*.[53] Indeed, as he suggested, one could argue that *Roe* was a far more "activist" decision than *Lochner*. First, unlike with the right to contract, there was no firm American intellectual or legal tradition supporting the right to terminate pregnancy. Second, while liberty of contract's scope was limited by the states' ability to exercise their police powers, *Roe* failed to recognize any meaningful limitation on the right to terminate pregnancy.

In the aftermath of *Roe*, Gunther's casebook increased its commentary on *Lochner* from one mundane page to seven pages discussing "what was wrong with *Lochner*."[54] The new *Lochner* material appeared in a chapter entitled "Substantive Due Process: Rise, Decline, Revival." Gunther presented *Lochner*, *Griswold*, and *Roe* as substantive due process cases in the same jurisprudential tradition, in an attempt to discredit the latter two cases.[55] As *Lochner* became a focal point of constitutional debate, the phrase "*Lochner* era" became increasingly common.[56] Gunther titled his casebook's subsection on pre–New Deal liberty of contract jurisprudence "The *Lochner* Era: Judicial Intervention and Economic Regulation."[57] The first appearance of the phrase "*Lochner* era" in a judicial opinion came in Supreme Court Justice Lewis Powell's opinion in *Moore v. City of East Cleveland* in 1977, citing Gunther.[58]

The most important event in establishing *Lochner* as the paradigmatic anticanonical economic substantive due process case, and in establishing the phrase "*Lochner* era" in the legal community's consciousness, was almost certainly the publication of Laurence Tribe's very influential treatise *American Constitutional Law* in 1978.[59] Tribe defined the "*Lochner* era" as having lasted from 1897 (*Allgeyer v. Louisiana*) to 1937 (*West Coast Hotel v. Parrish*). He spent more than twenty pages explaining why *Lochner* and its progeny—which, in his interpretation, did not include "civil liberties" cases like *Pierce, Meyer*, and *Gitlow v. New York*—had been wrongly decided. Tribe consistently used "*Lochner*" as shorthand for the Supreme Court's liberty of contract jurisprudence.[60] Tribe's treatise also advanced a modern liberal interpretation of *Lochner* with a lineage going back at least to Thomas Emerson's Supreme Court argument in *Griswold*. The *Lochner* Court, according to Tribe, properly adopted a strong role for the judiciary in protecting individual rights, but failed to understand that liberty of contract was obsolete in a modern industrial economy. Tribe contended that the "economic freedom" the Court had tried to protect "was more myth than reality."[61]

John Hart Ely, meanwhile, soon made his peace with modern liberal constitutional jurisprudence, if not immediately with *Roe*. He argued that this jurisprudence reflected the wisdom of *Carolene Products* footnote 4: Economic rights don't deserve more than minimal constitutional protection, but laws that infringe on fundamental personal liberties, or that seem to discriminate against historically oppressed groups such as African Americans, demand a high level of judicial scrutiny.[62]

The older generation of constitutional law professors, wedded to the traditional critique of the Supreme Court's due process jurisprudence, gradually retired. Their successors were far more comfortable with the idea of a strong judicial role in protecting individual rights. The younger generation was especially devoted to defending women's reproductive rights and therefore *Roe v. Wade*.

Meanwhile, conservative legal analysts overwhelmingly adopted the critique of "substantive due process" pioneered by Hugo Black in *Griswold*, with roots dating back to the Progressive critique of liberty of contract.[63] Conservatives argued that the Supreme Court should reassess its endorsement of *Griswold, Roe*, and other cases recognizing implicit fundamental rights under the Due Process Clause because they were in the same illegitimate tradition of judicial policymaking as *Lochner*.[64]

The leading proponent of this fusion between old-line Progressivism and modern conservatism, Robert Bork, was nominated to the Supreme Court in 1987. The Senate rejected his nomination after a well-organized campaign directed by a coalition of liberal interest groups. These groups effectively attacked Bork for his long-standing opposition to the Court's protection of the right to privacy in *Griswold*, which he argued had been just as wrongly decided as its "antecedents," *Pierce, Meyer, Adkins v. Children's Hospital*, and *Lochner*.[65] Since Bork, no Supreme Court nominee has argued that *Griswold* was wrongly decided, though conservative nominees have criticized Justice Douglas's "penumbras and emanations" reasoning.[66] Nevertheless, strong hostility to *Lochner* and its progeny, on originalist and anti-"judicial activism" grounds, remains bedrock conservative constitutional ideology.

The irony of the conservative originalist critique of *Lochner* is that the proponents of liberty of contract were themselves originalists, trying to adhere to what they saw as the constitutional understandings of the Fourteenth Amendment's Framers regarding individual liberty and the scope of the police power.[67] Originalist sentiments expressed by proponents of liberty of contract sometimes sound quite modern. Consider Justice Sutherland's dissent in *West Coast Hotel v. Parrish*:

> To say . . . that the words of the Constitution mean today what they did not mean when written—that is, that they do not apply to a situation now to which they would have applied then—is to rob that instrument of the essential element which continues it in force as the people have made it until they, and not their official agents, have made it otherwise.

Nevertheless, the early-twentieth-century version of originalism differed in significant ways from modern conservative originalism.[68] The originalism of a century ago was generally neither well theorized nor well explained by its judicial adherents, was far more intuitive and less grounded in historical research than modern originalism, and was much more likely to incorporate the natural rights tradition—but it was originalism nevertheless.

Progressives, by contrast, rarely undertook originalist critiques of liberty of contract.[69] During the liberty of contract era, the Supreme Court justices most associated with Progressivism overtly rejected originalism.[70] Unlike modern conservatives, Progressives generally blamed the Constitution and its implicit and explicit support for property rights and limited government, rather than "judicial activism," for the due process opinions they opposed. They argued that the Fourteenth Amendment should be interpreted in light of the needs of modern industrial society, regardless of "anachronistic" conceptions of liberty inherited from the Framers.[71] Indeed, Progressives invented and promoted the concept of a "living Constitution." Living constitutionalism is the antithesis of originalism; Progressives adopted it because they thought that, in general, the Constitution's text, history, and original intent and meaning supported their adversaries.

For obvious reasons, modern conservatives are loath to acknowledge that the Progressive critique of the liberty of contract cases that they have adopted was antioriginalist, and that there was a broad consensus in the early twentieth century that the Supreme Court's due process decisions were consistent with originalism. Indeed, conservatives sometimes argue that the demise of liberty of contract marked a triumph of originalist thinking over living constitutionalism,[72] when the truth is almost exactly the opposite.

With conservative jurists hostile to "substantive due process" as represented by *Lochner*, and the Supreme Court dominated by Republican appointees, the *Roe = Lochner* critique adopted by conservatives posed a threat to liberal due process precedents.[73] Liberal scholars therefore felt the need to explain why "the Court is not merely engaged in that most dread of all pursuits, 'Lochnerizing' . . . when, for example, it overturns state anti-abortion laws."[74]

Some liberal constitutionalists followed Tribe and Ely in arguing that the *Lochner*-era Court chose an appropriate role for the Court—defender of last resort of fundamental rights—but simply chose the wrong rights to emphasize. Instead of focusing on anachronistic contract rights, liberal academic luminaries argued, the Court should have concentrated on protecting the civil liberties necessary for a properly functioning modern liberal democracy.[75] These scholars argue that the Court eventually got it right and that *Lochner*, perhaps, should be recognized as a misstep on an otherwise sound path.

Another group of scholars, led by law professor Cass Sunstein, developed a more radical thesis. In an article called "*Lochner*'s Legacy" and in subsequent elaborations, Sunstein argued that the "*Lochner*-era" Court made two crucial errors in its liberty of contract jurisprudence. First, it understood the common law "to be a part of nature rather than a legal construct." Second, it sought to preserve what it saw as the "natural," "status quo" distribution of wealth against redistributive regulations.[76] Like other liberal scholars, Sunstein argued that his understanding of *Lochner* not only saved *Griswold* and *Roe* from the charge that they are *Lochner*'s illegitimate offspring, but also undermined the modern Supreme Court's rulings on issues such as affirmative action and campaign finance reform. Sunstein's work quickly came to dominate legal scholars' understanding of *Lochner*, but constitutional historians have properly dismissed it as ahistorical.[77]

Meanwhile, legal historians were producing their own corpus of *Lochner* revisionism that discredited various aspects of the conventional story inherited from the Progressives. For example, revisionists established that the Supreme Court had upheld the vast majority of laws that came before it, allowing significant, though not unlimited, room for the regulatory state's growth; that the Supreme Court was not wildly out of line with values widely accepted by the public before the Great Depression; and that the distributive consequences of the legislation the Court had invalidated were far more complex than the traditional "Court as the handmaiden of Big Business" story suggested.[78] The revisionist literature has inspired a smaller counter-revisionist literature.[79]

Perhaps the most significant myth demolished by revisionists was the notion that the origins of liberty of contract lay in "laissez-faire Social Darwinism."[80] Reaching a consensus as to what *did* motivate the Supreme Court to adopt liberty of contract has proved more difficult. Among the candidates proposed were natural rights and free labor ideology,[81] social contractarianism, opposition to paternalism, desire to establish a sphere of personal autonomy in an era of total war, hostility to "class legislation," and fealty to classical economic theory.[82] A consensus is emerging that the liberty of contract doctrine arose from a combination of hostility to "class legislation" and a desire to protect natural rights deemed fundamental to the development of American liberty.[83]

Meanwhile, several Supreme Court justices have adopted the Laurence Tribe/modern liberal perspective on *Lochner*. In *Planned Parenthood v. Casey*, in a section of a plurality opinion attributed to Justice Sandra Day O'Connor and joined by Justices David Souter and Anthony Kennedy,[84] O'Connor discussed why overruling *Lochner* was appropriate in 1937 but overruling *Roe* would not be appropriate in 1992. She explained that with regard to *Lochner*, "the Depression had come and, with it, the lesson that seemed unmistakable to most people by 1937, that the interpretation of contractual freedom protected in *Adkins* rested on fundamentally false factual assumptions about the capacity of a relatively unregulated market to satisfy minimal levels of human welfare."[85] *Lochner*'s error, then, was not using the Due Process Clause to protect unenumerated individual rights, but the Court's choice to protect liberty of contract.

Justice Souter, meanwhile, argued a few years later that *Lochner* had been correct to apply the Due Process Clause to prohibit arbitrary legislation, but unduly "absolutist" in its implementation of the relevant standard.[86] By contrast, according to Souter, *Meyer* and *Pierce* properly applied heightened scrutiny to truly important interests.[87] Despite his unvarnished endorsement of *Meyer* and *Pierce*, Souter often used *Lochner* as an epithet when he disagreed with his more conservative colleagues' opinions.[88] Most recently, Justice Kennedy's opinion in *Lawrence v. Texas* enthusiastically and unabashedly cited *Meyer* and *Pierce* as "broad statements of the substantive reach of liberty under the Due Process Clause."[89] Kennedy's majority opinion in *State Farm v. Campbell*, which placed strict substantive due process limitations on state punitive damages awards, suggests that he does not completely disavow meaningful review of government action that affects primarily economic interests.[90]

Conservative judges and scholars, for their part, continue to channel Progressive critiques of liberty of contract, and condemn *Lochner* for improper "judicial activism."[91] But even Justice Antonin Scalia, long the bellwether of elite conservative constitutional thought, has not challenged the incorporation doctrine even though, like *Lochner*, it involves protecting substantive rights via the Fourteenth Amendment's Due Process Clause. Nor, unlike Justice Black, has Scalia argued that the Due Process Clause only protects rights enumerated in the text of the Bill of Rights. Rather, he contends that only rights that are "so rooted in the traditions and conscience of our people as to be ranked as fundamental" are eligible for protection by the Due Process Clause.[92]

Meanwhile, a few leading libertarian legal scholars forcefully argue that *Griswold* and *Lochner* were both correctly decided.[93] Indeed, some have argued that *Lochner* was too timid and allowed too much room for government intervention in the economy.[94] While that is a distinctly minority position, even some prominent liberal scholars have argued that in completely abandoning liberty of contract, the Supreme Court has left important economic rights vulnerable to government overreaching.[95] And despite contrary Supreme Court precedent, lower federal courts occasionally invalidate draconian government regulations on occupations that seem to serve no legitimate public purpose.[96]

Nevertheless, and despite the flood of serious revisionist scholarship, *Lochner* is still primarily used as a symbol of one's jurisprudential opponents' perceived faults. Justice Scalia, dissenting in *Lawrence v. Texas*,[97] argued that the Fourteenth Amendment no more protects the right to engage in homosexual sodomy than it protects the right to work "more than 60 hours per week in a bakery."[98] In *United States v. United Foods*,[99] Justice Stephen Breyer, dissenting, criticized the majority for finding that the First Amendment imposes limits on government-coerced commercial speech. Breyer, citing *Lochner*, wrote: "I do not believe the First Amendment seeks to limit the Government's economic regulatory choices in this way—any more than does the Due Process Clause."[100] This sort of simplistic discourse about *Lochner* impoverishes our understanding of the Fourteenth Amendment and the influence of the liberty of contract cases on it, and brings no honor to the jurists who engage in it.

Focusing on the real *Lochner*, as opposed to the mythical *Lochner* of the constitutional anticanon, allows for the far more fruitful discussion of how the *Lochner* line of cases fits in with broader trends in American history, and influenced the evolution of judicial attitudes towards protecting rights under the Fourteenth Amendment. We have seen that *Lochner* and its progeny followed naturally from, but were much less radical than, earlier state court rulings protecting liberty of contract. These lower court opinions were not steeped in Social Darwinism, but had their roots in long-standing American intellectual traditions supporting natural rights and opposing class legislation.[101]

The Supreme Court's use of the Due Process Clause to protect a moderate version of liberty of contract was innovative but not terribly radical; the idea that the requirement of "due process of law" prohibits arbitrary government interference with substantive rights had a long pre-*Lochner* history in American constitutional thought. Contrary to the modern categorization of due process cases as either substantive or procedural, during the liberty of contract era "the ultimate meaning of due process was neither substantive nor procedural. . . . It protected individuals from the application of government authority that they never consented to be subjected to in the first place."[102]

Moreover, many liberty of contract cases don't fit neatly, if at all, into the crude "capitalists vs. workers" class conflict model that has inspired generations of *Lochner* critics. As the history of the *Lochner* case itself suggests, liberty of contract cases often either pitted the public as a whole against special interest groups seeking to gain economic advantage through favorable legislation, or pitted "out" groups struggling for economic survival against entrenched special interest groups that sought to exclude them from the marketplace.

Meanwhile, the origins of the modern Supreme Court's broad protection of civil liberties and civil rights can be traced to Lochnerian due process decisions such as *Adkins v. Children's Hospital* (1923), *Buchanan v. Warley* (1917), *Meyer v. Nebraska* (1923), *Pierce v. Society of Sisters* (1925), and *Gitlow v. New York* (1925). Justice Sutherland's opinion in *Adkins*, for example, anticipated by fifty years the modern view that working women are entitled to equal treatment with men, regardless of women's alleged physical and emotional disabilities. *Buchanan* held, over the fierce objections of Progressive critics, that residential segregation laws could not be justified by concerns over interracial tension and violence, miscegenation, or the alleged pathologies or inferiority of African Americans. *Meyer* and *Pierce* provided broad protection for unenumerated but important individual rights. They did so in the face of Progressive resistance and popular prejudice against the immigrants and Catholics who were the primary direct beneficiaries of these decisions. And *Gitlow* announced that the Supreme Court would henceforth protect the right of freedom of expression against state governments, a promise fulfilled in several other Fourteenth Amendment cases in the 1920s and 1930s.

Like *Lochner* and other liberty of contract cases, the cases noted above identified a threatened individual liberty, and refused to allow government infringement on that liberty unless the state could identify a valid police power interest in doing so. Indeed, in several of these cases protection of contractual and occupational freedom was intimately tied to other equalitarian and libertarian concerns.

Post–New Deal liberal jurisprudence segregated and ignored the economic aspects of these cases and reinterpreted them as "civil liberties" decisions, to distinguish them from discredited pre–New Deal natural rights–based decisions like *Lochner*. The post–New Deal Court also eliminated its predecessors' focus in due process cases on the scope of the police power, instead introducing balancing tests pitting the strength of the right asserted versus the importance of the asserted government interest.[103] But even after reinterpreting and elaborating on the old decisions, the Court did not reject their solicitude for equality and individual liberty.[104]

Liberty of contract's Progressive opponents worshipped at the altar of the police power, a power that mainstream Progressives believed included segregation laws, eugenics statutes, bans on interracial marriage, efforts to eliminate "defective" workers from the labor market, the coercive Americanization of immigrants through mandatory public schooling, and so on.[105] Today, even staunch judicial conservatives like Scalia refuse to defer to the legislature with anything like the alacrity urged by early-twentieth-century Progressives.[106]

Lochner's legacy, then, lives on in American constitutional law, in the application of various rights, enumerated and unenumerated, against the states via the Due Process Clause.[107] Justice Peckham's enunciation of an expansive liberty-protective interpretation of the clause in *Lochner* (and *Allgeyer*) begot Justice McReynolds's even more expansive opinion in *Meyer*, which in turn continues to serve as the constitutional foundation of various Fourteenth Amendment rights protected by the Supreme Court.[108] Contemporary Fourteenth Amendment civil liberties jurisprudence owes more to the views of Justices Harlan, Peckham, Sutherland, and McReynolds than to Holmes, Brandeis, and Frankfurter and their skepticism of constitutional protection for individual rights.

Conclusion

Alert readers will have noticed that I have titled this book *Rehabilitating* Lochner—as in improving *Lochner's* reputation—not *Defending* Lochner or *Restoring* Lochner. I argue that *Lochner* and liberty of contract jurisprudence more generally have been unfairly maligned, and their contribution to modern American constitutional law neglected.

Lochner historiography has been dominated by the perspective initially promoted by Progressive-era opponents of the liberty of contract doctrine. The Progressive outlook on constitutional law and related matters—a combination of support for the growth an administrative state dominated by experts insulated from both politics and the market, opposition to serious judicial review of the constitutionality of legislation, and indifference or hostility to "individualistic" civil liberties and the rights of minorities—is now anachronistic and finds no comfortable ideological home in modern American politics. Nevertheless, the mythical morality tale invented during the Progressive era for overtly ideological reasons, and elaborated upon ever since, continues to color our understanding of *Lochner* and other liberty of contract cases.

Though scholars over the years have added significant nuance to the received version of American constitutional history, modern liberal constitutionalists tend to see themselves as part of a generally consistent tradition tracing back to Progressives and New Dealers. The standard liberal version of constitutional history has relied on broad caricatures of the relevant historical actors: the good guys, starting with early-twentieth-century Progressive jurists, are said to have been champions of the little guy against the powerful, whether in the form of protecting civil liberties or of protecting the economically powerless against rapacious corporations. The liberals' historical bad guys are the "reactionary" justices of the Gilded Age and their successors into the early New Deal era, who are said to have substituted crass class interest or dogmatic laissez-faire ideology for constitutional principle.[1]

Modern conservative constitutionalists, meanwhile, though they dissent in some ways from the orthodox interpretation of American constitutional history, also want to see themselves as part of a seamless jurisprudential tradition, and they venerate some of the same Progressive heroes as their liberal adversaries do. The conservatives' preferred narrative revolves around a tradition of judicial restraint based on textualism, originalism, and respect for long-standing constitutional principle. In this tale the good guys are Holmes, Frankfurter, and other Supreme Court justices who are said to have properly put their political views to one side to enforce the Constitution as written.[2] The bad guys are the Court's "judicial activists," who purportedly made up the nonsensical doctrine of "substantive due process" to foist their political views on the American public. The original sin was that of the Court in the liberty of contract era, but the modern Court has failed to repent. Indeed, it has aggravated matters through additional judicial activism, substituting modern liberal-left social policy preferences for the laissez-faire prejudices of the earlier period.

For various reasons, including mere happenstance, the *Lochner* case became the key emblematic illustration of both of these stories, the one case that encapsulates everything about the bad guys' approach. These stories, however—both in terms of overall narrative and their specific depiction of the *Lochner* case—are demonstrably false. As shown in this book, the reality is much more complex and much more interesting. An accurate and nuanced view of the Supreme Court's pre–World War II due process jurisprudence does not allow for blithe categorization of justices who lived in a very different era, replete with ideological and political disputes and assumptions that are foreign and often barely comprehensible to modern scholars, into prescient heroes and narrow-minded villains.[3]

This also means that it would be a mistake to lionize the judicial supporters of liberty of contract in the early twentieth century, who had many flaws, if not necessarily the flaws attributed to them by their contemporary Progressive critics. I do, however, draw the following more modest conclusions from the material this book presents.

- The Supreme Court's liberty of contract decisions were far more deferential to regulatory legislation than the standard myth would have it, and were well within the realm of plausible constitutional interpretation, given existing precedents and prevailing contemporary understandings of the meaning and scope of the Due Process Clause.

- By providing more room for civil society and markets and restricting coercive regulation, Supreme Court decisions protecting liberty of contract were likely a net positive from the standpoint of their practical effects—especially once the liberty of contract doctrine's benign effects on sex and race equality and on civil liberties are taken into account—and they surely did not have the drastic negative practical consequences that generations of scholars have assumed.

- The first two points are complimentary: If the Supreme Court had been extremely activist and ideologically committed to a strong version of economic libertarianism enforced through constitutional interpretation, it would be more difficult to defend its decisions as either plausible interpretations of the Due Process Clause or—at least to nonlibertarians—as having benign consequences.

- Justice Harlan's dissent in *Lochner*, with its trenchant legal and factual analysis and its focus on the presumption of constitutionality in liberty of contract cases, is far more persuasive than Justice Holmes's more quotable but flippant counterpart. More generally, Harlan's jurisprudence challenges many of the stereotypes about the justices of the liberty of contract era. Harlan thought the police power broad enough to permit states to require limitations on the hours of bakers' labor, but not broad enough to permit either segregation laws or laws that favored organized labor by banning yellow-dog contracts. He was a proponent of natural rights and the liberty of contract doctrine, and also an advocate of applying the Bill of Rights to the states via the Fourteenth Amendment.

- Even if one disagrees with the outcome of some of the liberty of contract era's due process cases, the principle established in those cases—that the police power is not infinitely elastic—is a sound one, well rooted in long-standing American principle. Relatedly, the Court's due process jurisprudence during the liberty of contract era was preferable to the existing mainstream Progressive alternative emphasizing almost judicial total deference to legislation.

Given that I don't claim to provide any significant normative lesson for modern constitutional law, it's fair to ask why I think it's worth rehabilitating *Lochner*. Why not let *Lochner* be *Lochner*, so to speak, and let the case continue its important symbolic role in American constitutional debate, even if the underlying history isn't accurate?

One reason is the intrinsic value of having correct information in the history books, and, relatedly, the principle that history should not be misconstrued for political ends. The long-standing myth of a wildly activist, reactionary Supreme Court imposing a grossly unpopular laissez-faire ideology on the American people on behalf of large corporate interests—with little concern for precedent, constitutional text, or individual or minority rights—is far removed from historical reality. The academics who invented the prevalent mythology likely sought, consciously or not, to justify their preferred political outcomes. They promoted the notion that the liberty of contract cases had no origins in American tradition or in American constitutional thought, and were instead simply stalking horses for the economic elite's interests. This allowed advocates of the revolutionary New Deal and post–New Deal changes in constitutional interpretation to lump all the decisions of the pre–New Deal Supreme Court together.

Scores of books and articles state or imply that there is no significant difference between the "*Lochner*-era" commerce clause cases, due process cases, non-delegation cases, and so on. Rather, they purportedly were all different manifestations of the Court's reactionary "laissez-faire" jurisprudence. Conflating these doctrines allowed legal scholars—and, for that matter, Supreme Court justices—to elide debate over the meaning of the relevant constitutional provisions, and to reject out of hand the notion that the Old Court may have interpreted some of them correctly as a matter of text and history.

In short, supporters of the post–New Deal constitutional order—lawyers, historians, and political scientists—promoted the traditional *Lochner* story to shore up that order against residual or future opposition.[4] Modern conservatives have adopted major elements of this story as well, so that they can use *Lochner* to attack modern due process decisions they abhor, like *Roe v. Wade*. When scholars distort history to serve an agreeable governing ideology or to rally opposition to existing precedents that they dislike, their work richly deserves correction.[5]

As implied above, rehabilitating *Lochner* is also important because *Lochner* plays such an important role in modern constitutional law debates. For one thing, the *Lochner* myth reinforces the dubious notion that the Supreme Court is sometimes inclined to engage in aggressively activist behavior at extreme variance from public opinion. This notion seduces political activists to turn their attention away from political organizing and ideological persuasion and toward the courts.[6]

More important, *Lochner* serves as a uniquely important negative exemplar of constitutional error in constitutional law scholarship, op-ed columns, and blog posts, and even in Supreme Court decisions. When the justices and others use *Lochner* in this way, as shorthand for what they consider the "activist" sins of their opponents, they are substituting empty rhetoric for meaningful constitutional argument.

Replacing the mythical, evil *Lochner* with something closer to the real historical *Lochner* line of liberty of contract cases would deprive participants in debate over American constitutional law of this easy, but ultimately vacuous, rhetorical shortcut. A more accurate view of constitutional history would therefore lead to a more nuanced, civil, and constructive debate about modern constitutional law. And that's reason enough to rehabilitate *Lochner*.

NOTES

INTRODUCTION

1. Barry Friedman, for one, posits that *Lochner* has a *worse* reputation than *Dred Scott*. Barry Friedman, The Will of the People: How Public Opinion Has Influenced the Supreme Court and Shaped the Meaning of the Constitution 167 (2009).

2. *See* Victoria F. Nourse, *A Tale of Two* Lochners: *The Untold History of Substantive Due Process and the Idea of Fundamental Rights*, 97 Cal. L. Rev. 751, 754 (2009).

3. Senator Barack Obama, Speech re the Nomination of Justice Janice Rogers Brown to the D.C. Circuit Court of Appeals, June 8, 2005, available at http://www.barackobama .com/2005/06/08/remarks_of_us_senator_barack_0_1.php.

4. *See* Sujit Choudhry, *Worse than* Lochner?, in Access to Care, Access to Justice: The Legal Debate Over Private Health Insurance in Canada 75 (Collen M. Flood, et al. eds, 2005); Sujit Choudhry, *The* Lochner *Era and Comparative Constitutionalism*, 2 Int'l J. Const. L. 1, 15 (2004).

5. *See* Guy Miller Struve, *The Less-Restrictive-Alternative Principle and Economic Due Process*, 80 Harv. L. Rev. 1463 (1967).

6. *See generally* James W. Ely, Jr., *Economic Due Process Revisited*, 44 Vand. L. Rev. 213, 213 (1991). For recent reiteration of the traditional myth, see James MacGregor Burns, Packing the Court: The Rise of Judicial Power and the Coming Crisis of the Supreme Court (2009).

7. *See* Michael J. Phillips, The *Lochner* Court, Myth and Reality: Substantive Due Process from the 1890s to the 1930s, at 115 (2000); Jack M. Balkin, *"Wrong the Day it was Decided":* Lochner *and Constitutional Historicism*, 85 B. U. L. Rev. 677, 713 (2005); Nourse, *supra* note 2, at 756; *cf.* Lawrence M. Friedman, American Law in the 20th Century 24 (2002).

8. *See* ch. 7.

9. *See* ch. 1.

10. *See* ch. 2.

11. *See* ch. 3.

12. *See* chs. 3–6.

13. Allgeyer v. Louisiana, 165 U.S. 578, 589 (1897).

14. Howard Gillman, *Preferred Freedoms: The Progressive Expansion of State Power and the Rise of Modern Civil Liberties Jurisprudence*, 47 Pol. Res. Q. 623, 640 (1994).

15. *See* chs. 4–6.

16. *See* ch. 7.

17. Readers looking for a full-throated defense of libertarian constitutional jurisprudence will need to look such works as Randy E. Barnett, Restoring the Lost Constitution: The Presumption of Liberty (2003); Richard A. Epstein, Takings: Private Property and the Power of Eminent Domain (1985); Tim Sandefur, The Right to Earn a Living (2010); Bernard H. Siegan, Economic Liberties and the Constitution (1980).

CHAPTER ONE

1. For a very thorough attempt to show that "due process of law" has nothing to do with the substance of legislation, see John Harrison, *Substantive Due Process and the Constitutional Text*, 83 Va. L. Rev. 493 (1997).

2. John Hart Ely, Democracy and Distrust: A Theory of Judicial Review 18 (1980); *see also* Michael Stokes Paulsen, *Does the Constitution Prescribe Rules for Its Own Interpretation?*, 102 Nw. L. Rev. 857, 897 (2009) ("made-up, atextual invention"). Justice Scalia says that "substantive due process" is "babble." Vivek Krishnamurthy, *Live-Blogging: Nino Scalia*, http://the-reaction.blogspot.com/2006/11/live-blogging-nino-scalia.html.

3. *See* James W. Ely, Jr., The Guardian of Every Other Right: A Constitutional History of Property Rights 103–4 (2d ed. 1998); Lucas A. Powe, Jr., The Supreme Court and the American Elite, 1789–2008, at 169 (2009); G. Edward White, The Constitution and the New Deal 245 (2000); Howard J. Graham, *Procedure to Substance—Extra-Judicial Rise of Due Process, 1830–1860*, 40 Cal. L. Rev. 483 (1952); Wayne McCormick, *Economic Substantive Due Process and the Right of Livelihood*, 82 Ky. L. Rev. 397, 406–7 (1993–94); Kermit Roosevelt III, *Forget the Fundamentals: Fixing Substantive Due Process*, 8 U. Pa. J. Const. L. 883 (2006). Morton Horwitz argues that attacks on the substantive aspect of due process were "largely produced by later critical Progressive historians intent on delegitimizing the *Lochner* court." *See* Morton J. Horwitz, The Transformation of American Law, 1870–1960: The Crisis of Legal Orthodoxy 158 (1992). The notion that law is divided into "substantive" and "procedural" spheres was a product of the positivist revolution, specifically the attack on common law pleading. Thomas C. Grey, *Judicial Review and Legal Pragmatism*, 38 Wake Forest L. Rev. 473 (2003).

4. *See* Loren P. Beth, The Development of the American Constitution, 1877–1910, at 190 (1971); James MacGregor Burns, Packing the Court: The Rise of Judicial Power and the Coming Crisis of the Supreme Court 99 (2009); Archibald Cox, The Court and the Constitution 135 (1987); Gerald Gunther, Constitutional Law 432 (12th ed. 1991); A.H. Kelly & W.H. Harbison, The American Constitution: Its Origins and Development 498 (4th ed. 1970); Robert G. McCloskey, American Conservatism in the Age of Enterprise, 1865–1910, at 26–30 (1951); Wallace Mendelson, Capitalism, Democracy, and the Supreme Court 63 (1960); Frank R. Strong, Substantive Due Process of Law: A Dichotomy of Sense and Nonsense 95 (1986); Steven G. Calabresi, *Introduction*, in Originalism: A Quarter Century of Debate 13 (Steven G. Calabresi ed., 2007); Gary McDowell, *Debate on*

Judicial Activism, in The New Right v. the Constitution 109 (Stephen Macedo ed., 1987); Emily Bazelon, *The Supreme Court on Trial*, Slate, July 6, 2009. *See generally* Guy Miller Struve, *The Less-Restrictive-Alternative Principle and Economic Due Process*, 80 Harv. L. Rev. 1463 (1967) (proposing a moderate application of economic due process and criticizing the Court for completely abandoning constitutional review of economic regulations). Candice Dalrymple, Sexual Distinctions in the Law 3 (1987) ("That doctrine did not originate in the Constitution. It emerged in a series of Supreme Court opinions from the decade of the 1890s"); Gary D. Rowe, Lochner *Revisionism Revisited*, 24 L. & Soc. Inquiry 221, 242 (1999) (describing this understanding of *Lochner*).

5. The quote is from Larry Yackle, Regulatory Rights 75 (2007), but he is summarizing others' views. *Cf.* John P. Roche, *Entrepreneurial Liberty and the Fourteenth Amendment*, 4 Lab. Hist. 3, 27 (1963) (accusing Justice Rufus Peckham of "sardonic cruelty" in his *Lochner* opinion). This allegation continues to be popular despite the many revisionist books and articles explaining that the origins of the liberty of contract doctrine lie elsewhere. For examples of recent works that attribute the liberty of contract doctrine to Social Darwinism, see Angelo N. Ancheta, Scientific Evidence and Equal Protection of the Law 24–25 (2006); Craig R. Ducat, Constitutional Interpretation: Powers of Government 424 (2008); Norton Garfinkle, The American Dream vs. The Gospel of Wealth: The Fight for a Productive Middle-Class Economy 63 (2007); Phillip Jenkins, A History of the United States 168 (2007); Philip A. Klinkner & Rogers M. Smith, The Unsteady March: The Rise and Decline of Racial Equality in America 331 (2002); Ted Nace, Gangs of America: The Rise of Corporate Power and the Disabling of Democracy 126 (1995); David L. Faigman, Laboratory of Justice 86–90 (2004); William H. Rehnquist, The Supreme Court 109–10 (2001); Milton Ridvas Konvitz, Fundamental Liberties of a Free People: Religion, Speech, Press, Assembly xi (2001); Paul Kens, Lochner v. New York, in The Oxford Guide to United States Supreme Court Decisions 161 (Kermit L. Hall ed., 2001); Sidney A. Pearson, Jr., *Introduction*, in Woodrow Wilson, Constitutional Government in the United States xliii (Transaction Press reprint ed. 2002).

6. For overviews of the revisionist literature, see David E. Bernstein, Lochner *Era Revisionism, Revised:* Lochner *and the Origins of Fundamental Rights Constitutionalism*, 82 Geo. L.J. 1 (2003); Barry Cushman, *Some Varieties and Vicissitudes of Lochnerism*, 85 B.U. L. Rev. 881 (2005); Rowe, *supra* note 4; and Stephen A. Siegel, *The Revisionism Thickens*, 20 L. & Hist. Rev. 631 (2002). Prominent revisionist books include Mark Warren Bailey, Guardians of the Moral Order: The Legal Philosophy of the Supreme Court, 1860–1910 (2004); Barry Cushman, Rethinking the New Deal Court (1998); James W. Ely, Jr., The Chief Justiceship of Melville W. Fuller: 1888–1910 (1995); Richard A. Epstein, How the Progressives Rewrote the Constitution (2005); Owen Fiss, The Troubled Beginnings of the Modern State (1993); Howard Gillman, The Constitution Besieged: The Rise and Demise of *Lochner* Era Police Powers Jurisprudence (1993); Morton J. Horwitz, The Transformation of American Law, 1870–1960: The Crisis of Legal Orthodoxy (1992); Herbert Hovenkamp, Enterprise and American Law, 1836–1937 (1991); William E. Nelson, The Fourteenth Amendment (1988); Michael J. Phillips, The *Lochner* Court, Myth and Reality: Substantive Due Process from the 1890s to the 1930s (2000); G. Edward White, The Constitution and the New Deal (2000). Important early revisionist articles include

Michael Les Benedict, *Laissez-Faire and Liberty: A Re-Evaluation of the Meaning and Origins of Laissez-Faire Constitutionalism*, 3 L. & Hist. Rev. 293 (1985); William E. Forbath, *The Ambiguities of Free Labor: Labor and the Law in the Gilded Age*, 1985 Wis. L. Rev. 767; Alan Jones, *Thomas M. Cooley and "Laissez-Faire Constitutionalism": A Reconsideration*, 53 J. Am. Hist. 751 (1967); Charles W. McCurdy, *Justice Field and the Jurisprudence of Government-Business Relations: Some Parameters of Laissez-Faire Constitutionalism, 1863–1897*, 61 J. Am. Hist. 970 (1975); Charles W. McCurdy, *The Roots of "Liberty of Contract" Reconsidered: Major Premises in the Law of Employment, 1867–1937*, 1984 Sup. Ct. Hist. Soc'y Y.B. 20; William E. Nelson, *The Impact of the Anti-slavery Movement upon Styles of Judicial Reasoning in Nineteenth Century America*, 87 Harv. L. Rev. 513 (1974); Stephen A. Siegel, *Lochner Era Jurisprudence and the American Constitutional Tradition*, 70 N.C. L Rev. 1 (1991). Benedict's article, in particular, helped make *Lochner* revisionism a serious academic pursuit.

7. *See* Noga Morag-Levine, *Common Law, Civil Law, and the Administrative State: From Coke to* Lochner, 24 Const. Comm. 601 (2007). The judiciary had the authority to enforce the written constitution, and some prominent attorneys, including some Supreme Court justices, believed that the judiciary was also charged with enforcing America's unwritten constitution. *See, e.g.,* Calder v. Bull, 3 U.S. (3 Dall.) 386, 388 (1798).

8. *See, e.g.,* Sharpless v. Mayor of Philadelphia, 21 Pa. 147 (1853) (stating that the British Parliament's sovereignty was transferred to each state). *See generally* Frederick N. Judson, *Liberty of Contract Under the Police Power*, 14 Rep. A.B.A. 231, 231 (1891) (contrasting the "comprehensive and all-pervading police power of the States" with the "limited power of the Federal Government"). For a history of the police power, see Markus Dirk Dubber, The Police Power: Patriarchy and the Foundations of American Government (2005).

9. *See, e.g.,* Dartmouth College v. Woodward, 17 U.S. 518, 581–82 (1819) (recounting Daniel Webster's argument that only a "general law" may be the law of the land, and that laws "directly transferring the estate of one man to another" cannot be considered the law of the land); Gardner v. Village of Newburgh, 2 Johns. Ch. 162 (N.Y. 1816). For examples of early state court decisions arguing that for legislation to be considered a legitimate "law" subject to judicial enforcement, it must meet traditional natural/higher law normative standards, see Frederick Mark Gedicks, *An Originalist Defense of Substantive Due Process: Magna Charta, Higher-Law Constitutionalism, and the Fifth Amendment*, 58 Emory L.J. 586 (2009).

10. Stephen A. Siegel, *Lochner Era Jurisprudence and the American Constitutional Tradition*, 70 N.C. L Rev. 1, 59–60 (1991). On the origins of equal protection of the law as a constitutional value, see Philip A. Hamburger, *Equality and Diversity: The Eighteenth-Century Debate about Equal Protection and Equal Civil Rights*, 1992 Sup. Ct. Rev. 295.

11. James W. Ely, Jr., *The Oxymoron Reconsidered: Myth and Reality in the Origins of Substantive Due Process*, 16 Const. Comm. 315 (1999).

12. The most influential pre–Civil War due process opinion was *Wynehamer v. People*, 13 N.Y. 378 (1856), but the court did not fully articulate why it believed that due process of law includes the protection of substantive property rights. *See generally* Harrison, *supra* note 1, at 495 ("there is no *Marbury*, no *M'Culloch*, for substantive due process"). Recent scholarship has shown that there was really no "*Marbury*" for judicial

review either. The *Marbury* case only came to be seen as significant many decades after it was decided. Judges always assumed they had the implicit power to review the constitutionality of legislation, *Marbury* or no *Marbury*. *See* Philip Hamburger, Law and Judicial Duty (2008); Davison M. Douglas, *The Rhetorical Uses of* Marbury v. Madison: *The Emergence of a "Great Case"*, 38 Wake Forest L. Rev. 375 (2003).

13. Mark A. Graber, *Dred Scott* and the Problem of Constitutional Evil 64 (2006); *see also* Ryan C. Williams, *The (One and Only) Substantive Due Process Clause*, 120 Yale L.J. (forthcoming 2010). *See generally* Earl M. Maltz, *Fourteenth Amendment Concepts in the Antebellum Era*, 32 Am. J. Leg. Hist. 305 (1988).

14. 60 U.S. (How. 19) 393 (1857).

15. Robert Bork, The Tempting of America 32–33 (1987).

16. *See also* Graber, *supra* note 13, at 65; Rodney Mott, Due Process of Law 328 (1926); Alfred Hill, *The Political Dimension of Constitutional Adjudication*, 63 S. Cal. L. Rev. 1237, 1317 (1990); Williams, *supra* note 13.

17. Bloomer v. McQuewan, 55 U.S. 539, 553–54 (1852).

18. Graber, *supra* note 13, at 66.

19. *Id.* at 62–63.

20. *See* Williams, *supra* note 13.

21. *The National Liberty Convention*, Emancipator & Free American, Sept. 14, 1843.

22. Salmon Portland Chase & Charles Dexter Cleveland, Anti-Slavery Addresses of 1844 and 1845, at 86, 101 (1867).

23. "4. Resolved, That our fathers ordained the Constitution of the United States in order, among other great national objects, to establish justice, promote the general welfare, secure the blessings of liberty; but expressly denied to the federal government, which they created, a constitutional power to deprive any person of life, liberty, or property, without due legal process. 5. Resolved, That in the judgment of this convention Congress has no more power to make a slave than to make a king; no more power to institute or establish slavery than to institute or establish a monarchy. No such power can be found among those specifically conferred by the Constitution, or derived by just implication from them."

24. *The Antislavery Planks of the Republican National Platform (1856)*, in Sources in American Constitutional History 99 (Michael Les Benedict ed., 1996); *The Republican Party Platform (May 16, 1860)*, in 1 Documents of American History 363, 364 (Henry Steele Commager ed., 1973); *see also* Randy E. Barnett, Whence Comes Section One? The Abolitionist Origins of the Fourteenth Amendment (unpublished).

25. Thomas M. Cooley, A Treatise on the Constitutional Limitations Which Rest upon the Legislative Power of the States of the American Union iii (1868).

26. *Id.* at 174; *see also* State *ex rel.* St. Joseph & Denver City R.R. Co. v. Comm'rs of Nemaha Co., 7 Kan. 542, 555 (1871); People v. Salem, 20 Mich. 452, 473 (1870).

27. Loan Ass'n v. Topeka, 87 U.S. (20 Wall.) 655, 663 (1875); *see also* Hanson v. Vernon, 27 Iowa 28, 73 (1869) (Beck, J., concurring) ("There is, as it were, back of the written Constitution, an unwritten Constitution . . . which guarantees and well protects all the absolute rights of the people."); Cooley, *supra* note 25, at 93, 95, 175, 410–13.

28. Richard C. McMurtie, *A New Canon of Constitutional Interpretation*, 32 Am. L. Reg. & Rev. 1, 7 (1893).

29. A.V. Dicey, The Law of the Constitution 125 (2d ed. 1886); *see also* John W. Burgess, Political Science and Comparative Constitutional Law 228 (1890). "The glory of the founders of the United States," Dicey added, "is to have devised or adopted arrangements under which the Constitution became in reality as well as in name the supreme law of the land." Dicey, *supra*, at 145; *see also* John F. Dillon, The Laws and Jurisprudence of England and America 212–26 (1894).

30. Christopher G. Tiedeman, The Unwritten Constitution of the United States 77–78, 81 (1890).

31. *See* Michael G. Collins, *Before* Lochner: *Diversity Jurisdiction and the Development of General Constitutional Law*, 74 Tul. L. Rev. 1263 (2000).

32. 41 U.S. (16 Pet.) 1 (1842).

33. Railroad Comm'n Cases, 116 U.S. 307, 331 (1886) (rate regulation); Loan Association v. Topeka, 87 U.S. (20 Wall.) 655 (1874) (public purpose); Pumpelly v. Green Bay Co., 80 U.S. (13 Wall.) 166 (1871) (just compensation).

34. *See* William E. Nelson, The Fourteenth Amendment 171–72 (1988).

35. Slaughter-House Cases, 83 U.S. (16 Wall.) 36 (1872). For comprehensive discussions of *Slaughter-House*, see Michael A. Ross, Justice of Shattered Dreams: Samuel Freeman Miller and the Supreme Court During the Civil War Era (2003) and Jonathan Lurie & Ronald Ladde, The Slaughterhouse Cases: Regulation, Reconstruction and the Fourteenth Amendment (2003).

36. Slaughter-House Cases, 83 U.S. (16 Wall.) 36, (1872).

37. *See* City of Chicago v. Rumpff, 45 Ill. 90 (1867); City of Bloomington v. Wahl, 46 Ill. 489 (1868); Schuster v. Metro Board of Health, 49 Barb 450 (N.Y. 1867).

38. Slaughter-House Cases, 83 U.S. (16 Wall.) 36, 81 (1873).

39. *See* 3 Charles Warren, The Supreme Court in United States History 271 (1922).

40. 96 U.S. 97 (1877).

41. *Id.* at 102. *See generally* Nelson, *supra* note 34, at 158–59 (noting that one interpretation of Miller's opinion is that he agreed with Justice Field on the law, but disagreed about how to interpret the underlying facts).

42. Michael A. Ross, Justice of Shattered Dreams: Samuel Freeman Miller and the Supreme Court during the Civil War Era 253 (2003).

43. *See* Christopher Wolfe, The Rise of Modern Judicial Review 129 (1986).

44. Bertholf v. O'Reilly, 74 N.Y. 509 (1878).

45. 110 U.S. 516 (1884).

46. *Id.* at 531.

47. *Id.* at 532.

48. *Id.* at 535–36.

49. Mugler v. Kansas, 123 U.S. 623, 661 (1887); *cf.* The Sinking-Fund Cases, 99 U.S. 700, 738 (1878) (declaring that a statute transferring the property of A. to B. "is not legislation").

50. For acknowledgement of this point, see Ernst Freund, The Police Power 632 (1904); Lucius Polk McGehee, Due Process of Law under the Federal Constitution 311–12 (1906). *See generally* Charles A. Lofgren, The Plessy Case: A Legal-Historical Interpretation 89 (1987) ("the line between due process and equal protection was indistinct").

51. *See* Howard Gillman, The Constitution Besieged: The Rise and Demise of Lochner Era Police Powers Jurisprudence (1993); Nelson, *supra* note 34, at 176–81; Victoria F.

Nourse & Sarah A. Maguire, *The Lost History of Governance and Equal Protection*, 58 Duke L.J. 955, 963–66 (2009); Michael Les Benedict, *Laissez-Faire and Liberty*, 3 L. & Hist. Rev. 293 (1985).

52. Butchers' Union Slaughter-House & Live-Stock Landing Co. v. Crescent City Live-Stock & Slaughterhouse Co., 111 U.S. 746, 758 (1883) (Field, J., concurring).

53. *Id.* at 759. *See generally* Charles W. McCurdy, *Justice Field and the Jurisprudence of Government-Business Relations: Some Parameters of Laissez-Faire Constitutionalism, 1863–1897*, 61 J. Am. Hist. 970, 979–1004 (1975).

54. 109 U.S. 3, 24 (1883).

55. 129 U.S. 114, 124 (1889) ("[L]egislation is not open to the charge of depriving one of his rights without due process of law, if it be general in its operation upon the subjects to which it relates").

56. 139 U.S. 462, 468 (1891). *Accord* Caldwell v. Texas, 137 U.S. 692, 697 (1891); Florida Cent. & Peninsular R.R. Co. v. Reynolds, 183 U.S. 471, 478 (1902); Giozza v. Teirnan, 148 U.S. 657, 662 (1893).

57. Barbier v. Connolly, 113 U.S. 27 (1884).

58. *Id.* at 710–11. *See generally* Caleb Nelson, *Judicial Review of Legislative Purpose*, 83 N.Y.U. L. Rev. 1784 (2008).

59. Missouri Pacific Railway Co. v. Mackey, 127 U.S. 205 (1888).

60. 127 U.S. 678 (1888).

61. *Powell*, 127 U.S. at 686; *see* Geoffrey P. Miller, *Public Choice at the Dawn of the Special Interest State: The Story of Butter and Margarine*, 77 Cal. L. Rev. 83 (1989).

62. *Powell*, 127 U.S. at 687. As an indication of how forgiving the Court's test in *Powell* was, even Progressive Ernst Freund later criticized the Court for upholding the margarine law. Freund, *supra* note 50, at 57.

63. State v. Loomis, 22 S.W. 350 (Mo. 1893); State v. Goodwill, 10 S.E. 285, 288 (W. Va. 1889); *see also* Toledo, St. Louis & W. R.R. Co. v. Long, 82 N.E. 757 (Ind. 1907); Frorer v. People, 31 N.E. 395, 397–400 (Ill. 1892); Kellyville Coal Co. v. Harrier, 69 N.E. 927 (Ill. 1904).

64. Until 1914, the Supreme Court lacked jurisdiction to review state court decisions that invalidated legislation on federal constitutional grounds. In addition, as today, it lacked jurisdiction to review state court interpretations of state constitutions.

65. Freund, *supra* note 50, at 705.

66. *E.g.*, Connolly v. Union Sewer Pipe Co., 184 U.S. 540 (1902) (antitrust law that exempted only farmers and ranchers); Cotting v. Godard, 183 U.S. 79, 114–15 (1901) (Harlan, J., concurring for six justices) (state statute that regulated rates for some stock-yard companies but not for others); Gulf Coast & S.F. Ry. Co. v. Ellis, 165 U.S. 150 (1897) (statute that singled out railroad defendants for recovery of attorneys' fees).

67. *See* Mott, *supra* note 15, at 277–78; Nourse & Maguire, *supra* note 51.

68. *E.g.*, Am. Sugar Ref. Co. v. Louisiana, 179 U.S. 89, 92, 95 (1900); Atchison, Topeka & Santa Fe R.R. Co. v. Matthews, 174 U.S. 96 (1899). *See generally* Nourse & Maguire, *supra* note 51 (noting how rarely the Supreme Court invalidated laws as class legislation).

69. *E.g.*, District of Columbia v. Brooke, 214 U.S. 138, 142 (1909).

70. Truax v. Corrigan, 257 U.S. 312, 331–32 (1921).

71. *See* Nourse & Maguire, *supra* note 51.

72. *See* Barry Cushman, *Some Varieties and Vicissitudes of Lochnerism*, 85 B.U. L. Rev. 881, 926 (2005).

73. *See, e.g.,* Eubank v. City of Richmond, 226 U.S. 137 (1912); Dobbins v. Los Angeles, 195 U.S. 223 (1904). *See generally* Bradley C. Karkkainen, *The Police Power Revisited: Phantom Incorporation and the Roots of the Takings "Muddle"*, 90 Minn. L. Rev. 826 (2006).

74. Stephen A. Siegel, *Historism in Late Nineteenth-Century Constitutional Thought*, 1990 Wis. L. Rev. 1431, 1438.

75. Siegel, *supra* note 10, at 83; *see also* Lewis A. Grossman, *James Coolidge Carter and Mugwump Jurisprudence*, 20 L. & Hist. Rev. 577, 607 (2002); Alan R. Jones, The Constitutional Conservatism of Thomas McIntyre Cooley 359 (1987) . *See generally* Eric R. Claeys, *Blackstone's Commentaries and the Privileges or Immunities of United States Citizens: A Modest Tribute to Professor Siegan*, 45 San Diego L. Rev. 777, 789–96 (2008).

76. Slaughter-House Cases, 83 U.S. (16 Wall.) 36, 114, 115 (1872) (Bradley, J., dissenting).

77. *Id.* at 115, 119.

78. *See generally* William E. Forbath, *The Ambiguities of Free Labor: Labor and the Law in the Gilded Age*, 1985 Wis. L. Rev. 767, 782–86; Charles W. McCurdy, *The Liberty of Contract Regime in American Law, in* The State and Freedom of Contract 161, 165–79 (Harry N. Scheiber ed., 1998); William E. Nelson, *The Impact of the Antislavery Movement upon Styles of Judicial Reasoning in Nineteenth Century America*, 87 Harv. L. Rev. 513, 558–60 (1974). For broad historical discussions of the development of free labor ideology and its relationship to contract law, see Robert J. Steinfeld, The Invention of Free Labor: The Employment Relation in English and American Law and Culture, 1350–1870 (1991); Christopher L. Tomlins, Law, Labor, and Ideology in the Early American Republic 274–75 (1993).

79. *Slaughter-House Cases*, 83 U.S. at 110 (Field, J., dissenting).

80. *See, e.g., In re* Tie Loy, 26 F. 611, 613 (C.C.D. Cal. 1886); *In re* Sam Kee, 31 F. 680, 681 (C.C.N.D. Cal. 1887).

81. Butcher's Union Company v. Crescent City Company, 111 U.S. 746, 762 (1883) (Bradley, J., concurring); *see also* Powell v. Pennsylvania, 127 U.S. 678, 691–92 (1888) (articulating the right of a person "to follow such pursuits as may be best adapted to his faculties, and which will give to him the highest enjoyment") (Field, J., dissenting); *In re* Quong Woo, 13 F. 229, 233 (C.C.D. Cal. 1882) (Field, J.).

82. *See, e.g.,* Commonwealth v. Perry, 28 N.E. 1126, 1126–27 (Mass. 1891); Low v. Rees Printing Co., 59 N.W. 362, 366–68 (Neb. 1894); *In re* Jacobs, 98 N.Y. 98, 108–10 (1885); Godcharles v. Wigeman, 6 A. 354, 356 (Pa. 1886).

83. 2 N.E. 29, 33 (N.Y. 1885).

84. *In re* Jacobs, 98 N.Y. 98 (1885).

85. The law, in fact, was passed at the behest of the German-dominated Cigar Makers union to stifle competition from new Bohemian immigrants. H. M. Gitelman, *Adolph Strasser and the Origins of Pure and Simple Unionism*, 6 Lab. Hist. 71, 79–80 (1965); *Current Topics*, 31 Albany L.J. 81, 82 (1885); *The Week*, The Nation, Jan. 29, 1885, at 85; Editorial, N.Y. Times, Jan. 21, 1885, at 4.

86. P. S. Atiyah, The Rise and Fall of Freedom of Contract ch. 14 (1979); Michael J. Trebilcock, The Common Law of Restraint of Trade: A Legal and Economic Analysis

ch. 1 (1986); James W. Ely, Jr., *Economic Liberties and the Original Meaning of the Constitution*, 45 San Diego L. Rev. 673 (2008).

87. *See* Nelson, *supra* note 78.

88. Registering Co. v. Sampson, L.R., 19 Eq. 462 (1875).

89. Godcharles v. Wigeman, 6 A. 354 (Pa. 1886).

90. *Id.* at 356.

91. Editorial, *Immediate and Remote Liberty of Contract*, Dallas Morning News, Oct. 20, 1886, at 4.

92. People ex rel. Annan v. Walsh, 22 N.E. 682 (N.Y. 1889) (Peckham, J., dissenting).

93. *See, e.g.,* Commonwealth v. Perry, 28 N.E. 1126, 1126–27 (Mass. 1891).

94. *E.g.,* Frederick N. Judson, *Liberty of Contract Under the Police Power*, 25 Am. L. Rev. 871 (1891); D. H. Pingrey, *Limiting the Right to Contract*, 34 Cent. L. J. 91 (1892).

95. David Dudley Field, *American Progress in Jurisprudence*, 27 Am. L. Rev. 641 (1893). Cooley had expressed similar thoughts a decade and a half earlier. Thomas M. Cooley, *Limits to State Control of Private Business*, 1878 Princeton Rev. 233, 269.

96. Theodore W. Dwight, The Law of Persons and Personal Property 73 (Edward F. Dwight ed., 1894).

97. John F. Dillon, The Laws and Jurisprudence of England and America 203, 212, 226, 382 (1894).

98. Lawton v. Steele, 152 U.S. 133, 137 (1894).

99. Frisbie v. United States, 157 U.S. 160, 165 (1895).

100. Allgeyer v. Louisiana, 165 U.S. 578 (1897).

101. *Id.* at 589.

102. N. Sec. Co. v. United States, 193 U.S. 197, 351 (1904); Patterson v. Bark Eudora 190 U.S. 169, 173–79 (1903); United States v. Joint Traffic Ass'n, 171 U.S. 505, 572 (1898); Hopkins v. United States, 171 U.S. 578, 603 (1898).

103. *Allgeyer*, 165 U.S. at 590–91.

104. *See* Pollock v. Farmers' Loan & Trust Co., 157 U.S. 429, 607 (1895) (Field, J., concurring); Budd v. New York, 143 U.S. 517, 551 (1892) (Brewer, J., dissenting); Tiedeman, *supra* note 85, at vi–vii; David J. Brewer, *An Independent Judiciary as the Salvation of the Nation*, *in* N.Y. State Bar Ass'n, Proceedings of the New York State Bar Association 37, 37–47 (1893); Judson, *supra* 8, at 256–58.

105. Ely, *supra* note 6, at 78; Charles W. McCurdy, *The Roots of "Liberty of Contract" Reconsidered: Major Premises in the Law of Employment, 1867–1937*, 1984 Sup. Ct. Hist. Soc'y Y.B. 20, 33. For prominent examples of the traditional literature, see Sidney Fine, Laissez Faire and the General-Welfare State: A Study of Conflict in American Thought, 1865–1900, at 133 (1956); Arnold M. Paul, Conservative Crisis and the Rule of Law 223–39 (1960). Indeed, if anything the rise of the Supreme Court's liberty of contract doctrine is an example of ideological entrenchment by a winning political coalition, occurring after the Populist movement led by William Jennings Bryan was soundly defeated.

106. *See* David E. Bernstein, Lochner, *Parity and the Chinese Laundry Cases*, 41 Wm. & Mary L. Rev. 211 (1999).

107. Jacobson v. Massachusetts, 197 U.S. 11 (1905); *see* James W. Ely, Jr., *Rufus W. Peckham and Economic Liberty*, 62 Vand. L. Rev. 591, 622–23 (2009) (discussing *Jacobson*). Brewer and Peckham were by far the justices most likely to vote to invalidate state

legislation premised on the police power. *See* D. Grier Stephenson, *The Supreme Court and Constitutional Change:* Lochner v. New York *Revisited*, 21 Vill. L. Rev. 217, 234–36 (1976).

108. *See* Christopher Tomlins, *Necessities of State: Police, Sovereignty, and the Constitution*, 20 J. Pol'y Hist. 47, 54 (2007). *See generally* James Edwards Kerr, The *Insular Cases*: The Role of the Judiciary in American Expansionism (1982); Bartholomew H. Sparrow, The *Insular Cases* and the Emergence of American Empire (2006).

109. *See* Laura Kalman, *Eating Spaghetti with a Spoon*, 49 Stan. L. Rev. 1547, 1549 (1997) ("Judicial formalism . . . reflecting 'the entrenched faith in laissez faire,' emerged in cases such as *Lochner v. New York*").

110. Tiedeman, *supra* note 85, at vii.

111. *See* Herbert Spencer, Social Statics 9 (1848).

112. Tiedeman, *supra* note 85, at 457.

113. Pace v. Alabama, 106 U.S. 583 (1883).

114. *See* David N. Mayer, *The Myth of "Laissez-Faire Constitutionalism": Liberty of Contract During the* Lochner *Era*, 36 Hastings Con. L. Q. 217, 256 (2009).

115. *See* Ely, *supra* note 110, at 611; Siegel, *supra* note 10, at 14–16. Brewer once wrote, "The paternal theory of government is to me odious. The utmost possible liberty to the individual, and the fullest possible protection to him and his property, is both the limitation and the duty of government." Budd v. New York, 143 U.S. 517, 551 (1892) (Brewer, J., dissenting). As a state court judge, Peckham spoke of "the absolute liberty of the individual to contract regarding his own property." People *ex rel.* Annan v. Walsh, 22 N.E. 682, 687 (N.Y. 188) (Peckham, J., dissenting).

116. *See, e.g.*, Gardner v. Michigan, 199 U.S. 325, 335 (1905); Jacobson v. Massachusetts, 197 U.S. 11 (1905); Otis v. Parker, 187 U.S. 606, 611 (1903); Booth v. Illinois, 184 U.S. 425, 432 (1902); Knoxville Iron Co. v. Harbison, 183 U.S. 13, 22 (1901). *See generally* Charles Warren, *A Bulwark to the State Police Power: The United States Supreme Court*, 13 Colum. L. Rev. 667, 695 (1913).

117. *See* William F. Duker, *Mr. Justice Rufus W. Peckham: The Police Power and the Individual in a Changing World*, 1980 BYU L. Rev. 47, 48 (1980).

118. Ely, *supra* note 85, at 950; Siegel, *supra* note 10, at 2–22.

119. *See* Randy E. Barnett, Restoring the Lost Constitution: The Presumption of Liberty 211–18 (2004).

120. *See* Brian Z. Tamanaha, Beyond the Formalist-Realist Divide: The Role of Politics in Judging 100–101 (2009); William J. Novak, The *Legal Origins of the Modern American State*, in Looking Back at Law's Century 249, 262 (Austin Sarat, et al., eds., 2004).

CHAPTER TWO

1. *See* Matthew S. Bewig, *Lochner v. The Journeymen Bakers of New York: The Journeymen Bakers, Their Hours of Labor, and the Constitution*, 38 Am. J. Legal Hist. 413, 429–34 (1994).

2. *Unconstitutional*, Baker's J., May 6, 1905, at 1; *Bakeshop Legislation*, Baker's J., Sept. 1, 1897, at 52; *see also Bakers Lose at Law, But Not in Fact*, Am. Federationist, June 1905, at 361, 362.

3. Paul Kens, Judicial Power and Reform Politics: The Anatomy of *Lochner v. New York* 9 (1990); Matthew S. Bewig, *Laboring in the "Poisonous Gases": Consumption, Public Health, and the* Lochner *Court*, 1 NYU J. L. & Lib. 476, 484 (2005); Editorial, *Unconstitutional*, Baker's J., May 6, 1905, at 1; *Bakeshop Legislation*, Baker's J., Sept. 1, 1897, at 52; *Consumption Bred in Cellar Bakeries*, N.Y. Evening World, Aug. 10, 1905, at 5. Bernard Siegan points out that while inhaling flour dust was considered a health hazard, bakers only worked around flour dust for an hour or two a day, and only if their employer had not yet installed mixing machines. The hours law did not specifically address this problem. Bernard H. Siegan, Economic Liberties and the Constitution 137 (2d ed. 2006).

4. *The Demonstrations of the Bakers of New York and Brooklyn*, Baker's J., Apr. 27, 1895, at 1. Bakers' unions in Philadelphia, Boston, and Washington, D.C., also failed in their attempts to promote bakery legislation around this time. Stuart Bruce Kaufman, A Vision of Unity: The History of the Bakery and Confectionery Workers International Union 31 (1986).

5. *See* Dorothee Schneider, Trade Unions and Community: The German Working Class in New York City, 1870–1900, at 204–05 (1994). As late as May 1903, the *Baker's Journal's* editors estimated that at least half of union members nationwide were fluent in German and not English. *Two Journals*, Baker's J., May 30, 1903, at 1.

6. Tenth Annual Report of the Factory Inspectors of the State of New York 42 (1896); *Employes Alone Benefited*, Brooklyn Eagle, May 17, 1896, at 5.

7. *Now for the Ten-Hour Day*, Baker's J., Apr. 20, 1895, at 1; *see also* Factory Inspectors' Report, *supra* note 6, at 42–43.

8. Schneider, *supra* note 5, at 205. *For the Abolition of Saturday-Night and Sunday Work*, Baker's J., Oct. 15, 1897, at 102; *Non-Union Bakeries*, Baker's J., Aug. 19, 1905, at 1.

9. Kens, *supra* note 3, at 8; Paul Brenner, *The Formative Years of the Hebrew Bakers' Unions, 1881–1914*, 18 Yivo Ann. of Jewish Soc. Sci. 39, 41 (1983).

10. Dennis Hanlon, *Inspection of Bake-Shops*, in Ninth Annual Convention of the International Association of Factory Inspectors of North America 14–15 (1895); Brenner, *supra* note 9, at 42; *Complaints of the Bakers*, N.Y. Times, Nov. 21, 1895, at 9; *Employes Alone Benefited, supra* note 6.

11. *Employes Alone Benefited, supra* note 6.

12. *See* Kaufmann, *supra* note 4, at 27; Frank H. Brooks, *Ideology, Strategy, and Organization: Dyer Lum and the American Anarchist Movement*, 34 Lab. Hist. 57 (1993); Editorial, Liberty, Jan. 1899, at 5; *The San Francisco Dynamiters*, N.Y. Times, Dec. 18, 1885, at 1; Letter from Henry Weismann to California Gov. James H. Budd, June 24, 1895.

13. *Denies Opposing Loans to Allies*, N.Y. Times, July 30, 1915, at 4.

14. 2 Samuel Gompers, Seventy Years of Life and Labor: An Autobiography 4 (1925). For an account of a rabble-rousing speech by Weismann defending worker violence, see *Reds Wave Their Flag*, Chi. Trib., Nov. 9, 1891, at 1.

15. Kens, *supra* note 3, at 47–48. According to one source, Weismann started the *German American Bakers' Journal*, the bakers' union's original periodical, and started organizing for the union in 1885. William D. P. Bliss, et al., eds., The Encyclopedia of Social Reform 86 (1909). But another more contemporary source attributes the founding of the *Journal* to someone else. George E. McNeil, The Labor Movement: The Problem of Today 367–68 (1887).

16. *See The English Speaking Bakers*, N.Y. Times, July 15, 1893, at 1; *The Movement for Sanitary Bakeshops*, Baker's J., Mar. 23, 1895, at 1.

17. Brenner, *supra* note 9, at 64–65. Bernard Weinstein, secretary of the United Hebrew Trades, later took credit for bringing the story of the dying Jewish baker to public attention. Marina Balinska, The Bagel: The Surprising History of a Modest Bread 107–8 (2008).

18. Edward Marshall, *Bread and Filth Cooked Together*, N.Y. Press, Sept. 30, 1894, § 4, at 1; Henry Weismann, Letter to the Editor, N.Y. Press, Sept. 23, 1894. Similar stories were published in the *New York Recorder* at the urging of the English-speaking New York Local 80. Kaufman, *supra* note 4.

19. Marshall later spoke at a rally in favor of union-sponsored legislation, and promised to aid the union in this matter in any way he could. *See Brilliant and Imposing Demonstration of the Journeyman Bakers of New York*, Baker's J., May 25, 1895, at 1.

20. *The Bakeries Are All Right*, Brooklyn Eagle, May 12, 1896, at 4. For Weismann's reply, see *A Sharp Reply to Dr. Purdy*, Brooklyn Eagle, May 14, 1896, at 14.

21. *Big Bakers Back Audett*, Brooklyn Eagle, Feb. 23, 1896, at 22; *see* Factory Inspectors' Report, *supra* note 6, at 5; *Inspecting Bakeries in the State*, N.Y. Times, July 25, 1895, at 6. It should be noted, however, that one of the four state inspectors, Dennis Hanlon, was president of one of the union locals. Kaufmann, *supra* note 4, at 32.

22. *Employes Alone Benefited*, *supra* note 6.

23. *The Bakers' Bill Progressing*, Baker's J., Mar. 30, 1895, at 1.

24. Twelfth Annual Report of the Chief Factory Inspector of the State of New York (1898).

25. *See* People v. Lochner, 69 N.E. 373, 382 (N.Y. 1904).

26. *Id.*; *see also* Kens, *supra* note 3, at 44–59.

27. *The Bakers' Bill Progressing*, *supra* note 23.

28. The Condition of the Bakeshops and the Operative Bakers of New York, Brooklyn and Vicinity (Henry Weismann ed., Feb. 1895).

29. *The Bakers' Bill to be Signed by Governor Morton*, Baker's J., Apr. 20, 1895, at 2.

30. *Now for the Ten-Hour Day*, *supra* note 7.

31. Bewig, *supra* note 1, at 440.

32. *See Big Bakers Back Audett*, *supra* note 21.

33. *Id.*; Factory Inspectors' Report, *supra* note 6; *Employees Alone Benefited*, *supra* note 6; *The Ten-Hour Decision*, Bakers Rev., May 15, 1905, at 33; *A Ten-Hour Work Day*, Nat'l Baker, June 16, 1902, at 8.

34. *Employes Alone Benefited*, *supra* note 6.

35. *See* Bernard H. Siegan, Economic Liberties and the Constitution 117–18 (1980); Richard A. Epstein, *The Mistakes of 1937*, 11 Geo. Mason U.L. Rev. 5 (1988).

36. The National Association of Master Bakers, founded in 1898, explicitly endorsed sanitary laws like New York's. *Second Convention of the National Association of Master Bakers*, The Nat'l Baker, Sept. 15, 1899, at 9, 13; *see also* Fourth Annual Convention National Association of Master Bakers [Souvenir Program] 94–95 (1901).

37. *See A Voice in Favor of Bake Shop Laws in the Interest of the Baking Industry*, Baker's J., June 15, 1895, at 3; D. J. Hanlon, *Bakeshops*, in Twelfth Annual Report of the Factory Inspector, *supra* note 24, at 762, 765.

38. *The Baker's Bill to be Signed by Governor Morton, supra* note 29; Kens, *supra* note 3, at 58.

39. *Employees Alone Benefited, supra* note 6.

40. Paul Kens, Lochner v. New York: *Rehabilitated and Revised, But Still Reviled,* 1995 J. Sup. Ct. Hist. 31, 34; Baker's J., May 11, 1895, at 11; *Bakers Celebrate,* The Sun, May 19, 1895, at 4.

41. *The Baker's Bill to Be Signed by Governor Morton,* Baker's J., April 20, 1895, at 2.

42. N.Y. Laws Ch. 672 (1896); Hanlon, *supra* note 37, at 764; *The Amendments to the Baking Inspection Law of New York,* Baker's J., Jan. 22, 1896, at 1; *Bakers Appeal to the Governor,* N.Y. Times, Apr. 21, 1896; *War on Filthy Bakeries,* N.Y. Times, April 8, 1896, at 6; *Complaints of the Bakers,* N.Y. Times, June 25, 1895, at 8. As it turned out, several hundred of the basement bakeries managed to tunnel deeper underground to meet the height requirement. Hanlon, *supra.*

43. N.Y. Times, Feb. 6, 1896, at 16.

44. Albin E. Plarre, *Letter to Bakers' Helper,* Bakers' Helper, May 1905, at 444.

45. *Quoted in Triumphant,* Baker's J., Sept. 16, 1905.

46. Kens, *supra* note 3, at 98.

47. *Made the 10-Hour Law, Then Had it Unmade,* N.Y. Times, Apr. 19, 1905, at 1; Letter from Mary Weismann Lucy to Timothy Sandefur, Feb. 20, 2006. Before he graduated, Weismann was accused of practicing law without a license when he appeared in a civil action before a magistrate. Weismann claimed he appeared as an agent of attorney Carl Schurz. *Weisman* [sic] *Not a Lawyer,* Brooklyn Eagle, June 27, 1901, at 7.

48. Editorial, Liberty, Jan. 1899, at 5.

49. *See Two Master Bakers' Conventions,* Baker's J., Oct. 12, 1901, at 4; *Why All This Quarrel?,* Baker's J., Nov. 2, 1901, at 1. At a banquet celebrating the association's victory in *Lochner,* its treasurer gave an address mostly in German. *Celebration of Victory,* Bakers Rev., June 1905, at 41, 42. *Henry Weismann,* Baker's J., May 27, 1905, at 1; *see also The Traitors at Their Dirty Work in the Country Towns,* Baker's J., Apr. 1, 1898, at 5.

50. *The New York Boss Bakers' Bill Dead,* Baker's J., Apr. 15, 1898, at 292.

51. Hanlon, *supra* note 37, at 765; *Condition of Factories,* Brooklyn Eagle, Jan 24, 1898, at 7; *Hebrew Bakers Win,* New York Tribune, Jan. 13, 1901, at 1.

52. *The Ten-Hour Decision, supra* note 33, at 33; *National Association of Master Bakers,* Bakers' Rev., Sept. 15, 1903, at 31, 39; *The Ten-Hour Law,* Bakers Rev., Feb. 15, 1904, at 31.

53. *The Ten-Hour Decision, supra* note 33, at 33; *National Association of Master Bakers, supra* note 52, at 39; *Celebration of Victory, supra* note 49. New Jersey's bakeshop law, passed in 1896, also had a sixty-hours rule, but had a provision allowing for two hours daily of emergency overtime for extra pay. *The New Jersey Law,* Baker's J., Apr. 22, 1896, at 1.

54. *See More Agreements,* Baker's J., Apr. 15, 1902, at 1.

55. *The Ten-Hour Decision, supra* note 33, at 33; *National Association of Master Bakers, supra* note 52, at 39; *The Ten-Hour Law, supra* note 52.

56. Kaufmann, *supra* note 4, at 32.

57. Emil Braun, *Remarks at the United Master Bakers' Third Convention, May 27, 1902,* Bakers' Helper, June 1902, at 555.

58. Kaufman, *supra* note 4; *The Ten-Hour Decision, supra* note 33.

59. *Second Convention, supra* note 36.

60. *Master Bakers of New York State,* Bakers' Helper, Oct. 1901, at 25, 26.

61. *The Ten-Hour Law, supra* note 52. The latter article claims that the association also decided to find a test case at its 1901 convention, but a contemporary source states that the ten-hour law was discussed, but "no stand was taken." *Master Bakers of New York State,* Bakers' Helper, Oct. 1901, at 25, 16.

62. Chase E. Abbott, *The Advantages of Organization to Prevent Unjust Legislation,* Bakers Rev., Oct. 1905, at 42.

63. Hadley Arkes, Lochner v. New York *and the Cast of Our Laws, in* Great Cases in Constitutional Law 94, 104 (Robert P. George ed., 2000); *Boycotting a Bakery,* Utica Observer, Aug. 21, 1895, at 5; *Mrs. Joseph Lochner,* Utica Daily Press, April 23, 1908.

64. *Boycotting a Bakery, supra* note 63.

65. *Id.; The Lochner Boycott,* Utica Observer, Aug. 24, 1895, at 5; *see also* Baker's J., June 15, 1895.

66. *Boycotting a Bakery, supra* note 63.

67. Penal Law of the State of New York 698 (1911); *Baker Lochner Fined $20,* Utica Morning Herald, Dec. 22, 1899; Note, *Bakery Law of New York Unconstitutional,* 39 Am. L. Rev. 450, 450 (1905); *Decision Given in Labor Case,* Utica Herald Dispatch, Apr. 17, 1905; *The Ten-Hour Decision, supra* note 33.

68. In addition to the two prosecutions discussed in the text, while *People v. Lochner* was pending in the New York courts, he was arrested a third time for violating the hours law. *Baker Lochner: His Troubles,* Utica Herald Dispatch, July 7, 1903. This time, he was acquitted after arguing that the complaining baker had worked more than ten hours against his explicit orders to not do so to avoid "trouble with the union." *Jury Acquits Baker of Violating State Law,* Amsterdam Evening Recorder, Sept. 24, 1903; *Six Foot Baker was Chief Witness,* Syracuse J., Sept, 24, 1903, at 7; *Ten-Hour Bakery Law Sustained,* Bakers' Helper, March 1904, at 212.

69. *E.g.,* Utica Herald-Dispatch, March 17, 1900, at 5.

70. Penal Law, *supra* note 67 (reprinting the indictment). The indictment states that Lochner's previous offense was in 1895, but that is an error; it was 1899. *See Will Interest Many,* Utica Daily Press, Dec. 11, 1899.

71. Second Annual Report of the Department of Labor of the State of New York for the Twelve Months Ended September 30 1902, at 23 (1903); *Bakery Law of New York Unconstitutional,* 39 Am. L. Rev. 450, 450 (1905); *Court Kills Ten-Hour Law,* Buffalo Express, April 18, 1905; *Not Necessarily Melancholy,* Brooklyn Eagle, April 23, 1905, at 2.

72. *Personal,* Utica Sunday Tribune, June 11, 1899, at 13; Utica Observer, March 22, 1899, at 1 (advertisement). I'm assuming that "Aman Schmitter" (Lochner's on-again, off-again employee) and "Amand Schmitter" (owner of the Imperial Bakery, who traveled with Lochner) are the same person.

73. *Armand Schmitter,* Utica Observer, (exact date illegible 1941).

74. *The Ten-Hour Decision, supra* note 33. Lochner was active in the state bakers' association and attended the 1902 convention as an alternate delegate.

75. *See* chapter 1.

76. *See In re* Jacobs, 98 N.Y. 98 (N.Y. 1885).

77. People *ex rel.* Rodgers v. Coler, 59 N.E. 716 (N.Y. 1901).

78. *See generally* Felice Batlan, *A Reevaluation of the New York Court of Appeals: The Home, the Market, and Labor, 1885–1905,* 27 Law & Soc. Inquiry 489 (2002).

79. Kens, *supra* note 3, at 80–81.

80. People v. Lochner, 76 N.Y.S. 396 (N.Y. App. Div. 1902).

81. *Id.* at 401–2.

82. *Id.* at 401.

83. *See* People v. Lochner, 69 N.E. 373 (N.Y. 1904).

84. *Id.* at 379.

85. *Id.* at 379–81.

86. Editorial, *The Supreme Court and Chief Judge Alton B. Parker,* N.Y. Sun, Apr. 22, 1905, at 6. Nevertheless, the 1904 Democratic platform included a plank stating that "constitutional guarantees are violated whenever any citizen is denied the right to labor, acquire, and enjoy property." Michael Kammen, A Machine that Would Go of Itself: The Constitution in American Culture 193 (1986).

87. *Lochner,* 69 N.E. at 381 (Gray, J., concurring).

88. *Id.* at 382–84 (Vann, J., concurring).

89. *Id.* at 385–89 (O'Brien, J., dissenting).

90. The *New York Sun* praised this opinion for "casting doubt on the wisdom" of the law. Editorial, *The Constitutionality of the Bakers' Labor Law,* N.Y. Sun, Feb. 4, 1904, at 6.

91. *Lochner,* 69 N.E. at 389 (Bartlett, J., dissenting).

92. *Down With Ten-Hour-Law! Is the War-Cry of the Boss Bakers,* Baker's J., Feb. 27, 1904, at 1.

93. *Made the 10-Hour Law, Then Had it Unmade, supra* note 47; Plarre, *supra* note 44.

94. *Celebration of Victory, supra* note 49.

95. *See* chapter 1.

96. Holden v. Hardy, 169 U.S. 366 (1898); *see also* Atkin v. Kansas, 191 U.S. 207 (1903); St. Louis Consol. Coal Co. v. Illinois, 185 U.S. 203, 207 (1902); Knoxville Iron Co. v. Harbison, 183 U.S. 13, 22 (1901).

97. N. Sec. Co. v. United States, 193 U.S. 197, 351 (1904); Patterson v. Bark Eudora, 190 U.S. 169, 173–75 (1903); United States v. Joint Traffic Ass'n, 171 U.S. 505, 572–73 (1898); Allgeyer v. Louisiana, 165 U.S. 578, 589 (1897).

98. *See Atkin,* 191 U.S. at 220–24 (1903); *Knoxville Iron Co.,* 183 U.S. at 18–22; *Holden,* 169 U.S. at 388–98.

99. Soon Hing v. Crowely, 113 U.S. 703, 709 (1885).

100. *Id.*

101. Brief for the Plaintiff in Error, Lochner v. New York, 198 U.S. 45 (1905), at 8, 10–11, 15.

102. *Id.* at 41, 46.

103. *Id.* at 57–58.

104. *Id.* at 60.

105. Kens, *supra* note 3, at 113.

106. Brief for Defendants in Error, Lochner v. New York, 198 U.S. 45 (1905).

107. *Id.* at 14.

108. Lochner v. New York, 198 U.S. 45 (1905). Ernst Freund wrote, "To those acquainted with the earlier cases, the decision in *Lochner vs. New York* must have come

as a surprise." Ernst Freund, *Hours of Labor and the Supreme Court*, 13 J. Pol. Econ. 597, 598 (1905); *see also* James W. Ely, Jr., *Rufus W. Peckham and Economic Liberty*, 62 Vand. L. Rev. 591, 592 (2009); Noga Morag-Levine, *Common Law, Civil Law, and the Administrative State: From Coke to* Lochner, 24 Const. Comm. 601, 655 (2007).

109. *See* Atkin v. Kansas, 191 U.S. 207, 224 (1903).

110. *See* Charles Henry Butler, A Century at the Bar of the Supreme Court of the United States 172 (1942); John E. Semonche, Charting the Future: The Supreme Court Responds to a Changing Society, 1890–1920, at 181–82 (1978); Alan F. Westin, *The Supreme Court and Group Conflict: Thoughts on Seeing Burke Put Through the Mill*, 52 Am. Pol. Sci. Rev. 665, 667 n.3 (1958). Unfortunately, the docket sheet that might reveal the tally of the justices' initial conference vote on *Lochner's* outcome currently awaits cataloguing by the National Archives and is unavailable to researchers indefinitely. For now, whether one of the justices indeed switched his vote at the last minute, and if so why, remains a mystery.

111. *See* Am. Federationist, June 1905, at 363–64.

112. *See* Barry Cushman, *Some Varieties and Vicissitudes of Lochnerism*, 85 B.U. L. Rev. 881, 937 (2005). On the other hand, just a few years later Justice McKenna wrote an opinion expressing a rather narrow understanding of the scope of the Constitution's prohibition on class legislation. District of Columbia v. Brooke, 214 U.S. 138 (1909).

113. D. Grier Stephenson, *The Supreme Court and Constitutional Change:* Lochner v. New York *Revisited*, 21 Vill. L. Rev. 217, 232 n.78 (1976).

114. *See* Barry Friedman, *The History of The Countermajoritarian Difficulty, Part Three: The Lesson of* Lochner, 76 N.Y.U. L. Rev. 1383, 1418 (2001).

115. *Ex parte* Westerfield, 55 Cal. 550 (1880); People v. Gillson, 109 N.Y. 389, 399 (1888).

116. *See* Ernst Freund, *Limitation of Hours of Labor and the Federal Supreme Court*, 17 Green Bag 411, 417 (1905),

117. William E. Nelson: The Fourteenth Amendment: From Political Principle to Judicial Doctrine 199 (1988); *see also* Friedman, *supra* note 114, at 1419.

118. *Lochner*, 198 U.S. at 53.

119. *Id.*

120. A potential weakness in Peckham's argument is that he relied on mortality tables, which ignore morbidity. Bewig, *supra* note 3, at 494–95.

121. *Lochner*, 198 U.S. at 61.

122. Justice Peckham favorably cited a state case voiding a truck act, a type of legislation that the Supreme Court had already upheld over his and Brewer's dissent. Knoxville Iron Co. v. Harbison, 183 U.S. 13 (1901).

123. *See* Paul Kens, Lochner: *Tradition or Change in Constitutional Law*, 1 NYU J. L. & Liberty 404, 414 (2005). On the importance of presumptions in interpreting the Fourteenth Amendment, with specific reference to *Lochner*, see Randy E. Barnett, Restoring the Lost Constitution: The Presumption of Liberty 211–18 (2004).

124. *Lochner*, 198 U.S. at 65–68 (Harlan, J., dissenting).

125. *Id.* at 72, 73.

126. *Id.* at 76.

127. *Id.* (emphasis added).

128. Jeffrey Rosen, The Supreme Court: The Personalities and Rivalries that Defined America 113 (2007).

129. One could fill many pages with relevant citations, but a particularly stark example by a scholar who wrote an entire book about *Lochner* is Paul Kens, Judicial Power and Reform Politics: The Anatomy of *Lochner v. New York* 3–5, 67–71, 121 (1990).

130. *See* Howard Kaye, The Social Meaning of Modern Biology: From Social Darwinism to Sociobiology 33–34 (1985); Thomas C. Leonard, *Origins of the Myth of Social Darwinism: The Ambiguous Legacy of Richard Hofstadter's* Social Darwinism in American Thought, 71 J. Econ. Behavior & Org. 37 (2009); Joseph F. Wall, Lochner v. New York: *A Case Study in the Modernization of Constitutional Law*, in American Industrialization, Economic Expansion and the Law, 113, 132 (Joseph R. Frese & Jacob Judd, eds., 1981). *See generally* Mark Francis, Herbert Spencer and the Invention of Modern Life (2007).

131. Tom Grey and Randy Barnett have made the same point. Randy Barnett, *Is the Constitution Libertarian?*, 2008–09 Cato Sup. Ct. Rev. 9; Thomas C. Grey, *Judicial Review and Legal Pragmatism*, 38 Wake Forest L. Rev. 473, 500 n.120 (2003).

132. *Lochner*, 195 U.S. 48 (Holmes, J., dissenting).

133. *See* G. Edward White, Justice Oliver Wendell Holmes: Law and the Inner Self 325–26 (1993).

134. Not only did Harlan endorse the right to liberty of contract in *Lochner*, but three years later he authored a major liberty of contract opinion, Adair v. United States, 208 U.S. 161 (1908).

135. Bruce Ackerman agrees that liberty of contract jurisprudence reflected common, mainstream American understandings in the post-Reconstruction and pre–New Deal period. Bruce Ackerman, We the People: Transformations 255–78 (1998). Holmes's departure from standard American ideological assumptions is illustrated by his comment, "I see no meaning in the rights of man except what the crown will fight for." Letter from Oliver Wendell Holmes to Harold J. Laski (July 28, 1916), *reprinted in* 1 Holmes-Laski Letters 8 (Mark DeWolfe Howe ed., 1953).

136. *Bake Shop Law of the State of New York Prescribing Ten Hours a Day and Sixty Hours Week for Labor in Bakeries Declared Unconstitutional by United States Supreme Court*, Baker's J., Apr. 22, 1905, at 1.

137. *Unconstitutional*, Baker's J., May 6, 1905, at 1.

138. *The Decision of the United States Supreme Court on the Ten-Hour Law for Employees of Bakeries: The Passage and Provisions of the Law*, Baker's J., May 20, 1905, at 1.

139. *The Decision of the Supreme Court*, Baker's J., May 27, 1905, at 2.

140. *The Strike Situation*, Bakers Rev., June 1905, at 33.

141. *See Celebration of Victory*, *supra* note 49.

142. *Renegade as We Find Him in Books*, Baker's J., Sept. 16, 1905.

143. *Labor in the Bakeshop*, Nat'l Baker, June 1905, at 15.

144. *The Supreme Court Decision*, Nat'l Baker, May 1905, at 11.

145. *See Less Hours of Labor*, Baker's J., Nov. 10, 1900, at 1.

146. W. A. Evans, Cellar Bakeries and Their Dangers to Producers and Consumers (1910); Hazel Kyrk & Joseph Stancliffe Davis, The American Baking Industry 60–61, 108 (1925); Balinska, *supra* note 17, at 118. The bakers' union nevertheless claimed in 1910,

quite implausibly, that nonunion bakers still worked twelve hours a day, seven days a week in unsanitary conditions. *Staff of Life Causes Strife*, N.Y. Tribune, May 29, 1910, at 6.

147. *New Labor Laws Today*, N.Y. Tribune, Oct. 1, 1906, at 3.

148. *City's Bakeshops Sanitary*, The Sun, March 14, 1909, at 3; *see also How Your Brown, Crisp Loaf is Produced*, N.Y. Tribune, Sept. 25, 1909, at 19.

149. Robert McCloskey, The Modern Supreme Court 279 (1972).

150. 3 John Rogers Commons, et al., History of Labour in the United States 690 (1935).

151. *Current Topics*, 67 Albany L.J. 129, 129 (1905).

152. *Validity of State Regulation of Hours of Labor*, 60 Central L.J. 401, 403 (1905).

153. *E.g.*, Semonche, *supra* note 110, at 184; *but see* Barry Friedman, The Will of the People: How Public Opinion Has Influenced the Supreme Court and Shaped the Meaning of the Constitution 176 (2009).

154. Editorial, *Fussy Legislation*, N.Y. Times, Apr. 19, 1905, at 10.

155. Editorial, *Defying the Supreme Court*, N.Y. Sun, Apr. 19, 1905, at 6; *see also* Editorial, *The Supreme Court and Chief Judge Alton B. Parker*, N.Y. Sun, Apr. 22, 1905, at 6.

156. Editorial, *Reckless Criticism*, Wash. Post, Aug. 12, 1905, at 6.

157. Editorial, *Bakeshop Law Knocked Out*, L.A. Times, June 11, 1905, at 7; Editorial, *Stands by the Constitution*, L.A. Times, May 14, 1905, at 7.

158. Editorial, *A Check to Union Tyranny*, 80 Nation 346, 347 (1905).

159. *Quoted in* Bakers' Helper, May 1905, at 445.

160. *The Ten-Hour Day Unconstitutional*, X World's Work 6233 (1905).

161. *In Which the Right of Contract is Upheld*, Dallas Morning News, April 20, 1905, at 6.

162. *Not Necessarily Melancholy*, *supra* note 70; *see also A Decision for Free Labor and Free Contract*, Brooklyn Eagle, April 18, 1905, at 4.

163. *Supreme Court on the Ten-Hour Law*, Literary Digest, Apr. 29, 1905, at 613; Bakers' Helper, May 1905, at 445–47; *Hours of Labor Must Not be Restricted*, Philadelphia Inquirer, April 19, 1905, at 8; *Public Opinion Comment of Leading Newspapers on a Variety of Topics*, Baltimore American, Apr. 20, 1905, at 6 (quoting the *Philadelphia Record*); *see also* Note, *Bakery Law of New York Unconstitutional*, 39 Am. L. Rev. 450, 453 (1905) (praising the decision).

164. *See Bakers Lose at Law, But Win in Fact*, Am. Federationist, June 1905, at 363; *Labor Press on the Ten-Hour Law*, Literary Digest, May 6, 1905, at 654; *Constitutionality of the Ten-Hour Day*, Locomotive Engineers' Monthly J., May 1905, at 435; *Henry Weismann: Renegade Trade Unionist Gloats Over the Ten-Hour Decision*, Horseshoers' Magazine, May 1905, at 10.

165. *Labor Press*, *supra* note 164; Bakers' Helper, May 1905, at 445–47; *Iron Bands of Federal Constitution*, Baker's J., June 3, 1905, at 1. *see also* Editorial, *An Important Decision*, Salt Lake Tribune, April 23, 1905, § 2, at 4; Wilkes-Barre Times, April 20, 1905, at 4 (expressing mild criticism); *Reckless Criticism*, Wash. Post, Aug. 12, 1905, at 6 (discussing harsh criticism by the *New York World*).

166. *Quoted in* Bakers' Helper, May 1905, at 445.

167. For the traditional story line, see Kammen, *supra* note 86, at 193; Paul Finkelman, *Civil Rights in Historical Context: In Defense of* Brown, 118 Harv. L. Rev. 973 (2005).

CHAPTER THREE

1. *See* Wallace Mendelson, *The Influence of James B. Thayer upon the Work of Holmes, Brandeis, and Frankfurter*, 31 Vand. L. Rev. 71, 73 (1978).

2. E. Irving Smith, *The Legal Aspect of the Southern Question*, 2 Harv. L. Rev. 358, 375 (1889). For a similar take almost twenty years later, see Walter Clark, *Is the Supreme Court Constitutional?*, 63 Independent 723, 724 (1907).

3. Charles E. Shattuck, *The True Meaning of the Term "Liberty" in the Federal and State Constitutions Which Protect "Life, Liberty, and Property,"* 4 Harv. L. Rev. 365 (1891).

4. Richard C. McMurtrie, *A New Canon of Constitutional Interpretation*, 32 Am. L. Reg. & Rev. 1, 4 (1893).

5. *E.g.*, T. W. Brown, *Due Process of Law*, 32 Am. L. Rev. 14 (1898); Note, 11 Harv. L. Rev. 61 (1897); Note, 31 Am. L. Rev. 777, 778 (1897).

6. James B. Thayer, *The Origin and Scope of the American Doctrine of Constitutional Law*, 7 Harv. L. Rev. 129 (1893); *see also* Herbert Henry Darling, *Legislative Control Over Contracts of Employment: The Weavers' Fines Bill*, 6 Harv. L. Rev. 85, 85–97 (1892); C. B. Labatt, *State Regulation of the Contract of Employment*, 27 Am. L. Rev. 857, 863–64 (1893).

7. Mendelson, *supra* note 1, at 73; Edward A. Purcell, Jr., *Learned Hand: The Jurisprudential Trajectory of an Old Progressive*, 43 Buff. L. Rev. 873, 874, 885 (1995).

8. John C. Gray, *Some Definitions and Questions in Jurisprudence*, 6 Harv. L. Rev. 21, 24 (1892).

9. William D. Lewis, *Liberty and a Written Constitution*, 41 Am. L. Reg. 1064, 1070–71 (1893). *See generally* Eugene Wambaugh, *The Present Scope of Government*, 20 Rep. ABA 320 (1897).

10. Mendelson, *supra* note 1.

11. On the Court's deference to reformist legislation, see generally Charles Warren, *A Bulwark to the State Police Power: The United States Supreme Court*, 13 Colum. L. Rev. 667, 668–69 (1913); Charles Warren, *The Progressiveness of the United States Supreme Court*, 13 Colum. L. Rev. 294, 295 (1913); *Progressive Legislation, the Constitution, and the Supreme Court*, 2 Const. Rev. 19 (1918); Henry R. Seager, *The Attitude of American Courts Towards Restrictive Labor Laws*, 19 Pol. Sci. Q. 589 (1904).

12. *See, e.g.*, Ernst Freund, *Limitation of Hours of Labor and the Federal Supreme Court*, 17 Green Bag 411, 413 (1905).

13. For a discussion of how Progressive commentators misunderstood Holmes's *Lochner* dissent, see G. Edward White, The Constitution and the New Deal 252 (2000). On the free labor and anti–class legislation traditions, see chapter 1.

14. Roscoe Pound, *Mechanical Jurisprudence*, 8 Colum. L. Rev. 605, 616 (1908).

15. Lochner v. New York, 198 U.S. 45, 59 (1905). As discussed in chapter 2, these statistics were presented in Lochner's brief.

16. *See, e.g.*, Richard T. Ely, *Economic Theory and Labor Legislation*, 9 Am. Econ. Assoc. Q. 124, 144–46 (1908); Freund, *supra* note 12; Learned Hand, *Due Process of Law and the Eight-Hour Day*, 21 Harv. L. Rev. 495, 501–8 (1908); Pound, *supra* note 14, at 615–16.

17. Pound, *supra* note 14, at 616; *see also* Louis M. Greeley, *The Changing Attitude of the Courts Toward Social Legislation*, 5 U. Ill. L. Rev. 222, 223 (1910).

18. *See* Roscoe Pound, *"Liberty of Contract"*, 18 Yale L.J. 454, 464 (1909).

19. *See, e.g.*, Roscoe Pound, *Common Law and Legislation*, 21 Harv. L. Rev. 383 (1908); Pound, *supra* note 18, at 464.

20. *E.g.*, Benjamin N. Cardozo, The Nature of the Judicial Process 65 (1921).

21. *E.g.*, Edward S. Corwin, *The Doctrine of Due Process of Law Before the Civil War*, 24 Harv. L. Rev. 366 (1911). Charles Warren later joined Corwin's efforts. Charles Warren, *The New "Liberty" under the Fourteenth Amendment*, 39 Harv. L. Rev. 431 (1926); *see also* Robert P. Reeder, *The Due Process Clauses and the Substance of Individual Rights*, 58 U. Pa. L. Rev. 191, 217 (1910). On the Progressives' disinterest in originalist critiques of contemporary due process jurisprudence, see William G. Ross, A Muted Fury: Populists, Progressives and Labor Unions Confront the Courts, 1890–1937, at 64–65 (1994); White, *supra* note 13, at 256. For examples of arguments that courts should disavow adherence to precedent and framers' intent, see E. F. Albertsworth, *Program of Sociological Jurisprudence*, 8 ABA J. 393, 396 (1922); Pound, *supra* note 18, at 467.

22. *See* Louis D. Brandeis, *The Living Law*, 10 Ill. L. Rev. 463, 469 (1916).

23. Felix Frankfurter, *Child Labor and the Court*, The New Republic, July 26, 1922. Despite Corwin's originalist critique of the Court's Fourteenth Amendment jurisprudence, Corwin was not an originalist. *See* Cornell W. Clayton, *Edward S. Corwin as Public Scholar*, in The Pioneers of Judicial Behavior 289, 302–4 (Nancy Maveety ed., 2003).

24. Roscoe Pound, *Justice According to Law*, 13 Colum. L. Rev. 696, 706 (1913); Roscoe Pound, *The Scope and Purpose of Sociological Jurisprudence, Part II*, 25 Harv. L. Rev. 489, 515 (1912).

25. Robert E. Cushman, *The Social and Economic Interpretation of the Fourteenth Amendment*, 20 Mich. L. Rev. 737, (1922); Felix Frankfurter, *Hours of Labor and Realism in Constitutional Law*, 29 Harv. L. Rev. 353, 365 (1916); Thomas Reed Powell, *The Constitutional Issue in Minimum-Wage Legislation*, 2 Minn. L. Rev. 1, 18 (1917).

26. Thomas Grey, introduction to Christopher Tiedeman, The Unwritten Constitution of the United States at iii–vii (1974); Stephen A. Siegel, *Historicism in Late Nineteenth-Century Constitutional Thought*, 1990 Wis. L. Rev. 1431, 1528–32. *See generally* David N. Mayer, *The Jurisprudence of Christopher G. Tiedeman: A Study in the Failure of Laissez-faire Constitutionalism*, 55 Mo. L. Rev. 93 (1990).

27. Tiedeman abandoned his limited government ideology at the end of his career. Louise A. Halper, *Christopher G. Tiedeman, 'Laissez-faire Constitutionalism' and the Dilemmas of Small-scale Property in the Gilded Age*, 51 Ohio St. L.J. 1349, 1383 (1990).

28. *See, e.g.*, Steven J. Diner, A Very Different Age: Americans of the Progressive Era (1998); Maureen Flanagan, America Reformed: Progressives and Progressivisms, 1890s–1920s (2007); Richard Hofstader, The Age of Reform (1955); Michael E. McGerr, A Fierce Discontent: The Rise and Fall of the Progressive Movement in America (2003); Peter G. Filene, *An Obituary for "The Progressive Movement"*, 22 Am. Q. 20 (1970); Daniel T. Rodgers, *In Search of Progressivism*, 10 Revs. Am. Hist. 113 (1982).

29. Thomas Leonard, *American Economic Reform in the Progressive Era: What Beliefs Inclined the Progressives to Eugenics?*, 41 Hist. Pol. Econ. 109 (2009).

30. For scholars who agree with this assessment of Progressivism, see, e.g., James W. Ely, Jr., The Chief Justiceship of Melville W. Fuller, 1888–1910, at 68 (1996); Arthur A. Ekirch, The Decline of American Liberalism 171 (1980); William E. Forbath, *The White Court 1910–1921: A Progressive Court?*, in The United States Supreme Court: The Pursuit of Justice 172, 175 (Christopher Tomlins ed., 2005); Herbert Hovenkamp, *The Mind and Heart of Progressive Legal Thought*, 81 Iowa L. Rev. 149, 157 (2003); Leonard, *supra* note 29; David N. Mayer, *The Myth of "Laissez-Faire Constitutionalism": Liberty of Contract during the* Lochner *Era*, 36 Hastings Con. L.Q. 217, 219 n.12 (2009); G. Edward White, *From Sociological Jurisprudence to Realism: Jurisprudence and Social Change in Early Twentieth-Century America*, 58 Va. L. Rev. 999, 1003 (1972). H. L. Mencken, decidedly non-Progressive in his view of the proper role of government in American society, tartly defined a Progressive as "one who is in favor of more taxes instead of less, more bureaus and jobholders, more paternalism and meddling, more regulation of private affairs and less liberty." Baltimore Evening Sun, Jan. 19, 1926.

31. *See, e.g.*, George W. Alger, The Old Law and the New Order 241 (1913); Richard T. Ely, *Economic Theory and Labor Legislation*, 9 Am. Econ. Assoc. Q. 124, 146 (1908). *See generally* Mark A. Graber, Transforming Free Speech: The Ambiguous Legacy of Civil Libertarianism 11 (1992); David M. Rabban, Free Speech in Its Forgotten Years, 1870–1920, at 211 (1997).

32. *Quoted in* Gerald Gunther, Learned Hand 211 (1994); *see also* Felix Frankfurter, *Law and Order*, 10 Yale Rev. 233 (1920); Pound, *supra* note 18, at 457.

33. *E.g.*, Walter W. Cook, *Privileges of Labor Unions in the Struggle for Life*, 27 Yale L.J. 779, 783 (1918).

34. Christopher T. Wonnell, Lochner v. New York *as Economic Theory* 97 (University of San Diego, Public Law and Legal Theory, Working Paper No.24, 2000–2001), *available at* http://papers.ssrn.com/abstract=285433.

35. Editorial, *An Unseen Reversal*, New Republic, Jan. 9, 1915, at 7 (unsigned editorial by Hand); editorial, *The Red Terror of Judicial Reform*, The New Republic, Oct. 1, 1924 (unsigned editorial by Frankfurter); Melvin I. Urofsky, *The Brandeis-Frankfurter Conversations*, 1985 Sup. Ct. Rev. 299, 318, 325.

36. On sociological jurisprudence as a philosophy of law, see Charles L. Barzun, *Politics or Principle? Zechariah Chafee and the Social Interest in Free Speech*, 2007 BYU L. Rev. 259, 302–10 (2007). *See generally* N. E. H. Hull, Roscoe Pound and Karl Llewellyn: Searching for an American Jurisprudence (1997). Even Louis Brandeis is vulnerable to the charge that his fact-based dissents in liberty of contract cases were post-hoc rationalizations for his political preferences. G. Edward White, The American Judicial Tradition 176 (2d ed. 1991); *cf.* Thomas K. McCraw, Prophets of Regulation ch. 3 (1986).

37. Pound, *supra* note 18, at 458. More generally, Harlan wrote several opinions using the Due Process Clause to protect economic rights, which undoubtedly persuaded Progressives that he was not "one of them." *See* Berea College v. Kentucky , 211 U.S. 45, 58–70 (1908) (Harlan, J., dissenting); Chicago, B. & Q. R. Co. v. Chicago, 166 U.S. 226 (1897); *cf.* Butchers' Union Slaughter-House & Live-Stock Landing Co. v. Crescent City Live-Stock & Slaughterhouse Co., 111 U.S. 746 (1883) (Bradley, J., concurring) (Harlan joining Bradley's opinion).

38. Adair v. United States, 208 U.S. 161 (1908); Pound, *supra* note 18; *see* Linda Przybyszewski, *The Fuller Court 1888–1910: Property and Liberty*, in The United States Supreme Court: The Pursuit of Justice 147, 165 (Christopher Tomlins ed., 2005).

39. The Mind and Faith of Justice Holmes 143 (Max Lerner ed., 1943).

40. Benjamin N. Cardozo, The Nature of the Judicial Process 138 (1921).

41. *Id.*; Morton G. White, Social Thought in America: The Revolt against Formalism 108 (1957) (quoting Beard); Editorial, The New Republic, Dec. 11, 1915, at 132. Traditionalists, by contrast, attacked Holmes's opinion. One author wrote that if Holmes's views were to prevail, "constitutional government, in the sense in which it has been understood for a century and a half, will be at an end, and the doctrine of the police power will have been swallowed up in the capacious maw of unrestrained democracy." George W. Wickersham, *The Police Power, A Product of the Rule of Reason*, 27 Harv. L. Rev. 297, 316 (1914).

42. Pound, *supra* note 18, at 464.

43. Noble State Bank, 219 U.S. 104 (1911); *see* Gunther, *supra* note 32, at 211.

44. 219 U.S. 219 (1911); *see* Jeffrey Rosen, The Supreme Court: The Personalities and Rivalries that Defined America 98 (2007).

45. *See* William Cohen, At Freedom's Edge: Black Mobility and the Southern White Quest for Racial Control, 1861–1915 (1991).

46. *Bailey*, 219 U.S. at 245–46, 249–50 (Holmes, J., dissenting).

47. William E. Leuchtenburg, The Supreme Court Reborn: Constitutional Revolution in the Age of Roosevelt 19 (1995); *see also* Rosen, *supra* note 44, at 114; Melvin I. Urofsky, Louis D. Brandeis and the Progressive Tradition 145 (1981). Holmes wrote, "I hate facts." Letter from Oliver Wendell Holmes to Frederick Pollock (May 26, 1919), *reprinted* in 2 Holmes-Pollock Letters 13 (Mark DeWolfe Howe ed., 1961).

48. *See* Louis Menand, The Metaphysical Club (2002); Rosen, *supra* note 44, at 88, 104.

49. Howard Gillman, *Preferred Freedoms: The Progressive Expansion of State Power and the Rise of Modern Civil Liberties Jurisprudence*, 47 Pol. Res. Q. 623, 640 (1994).

50. Jerome Frank, Law and the Modern Mind 270–76 (1931); Gunther, *supra* note 32, at 162 (discussing Hand); Felix Frankfurter, *The Constitutional Opinions of Justice Holmes*, 29 Harv. L. Rev. 683 (1916); Roscoe Pound, *Sociology of Law and Sociological Jurisprudence*, 5 U. Toronto L.J. 1, 2–3 (1943); *see also* Felix Frankfurter, *The Zeitgeist and the Judiciary*, The Survey, Jan. 1913.

51. H. L. Mencken provided a more generous explanation. Progressives, "frantically eager to find at least one judge who was not violently and implacably" opposed to their theory of the Constitution, read into Holmes's opinions Progressive attitudes and ideas that were "foreign to his way of thinking." H. L. Mencken, *Mr. Justice Holmes*, Am. Mercury, May 1930.

52. Pound, *supra* note 18, at 484.

53. *See* chapter 2.

54. *E.g.*, Pound, *supra* note 14, at 621; Pound, *supra* note 18, at 470; Roscoe Pound, *Common Law and Legislation*, 21 Harv. L. Rev. 383, 405 (1908). *See generally* Herbert Croly, Progressive Democracy 137–40 (1914).

55. *See, e.g.*, Maureen A. Flanagan, America Reformed: Progressives and Progressivisms, 1890s–1920s, at 121 (2007); Morton J. Horwitz, The Transformation of American

Law, 1870–1960, at 29 (1992).; Duncan Kennedy, *Toward an Historical Understanding of Legal Consciousness: The Case of Classical Legal Thought in America*, 1850–1940, 3 Res. in L. & Soc. 3 (1980); Nat Stern, *State Action, Establishment Clause, and Defamation: Blueprints for Civil Liberties in the Rehnquist Court*, 57 U. Cin. L. Rev. 1175, 1212 (1989). At least one contemporary critic, however, recognized that the *Lochner* Court was not formalist, but was relying on its own conception of the underlying facts. Ernst Freund, *Constitutional Labor Legislation*, 4 Illinois L. Rev. 609, 620 (1910). For a rare dissent on this point in the post–New Deal period, see Robert E. Rodes, Jr., *Due Process and Social Legislation in the Supreme Court: A Post Mortem*, 33 Notre Dame Lawyer 5, 27 (1957). For recent criticism of Pound's claims, see Brian Z. Tamanaha, The Bogus Tale about the Legal Formalists 7 (unpublished manuscript 2008); *see also* Brian Z. Tamanaha, *Understanding Legal Realism*, 87 Tex. L. Rev . 731 (2009).

56. *See* Ely, *supra* note 30, at 73; Thomas C. Grey, *Judicial Review and Legal Pragmatism*, 38 Wake Forest L. Rev. 473, 475–76 (2003); Herbert Hovenkamp, *The Political Economy of Substantive Due Process*, 40 Stan. L. Rev. 379, 382–83 (1988); William P. Lapiana, *Thoughts and Lives*, 39 N.Y.L. Sch. L. Rev. 607, 624 (1994). Recent historical work expresses skepticism that any identifiable group of jurists were "formalists" in the sense their Progressive critics claimed. *See* Brian Z. Tamanaha, Beyond the Formalist-Realist Divide: The Role of Politics in Judging (2009); Bruce A. Kimball, *Langdell on Contracts and Legal Reasoning: Correcting the Holmesian Caricature*, 25 L. & Hist. Rev. 345 (2007); Bruce A. Kimball, *The Langdell Problem: Historicizing the Century of Historiography, 1906–2000*, 22 L. & Hist. Rev. 277 (2004).

57. The author thanks William Lapiana for this point. *See generally* Gilbert E. Roe, Our Judicial Oligarchy (1912).

58. *E.g.*, Roscoe Pound, *Scope and Purpose*, *supra* note 24, at 496–99.

59. Rosen, *supra* note 44, at 77. On Holmes and Social Darwinism, see, e.g., Albert W. Alschuler, Law Without Values: The Life, Work, and Legacy of Justice Holmes (2000); J. W. Burrow, *Holmes in His Intellectual Milieu, in* The Legacy of Oliver Wendell Holmes, Jr. 17, 25 (Robert W. Gordon ed., 1992); Yosel Rogat, *The Judge as Spectator*, 31 U. Chi. L. Rev. 213, 251 (1964); Joseph F. Wall, Lochner v. New York: *A Case Study in the Modernization of Constitutional Law*, in American Industrialization, Economic Expansion and the Law, 113, 133–35 (Joseph R. Frese & Jacob Judd, eds. 1981). On other justices' lack of Darwinism, see Ely, *supra* note 30, at 76; Herbert Hovenkamp, Enterprise and American Law, 1836–1937, at 99–100 (1991); Wall, *supra*, at 132; Bradley C. S. Watson, Living Constitution, Dying Faith: Progressivism and the New Science of Jurisprudence 62 (2009).

60. David W. Southern, The Progressive Era and Race: Reaction and Reform, 1900–1917, at 48–49 (2005); Watson, *supra* note 59, at 68–69; Herbert Hovenkamp, *Evolutionary Models in Jurisprudence*, 64 Tex. L. Rev. 645, 677–78 (1985).

61. On Pound's career in botany, see John Fabian Witt, Patriots and Cosmopolitans: Hidden Histories of American Law 218–19 (2007).

62. Herbert Hovenkamp, *Evolutionary Models in Jurisprudence*, 64 Tex. L. Rev. 645, 678–79 (1985).

63. Woodrow Wilson, The New Freedom 46 (1913).

64. Woodrow Wilson, Constitutional Government in the United States 22 (1908).

65. For a recent important contribution to the revisionist literature, see Thomas C. Leonard, *Origins of the Myth of Social Darwinism: The Ambiguous Legacy of Richard Hofstadter's* Social Darwinism in American Thought, 71 J. Econ. Behavior & Org. 73 (2009).

66. Thomas C. Leonard, *Mistaking Eugenics for Social Darwinism: Why Eugenics is Missing from the History of American Economics*, 37 Hist. Pol. Econ. 200 (2005).

67. Jack Balkin notes that postwar legal scholars tended to attribute to the pre–New Deal Supreme Court "the very opposite of those characteristics that supporters of the New Deal settlement wanted to believe about themselves." Jack M. Balkin, *"Wrong the Day It Was Decided:"* Lochner *and Constitutional Historicism*, 85 B.U. L. Rev. 677 (2005).

68. Rabban, *supra* note 31; Forbath, *supra* note 30, at 176; Jonathan O'Neill, *Constitutional Maintenance and Religious Sensibility in the 1920s: Rethinking the Constitutionalist Response to Progressivism*, 51 J. Church & State 1, 9–10 (2009).

69. Frank Goodnow, Social Reform and the Constitution v (1911).

70. *See* Stephen A. Siegel, *Let Us Now Praise Infamous Men*, 73 Tex. L. Rev. 661 (1995).

71. *E.g.*, Theodore Roosevelt, *Judges and Progress*, 100 Outlook 40, 43 (1912); Theodore Roosevelt, *Workman's Compensation*, 98 Outlook 49, 53 (1911); Theodore Roosevelt, Address at Carnegie Hall: The Right of the People to Rule, New York City, March 20, 1912, available at http://www.theodore-roosevelt.com/trrotptr.html. Judge Alton Parker, who wrote the New York Court of Appeals opinion affirming Joseph Lochner's conviction which was reversed by the Supreme Court, defended the Court from an earlier anti-*Lochner* attack by Roosevelt. N.Y. Tribune, Sept. 1, 1910, at 2.

72. W. F. Dodd, *Social Legislation and the Courts*, 28 Pol Sci. Q. 1, 5 (1913). For similar commentary, see Frederic R. Coudert, Certainty and Justice 57 (1914); Goodnow, *supra* note 69, at 329.

73. For a discussion of the reception these articles received, see Michael Allan Wolf, Charles Warren: Progressive, Historian 233 (unpublished PhD diss., Harvard Univ. 1991); *see also* Victoria F. Nourse, *A Tale of Two* Lochners: *The Untold History of Substantive Due Process and the Idea of Fundamental Rights*, 97 Cal. L. Rev. 751, 784 (2009).

74. Editorial, *A Great Court*, Outlook, July 4, 1914, at 508.

75. Felix Frankfurter, *Hours of Labor and Realism in Constitutional Law*, 29 Harv. L. Rev. 353, 369 (1916).

76. Keith E. Whittington, *Congress before the* Lochner *Court*, 85 B.U. L. Rev. 821, 830 (2005).

77. Act of Dec. 23, 1914, Pub. L. No. 63–224, 38 Stat. 790 (1914).

78. *See* Felix Frankfurter & James M. Landis, The Business of the Supreme Court: A Study in the Federal Judicial System 188–98 (1927). *Ives v. South Buffalo*, a New York decision invalidating a workers' compensation law, became an exaggerated (because it was not followed in other jurisdictions) symbol of state courts' hostility to reform legislation. *Ives*'s infamy was in part a product of bad timing; the day after the decision was announced, the infamous Triangle Shirt-Waist fire killed 146 workers, leading to a backlash in favor of legislative labor reform. *See* John Fabian Witt, The Accidental Republic: Crippled Workingmen, Destitute Widows, and the Remaking of American Law 171 (2004). State courts' willingness to invalidate legislation during the Progressive era has been greatly exaggerated. *See* Melvin I. Urofsky, *State Courts and Protective Legislation*

during the Progressive Era: A Reevaluation, 72 J. Am. Hist. 63, 64 (1985) Nevertheless, state courts did invalidate far more state legislation than did the U.S. Supreme Court. *See* William F. Dodd, *The Growth of Judicial Power*, 24 Pol. Sci. Q. 193, 198 (1909).

79. *See* Ross, *supra* note 21, at 160; *see also id.* at 20; Watson, *supra* note 59, at 119 (referring to *Lochner* as an "aberration"). Charles Warren wrote in 1913 that critics "who claim that the Court stands as an obstacle to 'social justice' legislation, if asked to specify where they find the evil of which they complain and for which they propose radical remedies, always take refuge in the single case of *Lochner v. New York*." Warren, *Progressiveness, supra* note 11, at 294.

80. *See* Barry Cushman, *The Secret Lives of the Four Horsemen*, 83 Va. L. Rev. 559 (1997).

81. Chas. Wolff Packing Co. v. Court of Industrial Relations, 262 U.S. 522 (1923) (unanimously holding that states could not require industrial disputes to be settled by government-imposed mandatory arbitration).

82. Adkins v. Children's Hosp., 261 U.S. 525 (1923).

83. *Id.*

84. Taft, campaigning as a private citizen for Republican presidential candidate Warren Harding, wrote in October 1920 that "there is no greater domestic issue in this election than the maintenance of the Supreme Court as the bulwark to enforce the guarantee that no man shall be deprived of his property without due process of law." Taft added that the sociological school of constitutional jurisprudence, represented by Justice Brandeis, threatened to "greatly impair our fundamental law." William H. Taft, *Mr. Wilson and the Campaign*, Yale Rev., Oct. 1920, at 19.

85. Village of Euclid v. Ambler Realty Co., 272 U.S. 365 (1926).

86. In two successive years, ABA presidents lamented the growth of government power and the failure of the courts to limit such growth. J. W. Davis, *Address of the President: Present Day Problems*, 48 Rep. ABA 198 (1923); Cordenio A. Severance, *Address of the President: The Constitution and Individualism*, 47 Rep. ABA 176 (1922).

87. Clarence Manion, *Liberty and the Police Power*, 3 Notre Dame L. 240, 240 (1927); Clarence Manion. *In Re Liberty: A Book and its Critic*, 4 Notre Dame L. 350 (1929); *cf.* Thomas James Norton, Losing Liberty Judicially (1928). *See generally* Michael Kammen, A Machine That Would Go of Itself, 208–54 (1988).

88. *See, e.g.*, Thomas James Norton, *National Encroachments and State Aggressions*, in American Bar Association, Report of the Fifteenth Annual Meeting of the American Bar Association 237 (1926).

89. This author follows Morton Horwitz in thinking that "it is best to see Legal Realism as simply a continuation of the reformist agenda of early-twentieth-century Progressivism." Horwitz, *supra* note 55, at 169.

90. *New State Ice v. Liebmann*, 285 U.S. 262 (1932); *see* White, *supra* note 21, at 277–81.

91. Paul L. Murphy, *Holmes, Brandeis and Pound: Sociological Jurisprudence as a Response to Laissez-Faire*, in Liberty, Property, and Government: Constitutional Interpretation before the New Deal 39, 56 (Ellen Frankel Paul & Howard Dickman, eds., 1989); *cf.* Richard A. Epstein, How Progressives Rewrote the Constitution 39 (2006); Michael J. Phillips, The *Lochner* Court, Myth and Reality 97–102 (2001).

92. *See* Mark Tushnet, The Rights Revolution in the Twentieth Century 20 (unpublished manuscript 2008).

93. Tex. & N.O. R.R. Co. v. Brotherhood of Railway & Steamship Clerks, 281 U.S. 548 (1930).

94. On Progressive commentators' hostility to the yellow dog contract cases, see Barbara H. Fried, The Progressive Assault on Laissez Faire: Robert Hale and the First Law and Economics Movement 33 (1998). On *Adkins*, see chapter 4.

95. 262 U.S. 522 (1923).

96. *See* Ken Kersch, Constructing Civil Liberties: Discontinuities in the Development of American Constitutional Law 159–67 (2004); Barry Friedman, *The History of the Countermajoritarian Difficulty, Part Three: The Lesson of* Lochner, 76 N.Y.U. L. Rev. 1383, 1441–47 (2001).

97. Urofsky, *supra* note 35, at 325.

98. Pound, *supra* note 18, at 454; *see also* Richard Olney, *Discrimination Against Union Labor—Legal?*, 42 Am. L. Rev. 161, 164 (1908).

99. 169 U.S. 366, 397 (1898).

100. These included laws forbidding the employment of children below the age of sixteen in certain hazardous occupations; regulating the hours of labor of both women and men in industrial occupations when overtime work was permitted; regulating the width of entries to coal mines; requiring coal mines to maintain wash houses for their employees at the request of twenty or more workers; making mining companies liable for their willful failure to furnish a reasonably safe place for workers; requiring that coal miners' pay be based on carloads of coal they produced; requiring railroads and mining companies to pay their employees in cash; requiring railroads to pay wages due an employee upon discharge regardless of contrary contractual agreement; requiring that coal produced by miners be weighed for payment purposes before it passes over a screen; giving preferences to citizens in public works employment; regulating the wages and hours of workers employed on public works projects; forbidding the payment of seamen's wages in advance; regulating the timing of wages paid to employees in specified industries; and mandating an eight-hour day for federal workers or employees of federal contractors. *See* David E. Bernstein, *Lochner's Legacy's Legacy*, 92 Tex L. Rev. 1 (2003).

101. Simpson v. O'Hara, 243 U.S. 629, 629–30 (1917); Bunting v. Oregon, 243 U.S. 426 (1917); Wilson v. New, 243 U.S. 332 (1917); Mountain Timber Co. v. Washington, 243 U.S. 219 (1917); Hawkins v. Bleakly, 243 U.S. 210 (1917); N.Y. Cent. R.R. Co. v. White, 243 U.S. 188 (1917).

102. *See* chapter 2.

103. Adair v. United States, 208 U.S. 161 (1908); Coppage v. Kansas, 236 U.S. 1 (1915); *see also* Hitchman Coal & Coke Co. v. Mitchell, 245 U.S. 229 (1917) (upholding an injunction preventing a union from trying to organize workers bound by a yellow-dog contract).

104. *E.g.*, Robert L. Hale, *Law Making by Unofficial Minorities*, 20 Colum. L. Rev. 451, 452 (1920); Morris R. Cohen, *Property and Sovereignty*, 13 Cornell L.Q. 8 (1927). *See generally* Thomas C. Leonard, *More Merciful and Not Less Effective: Eugenics and American Economics in the Progressive Era*, in The Street Porter and the Philosopher: Conversations on Analytical Egalitarianism 358, 370 (Sandra J. Peart & David M. Levy,

eds., 2008). Most modern economists believe that in a competitive labor market, workers' wages track their marginal productivity. *See, e.g.,* Howard Dickman, Industrial Democracy in America: Ideological Origins of National Labor Relations Policy 179 (1987); Campbell R. McConnell, Economics 651–53 (10th ed. 1987); Lloyd G. Reynolds, et al., Labor Economics and Labor Relations 301, 314 (1986); Solomon Fabricant, A Primer on Productivity 103 (1969); Martin S. Feldstein, Did Wages Reflect Growth in Productivity? National Bureau of Economic Research Working Paper 13953 (2008).

105. *E.g.,* Thomas Reed Powell, *Collective Bargaining Before the Supreme Court,* 33 Pol. Sci. Q. 405 (1918).

106. Herbert Croly, The Promise of American Life 387 (1911).

107. *See* David E. Bernstein, Only One Place of Redress: African Americans, Labor Regulations and the Courts from Reconstruction to the New Deal (2001); Charles Wesley, Negro Labor In The United States ch. 9 (1927); Frank Wolfe, Admission To American Trade Unions ch. 6 (1912).

108. Even some Progressives devoted to civil rights believed that unions, regardless of their discriminatory policies, needed to be nurtured because they represented workers', including African American workers', only long-term hope of prosperity. W. E. B. Du Bois, for example, hired members of a labor union that excluded African Americans to print the NAACP's *Crisis* magazine. He hoped that unions would become more enlightened on racial issues as their power grew. *See* Paul D. Moreno, Black Americans and Organized Labor: A New History 92 (2006). Du Bois eventually became sufficiently frustrated with union intransigence on civil rights matters that despite his socialist outlook he urged African Americans to cooperate with capitalists against labor unions. W. E. B. Du Bois, *The Denial of Economic Justice to Negroes,* The New Leader, Feb. 9, 1929, at 43, 46.

109. David W. Park, "Compensation or Confiscation?": Workmen's Compensation and Legal Progressivism, 1898–1917, at 749–50 (2000) (unpublished PhD diss., Univ. of Wisconsin). Justice Harlan, who wrote the yellow-dog contract opinion in *Adair v. United States,* had made it clear that he believed that the proper reaction of the government to an improper monopoly was to break up the monopoly, not to establish a new one. Carroll v. Greenwich Ins. Co. of N.Y., 199 U.S. 401, 413–14 (1905). In 1914, former president and future Chief Justice William Howard Taft complained that the "great political power that labor combinations are believed to exercise has enabled them successfully to press upon legislatures the idea that they are politically a privileged class." *Address of the President,* annual meeting of the American Bar Association, Oct. 1914, reprinted in 34 Can. L. Times 1039 (1914).

110. *See* Park, *supra* note 109. Howard University professor and civil rights activist Kelly Miller, for example, wrote that "what the trusts are to capital, trade unions are to labor." Kelly Miller, *The City Negro: Industrial Status,* 30 Southern Workman 340 (1903). Such attitudes were widely shared among African American intellectuals and workers. *See* Bernstein, *supra* note 107; Eric Arnesen, *"The Quicksands of Economic Insecurity": African Americans, Strikebreaking, and Labor Activism in the Industrial Era,* in The Black Worker: Race, Labor, and Civil Rights since Emancipation 41 (Eric Arnesen ed., 2007).

111. Coppage v. Kansas, 236 U.S. 1, 14 (1915).

112. *See* chapter 4.

113. Adkins v. Children's Hosp., 261 U.S. 525, 560 (1923).

114. *Id.*; Wilson v. New, 243 U.S. 332, 387–88 (1917) (Pitney, J., dissenting); *see* Samuel Gompers, *The Workers and the Eight Hour Work Day*, in Labor and the Common Welfare, American Labor: From Conspiracy to Collective Bargaining 16 (Samuel Gompers & Hayes Robbins, eds., reprint ed. 1969); Samuel Gompers, *Judicial Vindication of Labor's Claims*, 7 American Federationist, 283, 284 (1901).

115. *See* David E. Bernstein & Thomas C. Leonard, *Excluding Unfit Workers: Social Control versus Social Justice in the Age of Economic Reform*, 72 L. & Contemp. Probs. 177 (2009).

116. *Id.*

117. Brief for Defendants in Error upon Reargument, Simpson v. O'Hara, 243 U.S. 629 (1917), at A35.

118. Thomas Reed Powell, *Major Constitutional Issues in 1920–1921*, 36 Pol. Sci. Q. 469, 494 (1921); *see also* Samuel A. Goldberg, *The Unconstitutionality of Minimum Wage Legislation*, 71 U. Pa. L. Rev. 360, 364 (1923). This particular parade of horribles was not so imaginary; the federal government has set maximum wages nationally at least three times since 1933. *See* Hugh Rockoff, Drastic Measures: A History of Wage and Price Controls in the United States 200–233 (1984).

119. *See* Dorothy Ross, The Origins of American Social Science 145 (1991). *See generally* Kersch, *supra* note 96, at 171–72.

120. *See, e.g.*, Adkins v. Children's Hosp., 261 U.S. 525, 560 (1923); Henry Billings Brown, *The Distribution of Property*, 27 Am. L. Rev. 656 (1893); William H. Taft, *The Right of Private Property*, 3 Mich. L. Rev. 222 (1894). Modern economic historians believe that the anti-Progressives had the better of the argument. *See, e.g.*, Albert Rees, Real Wages in Manufacturing 1890–1914, at 120–21 (1961); Herbert Hovenkamp, *Labor Conspiracies in American Law, 1880–1930*, 66 Tex. L. Rev. 919, 931 (1988).

121. Edward A. Purcell, Brandeis and the Progressive Constitution 16 (2000); Barzun, *supra* note 36, at 310.

CHAPTER FOUR

1. Bradwell v. Illinois, 83 U.S. (16 Wall.) 130 (1873).

2. 83 U.S. (16 Wall.) 36 (1873).

3. *Id.* at 141 (Bradley, J., concurring).

4. Commonwealth v. Hamilton Manufacturing, 120 Mass. 383 (1876).

5. Ritchie v. People, 40 N.E. 453 (Ill. 1895); *see* Frances E. Olsen, *From False Paternalism to False Equality: Judicial Assaults on Feminist Community, Illinois, 1869–1895*, 84 Mich. L. Rev. 1518, 1520 (1986).

6. Brief for the Defendant in Error, Ritchie v. People, 40 N.E. 453 (Ill. 1895), at 46.

7. Brief for the Plaintiffs in Error, Ritchie v. People, 40 N.E. 453 (Ill. 1895), at 7–12, 48.

8. *Ritchie*, 40 N.E. at 458; *see also* Nancy S. Erickson, Muller v. Oregon *Reconsidered: The Origins of a Sex-Based Doctrine of Liberty of Contract*, 30 Lab. Hist. 228, 241 (1989). Historian Kathryn Kish Sklar concludes that while "[s]upport for the law by those it was designed to protect is difficult to gauge," support for the law among women who

would be affected by it was clearly far from unanimous. Kathryn Kish Sklar, Florence Kelly and the Nation's Work 262–64 (1995).

9. *See* Erickson, *supra* note 8, at 236 (1989); Lori Ann Kran, Gendered Law: A Discourse Analysis of Labor Legislation, 1890–1930, at 49–50 (PhD diss., Univ. of Mass. 1993).

10. Florence Kelley, Some Ethical Gains through Legislation 141 (1910). For other negative commentary on *Ritchie*, see Ernst Freund, The Police Power § 313, at 298 (1904); Comment, 4 Yale L.J. 200, 201 (1895). The latter article argued that "the incessant jar and rumble of machinery" could injure a woman's reproductive capacity, and "it is the duty of the state to protect posterity."

11. F. J. Stimson, Handbook to the Labor Law of the United States 64–65 (1896).

12. *Quoted in* Sklar, *supra* note 8, at 282.

13. Nancy Woloch, *Muller v. Oregon*: A Brief History with Documents 34–35 (1996).

14. Julie Novkov, Constituting Workers, Protecting Women: Gender, Law, and Labor in the Progressive Era and New Deal Years 80 (2001); Nancy Woloch, *Muller v. Oregon*: A Brief History with Documents 28 (1996).

15. Leading reformer Mary Van Kleeck, for example, wrote, "We are interested in the protection of women workers by wage legislation at this time, not particularly because they are women, but because they are underpaid workers and underpayment is a social menace whether the worker be a man or woman, but it happens that the condition pressed most heavily upon women at this time." *Quoted in* Elizabeth Faulkner Baker, *At the Crossroads in the Legal Protection of Women in Industry*, 143 Annals of the Am. Academy of Pol. & Soc. Sci. 265, 267 (1929); *see* Vivien Hart, Bound by Our Constitution: Women, Workers, and the Minimum Wage 93 (1994); Landon R. Y. Storrs, Civilizing Capitalism 42 (2000); Woloch, *supra* note 14, at 9.

16. Kathryn Kish Sklar, *Two Political Cultures in the Progressive Era: The National Consumers' League and the American Association for Labor Legislation*, in U.S. History as Women's History: New Feminist Essays 36, 41(Kinda K. Kerber, et al., eds., 1995). *See generally* Sklar, *supra* note 8.

17. Novkov, *supra* note 14, at 96, 209–11; Thomas C. Leonard, *Protecting Family and Race: The Progressive Case for Regulating Women's Work*, 64 Am. J. Econ. & Sociology 758, 759 (2005). The family wage idea was especially prevalent among Progressive reformers. *See* Linda Gordon, *Social Insurance and Public Assistance: The Influence of Gender in Welfare Thought in the United States, 1890–1935*, 97 Am. Hist. Rev. 19, 47 (1992).

18. *See, e.g.,* Elizabeth Faulkner Baker, *Do Women in Industry Need Special Protection? We Need More Knowledge*, The Survey, Feb. 15, 1926, at 531, 532; Frances Perkins, *Do Women in Industry Need Special Protection? Yes*, The Survey, Feb. 15, 1926, at 529; Frank Taussig, *Minimum Wages for Women*, Q. J. Econ., May 30, 1916, at 411, 441. *See generally* Claudia Goldin, Understanding The Gender Gap: An Economic History Of American Women 198 (1990) (recounting that many advocates of protective legislation for women saw such legislation as "an indispensable substitute for collective action by women workers"); Daniel P. Bryden, *Brandeis's Facts*, 1 Const. Comment. 281, 287 (1994) (suggesting that women "were in no position to demand high wages or ideal working conditions").

19. Holden v. Hardy, 169 U.S. 366, 398 (1898).

20. Wenham v. State, 91 N.W. 421 (Neb. 1902); Commonwealth v. Beatty, 15 Pa. Super. 5 (1990); State v. Buchanan, 70 P. 52 (Wash. 1902).

21. *Wenham*, 91 N.W. at 424–25.

22. People v. Williams, 81 N.E. 778, 780 (N.Y. 1907); *see also* Burcher v. People, 14 Colo. 495 (1907) (overturning a law setting eight hours as the legal limit for women and children working in laundries). For favorable commentary on *Williams*, see Recent Cases, 20 Harv. L. Rev. 653 (1907).

23. Florence Kelley, *Wage-Earning Women in War Time: The Textile Industry*, 1 J. Industrial Hygiene 276 (1919).

24. State v. Muller, 85 P. 855 (Ore. 1906). *See generally* Barbara Allen Babcock, et al., Sex Discrimination and the Law 97–99 (2d. ed. 1995).

25. Elaine Zahnd Johnson, Protective Legislation and Women's Work: Oregon's Case Ten-Hour Law and the *Muller v. Oregon* Case, 1900–1913, at 228 (Ph.D. diss. Univ. Ore. 1982).

26. Brief for the State of Oregon, Muller v. Oregon, 208 U.S. 412 (1908), in Landmark Briefs and Arguments of the Supreme Court of the United States 37 (Phillip B. Kurland & Gerhard Casper, eds., 1975).

27. *Id.*

28. Woloch, *supra* note 14, at 28.

29. Novkov, *supra* note 14, at 108.

30. This summary is adapted from Erickson, *supra* note 8, at 247. The entire brief can be found at http://www.law.louisville.edu/library/collections/brandeis/node/235.

31. Woloch, *supra* note 14 at 32.

32. Melvin I. Urofsky, Louis D. Brandeis and the Progressive Tradition 53 (1981).

33. Owen Fiss, The Troubled Beginnings of the Modern State 175 (1993) ("hodgepodge"); Michael Rustad & Thomas Koenig, *The Supreme Court and Junk Social Science: Selective Distortion in Amicus Briefs*, 72 N.C. L. Rev. 91, 106 & n.63 (1993) ("junk social science"); Clyde Spillinger, *Revenge of the Triple Negative: A Note on the Brandeis Brief in* Muller v. Oregon, 22 Const. Comment. 5, 7 (2005) ("biased and amateurish"). Some of the evidence presented in the brief was nonsensical, even by the standards of the day. The brief reports that "there is more water" in women's blood than in men's, and that women therefore are "inferior to men" in certain physical tasks, and also that women's knees are constructed in such a way as to prevent them from engaging in difficult physical tasks. Brief for Defendant in Error, Muller v. Oregon, 208 U.S. 412 (1908), at 19–21.

34. Brief for Plaintiff in Error, Muller v. Oregon, 208 U.S. 412 (1908), at 29–30.

35. *Id.* at 34; Bryden, *supra* note 18, at 293.

36. Woloch, *supra* note 14, at 34–35.

37. *Quoted in* Robert D. Johnston, The Radical Middle Class 22 (2003). Even women who supported protective laws at times approached them with some skepticism. For example, in 1906, a female economist cautioned in the *Journal of Political Economy* that protective "legislation is not enacted exclusively, or even primarily, for the benefit of women themselves." S. P. Breckinridge, *Legislative Control of Women's Work*, 14 J. Pol. Econ. 107, 108 (1906).

38. Muller v. Oregon, 208 U.S. 412 (1908).

39. *See, e.g.*, Budd v. New York, 143 U.S. 517, 551 (1892) (Brewer, J., dissenting) ("The paternal theory of government is to me odious. The utmost possible liberty to the individual, and the fullest possible protection to him and his property is both the limitation and the duty of government.")

40. *See* Michael J. Brodhead, David J. Brewer: The Life of a Supreme Court Justice 1837–1910 (1994).

41. *Muller*, 208 U.S. 412.

42. *Id.* at 419–20.

43. *Id.* at 421–22.

44. *Id.* at 422.

45. David J. Brewer, *The Legitimate Exercise of the Police Power on the Protection of Healthy Women*, Charities and the Commons, Nov. 8, 1908, at 21.

46. *See* Jacob Andrew Lieberman, Their Sisters' Keepers: The Women's Wage and Hours Movement in the United States, 1890–1925, at 126–29 (unpublished PhD diss. Columbia Univ. 1971).

47. Florence Kelley, *The New Woman's Party*, The Survey, March 5, 1921, at 828, 829.

48. On the history and influence of maternalism, see Theda Skocpol, Protecting Soldiers and Mothers: The Political Origins of Social Policy in the United States (1992).

49. Alice Kessler-Harris, In Pursuit of Equity: Women, Men, and the Quest for Economic Citizenship in 20th-Century America 33 (2001).

50. *Quoted in* David A. Moss, Socializing Security: Progressive-Era Economists and the Origins of American Social Policy 111 (1996).

51. *Quoted in* Sarah Eisenstein, Give Us Bread but Give Us Roses: Working Women's Consciousness in the United States, 1890 to the First World War 22 (1983).

52. *See* Moss, *supra* note 50, at 111–12.

53. Elizabeth Faulkner Baker, Protective Labor Legislation: With Special Reference to Women in the State of New York 437 (1925).

54. Jennifer Friesen & Ronald K.L. Collins, *Looking Back on* Muller v. Oregon, 69 ABA J. 472 (1983).

55. *E.g.*, Alice Hamilton, *Protection for Women Workers*, 72 The Forum 152, 153 (1924); *see also* Susan Lehrer, Origins of Protective Labor Legislation for Women, 1905–1925, at 165 (1987); Sandra F. Van Burkleo, "Belonging to the World": Women's Rights And American Constitutional Culture 216–17 (2001); Storrs, *supra* note 15, at 51; Bryden, *supra* note 18, at 317–19.

56. Thomas Reed Powell, *The Constitutional Issue in Minimum-Wage Legislation*, 2 Minn. L. Rev. 1, 17 (1917).

57. State of New York, 5 Fourth Report of the Factory Investigating Commission 2884 (1915) (testimony of Louis D. Brandeis).

58. Louisa Harding, *Male Socialism*, The Women's Standard, April 1908, at 2.

59. *Id.*

60. *Pertinent Inquiries*, The Woman's Tribune, May 9, 1908, at 19.

61. *Special Legislation for Women*, The Woman's Tribune, Feb. 29, 1908, at 16; *see also Against Justice Brewer's Decision*, The Woman's Tribune, May 9, 1908, at 19.

62. Bosley v. McLaughlin, 236 U.S. 385, 392–94 (1915); Miller v. Wilson, 236 U.S. 373, 379–82 (1915); Riley v. Massachusetts, 232 U.S. 671, 679–81 (1914); *see also* Hawley v. Walker, 232 U.S. 718 (1914).

63. W. C. Ritchie & Co. v. Wayman, 91 N.E. 695 (Ill. 1910).

64. People v. Charles Schweinler Press, 24 N.Y. 395, 401 (1915). For a discussion of the origins of the New York night work law, see John Thomas McGuire, *Making the Case for Night Work Legislation in Progressive Era New York, 1911–1915,* 5 J. Gilded Age & Progressive Era 1 (2006).

65. Novkov, *supra* note 14, at 139.

66. People v. Schweinler, 213 N.Y. 395, 409 (1915).

67. 243 U.S. 629 (1917).

68. Brief for Defendants in Error upon Reargument, Stettler v. O'Hara, at 330.

69. *Id.* at 671 (quoting State of New York, I Fourth Report of the Factory Investigating Commission 43–43 (1915)).

70. *Quoted in* Alpheus Thomas Mason, The Supreme Court from Taft to Warren 31 (1968).

71. *Quoted in* Rebecca J. Mead, *"Let the Women Get Their Wages as Men Do": Trade Union Women and the Legislated Minimum Wage in California,* 67 Pac. Hist. Rev. 318, 321–22 (1998).

72. Baker, *supra* note 53, at 336, 425–26; Alice Kessler-Harris, Out of Work: A History of Wage-Earning Women in the United States 193–94 (1982); Lehrer, *supra* note 55, at 167; Maureen Wiener Greenwald, Women, War and Work: The Impact of World War I on Women Workers in the United States ch. 4 (1980).

73. *Quoted in* Moss, *supra* note 50, at 113.

74. Baker, *supra* note 53, at 190.

75. *See* Gail Laughlin, *Why an Equal Rights Amendment,* 11 Equal Rights 61 (1924) (quoting a 1920 resolution of the Federation).

76. *Quoted in* Rheta Childe Door, *Should There Be Labor Laws for Women? No,* Good Housekeeping, Sept. 1925, at 52, 164.

77. Nancy F. Cott, *Feminist Politics in the 1920's: The National Woman's Party,* 71 J. Am. Hist. 43 (1984).

78. *See* Joan G. Zimmerman, *The Jurisprudence of Equality: The Women's Minimum Wage, the First Equal Rights Amendment, and* Adkins v. Children's Hospital, *1905–1923,* 78 J. Am. Hist. 188 (1991).

79. Cott, *supra* note 77, at 56–60.

80. Meredith Tax, The Rising of the Women 201 (1980); Cott *supra* note 77, at 62.

81. Novkov, *supra* note 14, at 183, 198–99.

82. Lehrer, *supra* note 49, at 161–63, 213–14. *See* Suzanne La Follette, Concerning Women 175–84 (1926) (discussing her opposition to all protective legislation).

83. Hart, *supra* note 15, at 78; Kessler-Harris, *supra* note 72, at 69.

84. Hart, *supra* note 15, at 69, 83. Blanche Crozier, Note, *Constitutional Law: Regulation of Conditions of Employment of Women. A Critique of* Muller v. Oregon, 15 B.U. L. Rev. 276, 287 (1935). California's 1913 minimum-wage law was an exception. Mead, *supra* note 71, at 323.

85. Clara M. Beyer, History of Labor Legislation for Women in Three States 2 (1929); *see also* Cott, *supra* note 77, at 61; Lehrer, *supra* note 55, at 159; Kessler-Harris, *supra* note 72, at 201–5; Novkov, *supra* note 14, at 212; Jane Norman Smith, *Hours Legislation for Women Only*, Equal Rights, Jan. 16, 1932, at 396, 396.

86. Leonard, *supra* note 17, at 770–72.

87. Florence Kelley, *Minimum Wage Boards*, 17 Am. J. Sociology 303, 304 (1911); *see* Leonard, *supra* note 17.

88. Marilyn Power, *Parasitic-Industries Analysis and Arguments for a Living Wage for Women in the Early Twentieth-Century United States*, 5 Feminist Econ. 61 (1999). For contemporary criticism of the parasitic-industries argument, see F. W. Taurig, *Minimum Wages for Women*, Q. J. Econ., May 1916, at 411.

89. Novkov, *supra* note 14, at 200. Other advocates of protective laws, however, continued to rely on "fundamental" "physical and biological differences between men and women" as a rationale for protective laws. *E.g.*, Frances Perkins, *Do Women in Industry Need Special Protection? Yes*, The Survey, Feb. 15, 1926, at 529, 530.

90. John McGuire, *From the Courts to the State Legislatures: Social Justice Feminism, Labor Legislation, and the 1920s*, 45 Lab. Hist. 225, 230 (2004).

91. I Brief for Appellants, Adkins v. Children's Hosp., 261 U.S. 525 (1923), at xliv.

92. *See* Zimmerman, *supra* note 78, at 220.

93. *E.g.*, Adkins v. Children's Hospital, 261 U.S. 525, 564 (1923) (Taft, C. J., dissenting); 3 Charles Warren, The Supreme Court in United States History 463 (1922); Edward S. Corwin, *Social Insurance and the Constitution*, 26 Yale L.J. 431, 432 (1917); Samuel A. Goldberg, *The Unconstitutionality of Minimum Wage Legislation*, 71 U. Pa. L. Rev. 360, 364 (1923); Francis B. Sayre, *The Minimum Wage Decision*, Survey, May 1, 1923, at 150. *See generally* Victoria F. Nourse, *A Tale of Two* Lochners: *The Untold History of Substantive Due Process and the Idea of Fundamental Rights*, 97 Cal. L. Rev. 751, 769 n.103 (2009) (providing additional citations).

94. *See, e.g.*, Charles K. Burdick, The Law of the American Constitution: Its Origin and Development 582 (1922).

95. Adkins v. Children's Hosp., 261 U.S. 525, 557 (1923).

96. *Id.* at 542–43.

97. *Id.* at 556–57.

98. *Quoted in* Baker, *supra* note 53, at 98.

99. Florence Kelley, *Progress of Labor Legislation for Women*, in Proceeedings of the National Conference of Social Work 114 (1923).

100. Editorial, *The Legal Right to Starve*, New Republic, May 2, 1923, at 254; *see also* Samuel Gompers, *Usurped Power*, The Survey, May 15, 1923, at 221; Barbara N. Grimes, Comment, *Minimum Wage for Women*, 11 Cal. L Rev. 353 (1923); Note, *The Unconstitutionality of Minimum Wage Legislation*, 71 U. Penn. L. Rev. 360 (1923).

101. Ira Jewell Williams, *Minimum Wage Laws: Are They Compatible With American Concepts of What is of the Essence of Freedom?*, 9 Const. Rev. 195, 198 (1925).

102. Charles Cheney, *Editorial*, Survey, May 19, 1923, at 220; *see also* Rheta Childe Dorr, *Should There Be Labor Laws for Women? No*," Good Housekeeping, Sept. 1925, at 52.

103. Brief Amicus Curiae, National Woman's Party, et al., Tipaldo *ex rel.* Morehead v. New York, 298 U.S. 587 (1936), at 34.

104. Doris Stevens, *Suffrage Does Not Give Equality*, 72 The Forum 145, 151 (1924).

105. William E. Leuchtenberg, *The Case of the Chambermaid and the Nine Old Men*, American Heritage, Dec. 1986, at 33, 35.

106. *See* Joan Hoff, A Legal History of U.S. Women 203 (1990) ("male bias and corporate favoritism); Sandra Van Burkleo, "Belonging to the World": Women's Rights and American Constitutional Culture 229 (2001) (a rhetorical means to preserve "laissez-faire jurisprudence"); Storrs, *supra* note 15, at 48 ("disingenuous"); Sybil Lipschultz, *Hours and Wages: The Gendering of Labor Standards in America*, 8 J. Women's Hist. 114, 127 (1996) (Sutherland "made a farce of women's equality"); Zimmerman, *supra* note 78, at 219–20 (accusing Sutherland of insincerity). For more sympathetic portrayals of Sutherland's opinion in *Adkins*, see Hadley Arkes, The Return of George Sutherland (1994); Bryden, *supra* note 18.

107. *See* George Sutherland, *Women Suffrage*, 10 Green Bag 2d 387 (2007) (reprinting speech of Senator George Sutherland at the Woman Suffrage Meeting, Belasco Theater, Dec. 13, 1915); *see also* 51 Cong. Rec. 3598–3601 (statement of Sen. Sutherland); 53 Cong. Rec. 11,318 (1916) (statement of Sen. Sutherland); 53 Cong. Rec. 75 (statement of Sen. Sutherland).

108. Phillipa Strum, Louis D. Brandeis: Justice for the People 127–31 (1984).

109. Reva B. Siegel, *She the People: The Nineteenth Amendment, Sex Equality, Federalism, and the Family*, 115 Harv. L. Rev. 947 (2002).

110. Radice v. New York, 264 U.S. 292, 293–95 (1924).

111. Melvin I. Urofsky, *The Brandeis-Frankfurter Conversations*, 1985 Sup. Ct. Rev. 299, 330.

112. *E.g.*, Hoff, *supra* note 106, at 205.

113. Donham v. West Nelson Mfg. Co., 273 U.S. 65 (1927); Murphy v. Sardell, 269 U.S. 530 (1925).

114. *See generally* Jane Norman Smith, *Wage Laws Result in Unemployment*, The Survey, Feb. 4, 1933, at 5.

115. 291 U.S. 502 (1934).

116. Morehead v. New York *ex rel.* Tipaldo, 298 U.S. 587 (1936).

117. *Quoted in* Leuchtenberg, *supra* note 105, at 36.

118. Historians, however, have cast serious doubt on the idea that Roberts's "switch" was motivated by political considerations. Barry Cushman, Rethinking the New Deal Court: The Structure of a Constitutional Revolution (1998); Richard D. Friedman, *Switching Time and Other Thought Experiments: The Hughes Court and Constitutional Transformation*, 142 U. Pa. L. Rev. 1891, 1897 (1994); *but cf.* Michael S. Ariens, *A Thrice-Told Tale, or Felix the Cat*, 109 Harv. L. Rev. 620 (1993).

119. West Coast Hotel Company v. Parrish, 300 U.S. 379 (1937).

120. *Id.* at 398–400.

121. *Id.* at 399–400.

122. *Id.* at 394–95.

123. *Id.* at 411–13 (Sutherland, J., dissenting). An unidentified woman wrote to Sutherland: "May I say that the minority opinion handed down in the Washington mini-

mum wage case is, to me, what the rainbow was to Mr. Wordsworth? . . . You did my sex the honor of regarding women as persons and citizens." *Quoted in* William E. Leuchtenburg, The Supreme Court Reborn: Constitutional Revolution in the Age of Roosevelt 176 (1995).

124. Goesart v. Cleary, 335 U.S. 464 (1948).

125. Sally J. Kenney, For Whose Protection? Reproductive Hazards and Exclusionary Policies in the United States and Britain 48 (1992); Dianne Avery, *The Great American Makeover: The Sexing Up and Dumbing Down of Women's Work after* Jespersen v. Harrah's Operating Company, Inc., 42 U.S.F. L. Rev. 299, 303–5 (2007).

126. Dorothy Sue Cobble, Dishing It Out: Waitresses and Their Unions in the Twentieth Century 166 (1991).

CHAPTER FIVE

1. Bruce Ackerman, We the People 147 n. * (1992); Derrick A. Bell, Silent Covenants 84 (2004); Cass Sunstein, The Partial Constitution 45 (1993); *see also* Owen Fiss, History of the Supreme Court of the United States: Troubled Beginnings of the Modern State, 1888–1910, at 362 (1993).

2. Recently, several scholars have recognized these conflicts. *See* Mark Tushnet, *Race, State, Market, and Civil Society in Constitutional History,* in Constitutionalism and American Culture 359, 367 (Sandra F. VanBurkleo et al., eds., 2002); Hans J. Hacker & William D. Blake, *The Neutrality Principle: The Hidden Yet Powerful Legal Axiom at Work in Brown versus Board of Education,* 8 Berkeley J. Afr.-Am. L & Pol'y 5, 22 (2006).

3. Richard A. Epstein, Forbidden Grounds 102–7 (1992); Barton J. Bernstein, Plessy v. Ferguson: *Conservative Sociological Jurisprudence,* 48 J. Negro Hist. 196 (1963); Michael J. Klarman, *Constitutional Fact/Constitutional Fiction: A Critique of Bruce Ackerman's Theory of Constitutional Moments,* 44 Stan. L. Rev. 759, 787 (1992); Mark Tushnet, Plessy v. Ferguson *in Libertarian Perspective,* 16 L. & Phil. 245 (1997).

4. *See* Howard N. Rabinowitz, *More than the Woodward Thesis: Assessing The Strange Career of Jim Crow,* 75 J. Am. Hist. 842, 850 (1988). Michael Klarman lists and describes sources that discuss the extent of integration in the South when *Plessy* was decided in Brown, *Originalism, and Constitutional Theory: A Response to Professor Mc-Connell,* 81 Va. L. Rev. 1881, 1882 n.7 (1995).

5. Rabinowitz, *supra* note 4. For a discussion of the relevant political economy, see Jennifer Roback, *Racism as Rent Seeking,* 27 Econ. Inquiry 661 (1989). For a discussion of factors that encouraged legislators to pass segregation laws, see Michael J. Klarman, From Jim Crow to Civil Rights: The Supreme Court and the Struggle for Racial Equality 18 (2004).

6. *See* James W. Ely, Jr., Railroads and American Law 138–43 (2001); Barbara Young Welke, Recasting American Liberty: Gender, Race, Law, and the Railroad Revolution, 1865–1920, at 356–59 (2001).

7. Edward L. Ayers, The Promise of the New South: Life After Reconstruction 144 (1992); Charles A. Lofgren, The Plessy Case: A Legal-Historical Interpretation 28 (1987); V. F. Nourse & Sarah A. Maguire, *The Lost History of Governance and Equal Protection,* 58 Duke L.J. 955, 985–86 (2009).

8. Lofgren, *supra* note 7, at 41; Rebecca J. Scott, *Public Rights, Social Equality, and the Conceptual Roots of the* Plessy *Challenge*, 106 Mich. L. Rev. 777, 798 (2008).

9. Theodore W. Dwight, The Law of Persons and Personal Property 75 (Edward F. Dwight ed., 1894).

10. Plessy v. Ferguson, 163 U.S. 537, 551–52 (1896) (distinguishing social rights from political and civil rights).

11. Pace v. Alabama, 106 U.S. 583 (1883). For the argument that the *Pace* precedent made *Plessy* a doctrinally easy case, see Jack M. Balkin, *"Wrong the Day it was Decided":* Lochner *and Constitutional Historicism*, 85 B.U. L. Rev. 677, 707 (2005); Klarman, *supra* note 5, at 21.

12. *See* chapter 1; Klarman, *supra* note 5, at 21; Lofgren, *supra* note 7, at 80; Richard S. Kay, *The Equal Protection Clause in the Supreme Court: 1873–1903*, 29 Buff. L. Rev. 667, 696 (1980).

13. The Court wrote, "Legislation is powerless to eradicate racial instincts, or to abolish distinctions based upon physical differences." *Plessy*, 163 U.S. at 550. The Court endorsed the separate-but-equal standard in later cases, but it played no role in the majority's reasoning in *Plessy*. *See* Benno C. Schmidt, Jr., *Principle and Prejudice: The Supreme Court and Race in the Progressive Era Part 1: The Heyday of Jim Crow*, 82 Colum. L. Rev. 444, 468–69 (1982).

14. *Plessy*, 163 U.S. at 551; *see* Epstein, *supra* note 3, at 107; John E. Semonche, Charting the Future: The Supreme Court Responds to a Changing Society 83 (1978); Tushnet, *supra* note 2, at 367.

15. Lofgren, *supra* note 7, at 24; Klarman, *supra* note 5, at 23; Welke, *supra* note 6, at 351.

16. *See* Klarman, *supra* note 5, at 23.

17. *Plessy*, 163 U.S. at 557 (Harlan, J., dissenting).

18. *Id.* at 559.

19. *See* Fiss, *supra* note 1, at 357; Tushnet, *supra* note 2, at 367.

20. Michael Klarman, *The* Plessy *Era*, 1998 Sup. Ct. Rev. 303, 336.

21. 211 U.S. 45 (1908).

22. Brief for Plaintiff in Error, 211 U.S. 45 (1908), at 10.

23. *Id.* at 11–23.

24. *Id.* at 25; *see also* Klarman, *supra* note 5, at 23.

25. Brief for Plaintiff in Error, *supra* note 22, at 24.

26. *Id.* at 40.

27. *Id.* at 2.

28. *See* Charles Magnum, Jr., The Legal Status of the Negro 103 (1940) (suggesting that this evasion was intentional).

29. *Berea College*, 211 U.S. at 67 (Harlan, J., dissenting).

30. *Berea College*, 211 U.S. at 67–68 (quoting Allgeyer v. Louisiana, 165 U.S. 578, 589 (1897)).

31. *Id.* at 68.

32. Editorial, *The Berea College Case*, 13 Va. L. Reg. 643 (1908); Andrew Alexander Bruce, *The* Berea College *Decision and the Segregation of the Colored Races*, 68 Central

L.J. 137, 142 (1909); Note, *Constitutionality of a Statute Compelling the Color Line in Private Schools*, 22 Harv. L. Rev. 217, 218 (1909).

33. Editorial, *supra* note 32, at 644; Charles Warren, *A Bulwark to the State Police Power: The United States Supreme Court*, 13 Colum. L. Rev. 667, 695 (1913); 12 Law Notes 163, 163 (1908); *see also* Note, *Constitutionality of a Statute Compelling the Color Line in Private Schools*, 22 Harv. L. Rev. 217 (1909). Years later, Warren criticized Harlan's attempt to expand the constitutional definition of "liberty" in his *Berea College* dissent. Charles Warren, *The New "Liberty" under the Fourteenth Amendment*, 39 Harv. L. Rev. 431, 451 (1926).

34. David Currie, *The Constitution in the Supreme Court: 1910–1921*, 1985 Duke L.J. 1111, 1136. *Berea College's* author, Justice Brewer, a strong antistatist and, for his day, a liberal on racial issues, may have intentionally sought to leave room for future challenges to segregation laws. *See* Alexander M. Bickel & Benno C. Schmidt, Jr., The Judiciary and Responsible Government 1910–21, at 736 (1985); J. Gordon Hylton, *The Judge Who Abstained in* Plessy v. Ferguson: *Justice David Brewer and the Problem of Race*, 61 Miss. L.J. 315 (1991).

35. *Berea College*, 211 U.S. at 54.

36. *See* Roger L. Rice, *Residential Segregation by Law, 1910–1917*, 34 J. So. Hist. 179, 180–83 (1968); Klarman, *supra* note 5, at 79; Bickel & Schmidt, *supra* note 34, at 791; Morton Keller, Regulating a New Society: Public Policy and Social Change in America, 1900–1933, at 265–66 (1994); Christopher Silver, *The Racial Origins of Zoning: Southern Cities from 1919–1940*, 6 Plan. Persp. 189 (1991).

37. Carl V. Harris, *Reforms in Government Control of Negroes in Birmingham, Alabama, 1890–1920*, 38 J.S. Hist. 567, 571 n.10 (1972); Silver, *supra* note 36, at 191.

38. Desmond King, Separate and Unequal: Black Americans and the U.S. Federal Government 21 (1995); *see* John Louis Recchiuti, Civic Engagement: Social Science and Progressive-Era Reform in New York City ch. 7 (2007). The NAACP, for example, was founded by a coalition of Progressives and classical liberals.

39. Simply put, "In the era of Jim Crow, the connection between being a partisan of progress . . . and a proponent of racial equality or antiracism had long since been severed. . . . Antiracism at this time, simply put, was not part of the definition of what it meant to be a reformer." Ken I. Kersch, Constructing Civil Liberties: Discontinuities in the Development of American Constitutional Law 91 (2004); *see also* Lofgren, *supra* note 7, at 110; David W. Southern, The Malignant Heritage: Yankee Progressives and the Negro Question, 1901–1914, at 48–49 (1968); David W. Southern, The Progressive Era and Race: Reaction and Reform, 1900–1917, at 5 (2005); C. Vann Woodward, The Origins of the New South, 1877–1913, at 369–95 (1951); William E. Forbath, *The White Court 1910–1921: A Progressive Court?*, in The United States Supreme Court: The Pursuit of Justice 172, 191–96 (Christopher Tomlins ed., 2005).

40. *See* Dewey W. Grantham, Jr., *The Progressive Movement and the Negro*, 54 S. Atlantic Q. 461, 472 (1954).

41. Thomas F. Gossett, Race: The History of an Idea in America 154–74 (1963); Kersch, *supra* note 39, at 326; Donald G. Nieman, Promises to Keep: African Americans and the Constitutional Order, 1776 to Present 101 (1991); Charles Crowe, *Racial Violence*

and Social Reform: Origins of the Atlanta Riot of 1906, 53 J. Negro. Hist. 234, 245 (1968); Dewey W. Grantham, Jr., *The Progressive Movement and the Negro,* 54 S. Atlantic Q. 461, 472 (1954); Randall Kennedy, *Race Relations Law and the Tradition of Celebration: The Case of Professor Schmidt,* 86 Colum. L. Rev. 1622, 1632 (1986).

42. Garrett Power, *Apartheid Baltimore Style: The Residential Segregation Ordinances of 1910–1913,* 42 Md. L. Rev. 297 (1983).

43. *See* Melvin I. Urofsky, Louis D. Brandeis: A Life 640 (2009); William G. Ross, A Muted Fury: Populists, Progressives and Labor Unions Confront the Courts, 1890–1937, at 66 (1994); Christopher A. Bracey, *Louis Brandeis and the Race Question,* 52 Ala. L. Rev. 859 (2001); Garrett Power, *Advocates at Cross-Purposes: The Briefs on Behalf of Zoning in the Supreme Court,* 1997 J. Sup. Ct. Hist. (Vol. II) 79, 85; Larry M. Roth, *The Many Lives of Louis Brandeis: Progressive Reformer. Supreme Court Justice. Avowed Zionist and a Racist?,* 34 Southern U. L. Rev. 123, 151–63 (2007).

44. State v. Gurry, 88 A. 546 (Md. 1913); Carey v. City of Atlanta, 84 S.E. 456 (Ga. 1915). The North Carolina Supreme Court held that a local segregation law was unconstitutional because it was beyond the power granted to municipalities by the state constitution. State v. Darnell, 81 S.E. 338 (N.C. 1914).

45. Harden v. City of Atlanta, 93 S.E. 401 (Ga. 1917); Hopkins v. City of Richmond, 86 S.E. 139 (Va. 1915). For a detailed discussion of state court opinions on residential segregation laws, see A. Leon Higginbotham, Jr., et al., *De Jure Housing Segregation in the United States and South Africa: The Difficult Pursuit for Racial Justice,* 1990 U. Ill. L. Rev. 763, 807–62.

46. 245 U.S. 60 (1917).

47. George C. Wright, *The NAACP and Residential Segregation in Louisville, Kentucky, 1914–1917,* 78 Reg. Ky. Hist. Soc'y 39, 41 (1980).

48. *Quoted in id.* at 47.

49. Bickel & Schmidt, *supra* note 34, at 794.

50. Harris v. City of Louisville, 177 S.W. 472, 476 (Ky. 1915).

51. *See generally* Klarman, *supra* note 5, at 63; Henry Blumenthal, *Woodrow Wilson and the Race Question,* 48 J. Negro Hist. 1, 6 (1963); Cleveland M. Green, *Prejudices and Empty Promises: Woodrow Wilson's Betrayal of the Negro,* 1910–1919, 87 Crisis 380 (1980); Nancy J. Weiss, *The Negro and the New Freedom: Fighting Wilsonian Segregation,* 84 Pol. Sci. Q. 61, 61 (1969); Morton Sosna, *The South in the Saddle: Racial Politics During the Wilson Years,* 54 Wisc. Mag. Hist. 30 (1970).

52. Indeed, just before the Court decided *Buchanan,* the Georgia Supreme Court relied on *Plessy* in holding that residential segregation laws were constitutional as reasonable exercises of the police power. Harden v. City of Atlanta, 93 S.E. 401, 402–3 (Ga. 1917).

53. Charles Warren, *A Bulwark to the State Police Power: The United States Supreme Court,* 13 Colum. L. Rev. 667, 668 (1913).

54. Welke, *supra* note 6, at 351–52; Joseph Gordon Hylton, *Prelude to* Euclid: *The United States Supreme Court and the Constitutionality of Land Use Regulation, 1900–1920,* 3 Wash. U. J.L. & Pol'y 1 (2000).

55. *See* Michael J. Phillips: The *Lochner* Court: Myth and Reality (2000); David E. Bernstein, Lochner *Era Revisionism, Revised:* Lochner *and the Origins of Fundamental Rights Constitutionalism,* 92 Geo. L.J. 1 (2003); Robert E. Cushman, *The Social and Eco-*

nomic Interpretation of the Fourteenth Amendment, 20 Mich. L. Rev. 737, 757 (1922); Charles Warren, The Progressiveness of the United States Supreme Court, 13 Colum. L. Rev. 294 (1913).

56. For relevant law review commentary, see James F. Minor, Constitutionality of Segregation Ordinances, 18 Va. L. Reg. 574 (1912); Warren B. Hunting, The Constitutionality of Race Distinctions and the Baltimore Negro Segregation Ordinance, 11 Colum. L. Rev. 24 (1911); Municipal Segregation Ordinances, 3 Va. L. Rev. 304 (1915); Separating Residences of White and Colored Races, 21 Ohio L. Rep. 353, 355 (1914); Segregation of Races, 1 Va. L. Rev. 333, 335 (1914); Note, Constitutional Law: Segregation Ordinance, 63 U. Pa. L. Rev. 895, 897 (1915).

57. Note, The Constitutionality of Segregation Ordinances, 12 Mich. L. Rev. 215, 217 (1914)

58. Myers v. Anderson, 238 U.S. 368 (1915); Guinn v. United States, 238 U.S. 347, 364–65 (1915); McCabe v. Atchison, T. & S.F. Ry. Co., 235 U.S. 151 (1914); United States v. Reynolds, 235 U.S. 133 (1914); Bailey v. Alabama, 219 U.S. 219 (1911).

59. Brief for Defendant in Error at 13, Buchanan v. Warley, 245 U.S. 60 (1917).

60. Id. at 118, 119.

61. C. B. Blakely, The History of the Louisville Segregation Case 12 (1917).

62. Supplemental and Reply Brief for Defendant in Error on Rehearing at 123, Buchanan v. Warley, 245 U.S. 60 (1917).

63. The Court acknowledged that "property may be controlled in the exercise of the police power in the interest of the public health, convenience, or welfare." Buchanan, 245 U.S. at 74.

64. Id. at 78–79 (emphasis added).

65. Buchanan, 245 U.S. at 81.

66. Id. at 82.

67. Bickel & Schmidt, supra note 34, at 814.

68. Kull, supra note 81, at 141; see also Mark Tushnet, Red, White and Blue: A Critical Analysis of Constitutional Law 42 (1998); Hacker & Blake, supra note 2, at 51.

69. See chapter 3.

70. See Randall Kennedy, Race Relations Law and the Tradition of Celebration, 86 Colum. L. Rev. 1622, 1642–44 (1986).

71. Quoted in Albert W. Alschuler, Law without Values: The Life, Work, and Legacy of Justice Holmes 56 (2002).

72. Bickel & Schmidt, supra note 34, at folio following 592.

73. A. Leon Higginbotham, Shades of Freedom: Racial Politics and Presumptions of the American Legal Process 126 (1996); John R. Howard, The Shifting Wind: The Supreme Court and Civil Rights from Reconstruction to Brown 192 (1999).

74. See, e.g., David Beito & Linda Royster Beito, Black Maverick: T. R. M. Howard's Fight for Civil Rights and Economic Power (2009).

75. Arthur T. Martin, Segregation of Residences of Negroes, 32 Mich. L. Rev. 721, 723–24 (1934).

76. Klarman, supra note 5, at 262; see also William A. Fischel, Why Judicial Reversal of Apartheid Made a Difference, 51 Vand. L. Rev. 977, 981 (1998).

77. E.g., John Wertheimer & Michael Daly, State v. William Darnell: The Battle over

De Jure Housing Segregation in Progressive Era Winston-Salem, in "Warm Ashes": Issues in Southern History at the Dawn of the Twenty-First Century 255, 257 (W. B. Moore et al., eds., 2003).

78. *See generally* James W. Ely, Jr., *Reflections on* Buchanan v. Warley, *Property Rights, and Race*, 51 Vand. L. Rev. 953, 955 (1998); William Fischel, *Rethinking* Buchanan v. Warley, 51 Vand. L. Rev. 975 (1998).

79. *See* Carol Rose, Shelley v. Kraemer, in Property Stories 169, 174 (Gerald Korngold & Andrew P. Morris, eds., 2004).

80. For a recent work that dismisses *Buchanan* as a mere property decision with little relevance to the rights of African-Americans, see Lucas A. Powe, Jr., The Supreme Court and the American Elite, 1789–2008, at 189 (2009).

81. Bickel & Schmidt, *supra* note 34, at 799; Andrew Kull, The Colorblind Constitution 139 (1992).

82. This principle was to play a crucial role in the Court's important 1920s civil liberties precedents. Farrington v. Tokushige, 273 U.S. 284 (1927); Pierce v. Soc'y of Sisters, 268 U.S. 510 (1925); Meyer v. Nebraska, 262 U.S. 390 (1923); *see* chapter 6.

83. Note, *Constitutionality of Race Segregation*, 18 Colum. L. Rev. 147 (1918).

84. Comment, *Unconstitutionality of Segregation Ordinances*, 27 Yale L.J. 393, 397 (1918).

85. Note, *Constitutionality of Segregation Ordinances*, 16 Mich. L. Rev. 109, 111 (1917).

86. Note, *Race Segregation Ordinance Invalid*, 31 Harv. L. Rev. 475 (1917).

87. *Id.* at 479.

88. Howard Lee McBain, The Living Constitution 78 (1927). For additional criticism of *Buchanan*, see George D. Hott, *Constitutionality of Municipal Zoning and Segregation Ordinances*, 33 W. Va. L.Q. 348, 348–49 (1927); Arthur T. Martin, *Segregation of Residences by Negroes*, 32 Mich. L. Rev. 721, 731 (1934). Mark Tushnet notes that *Buchanan* could have been decided as a case about depriving whites of their social right to live away from African-Americans. Mark Tushnet, The Rights Revolution in the Twentieth Century 15 (2009).

89. *See* Bernard H. Nelson, The Fourteenth Amendment and the Negro Since 1920, at 163 (1946).

90. Euclid v. Ambler Realty Co., 272 U.S. 365 (1926).

91. Clement E. Vose, Caucasians Only 52 (1959).

92. City of Richmond v. Deans, 281 U.S. 704 (1930); Harmon v. Tyler, 273 U.S. 668 (1927).

93. Chaires v. City of Atlanta, 164 Ga. 755 (1926); *see also* Yu Cong Eng v. Trinidad, 271 U.S. 50 (1926) (invalidating a law in the Philippines forbidding merchants to keep their business records in Chinese).

94. Nelson, *supra* note 89, at 163; Louis R. Harlan, Booker T. Washington: The Wizard of Tuskegee 1901–1915, at 247 (1983).

95. Mark Tushnet, Laying the Groundwork: From *Plessy* to *Brown* 12 (n.d., unpublished manuscript).

96. *See* Davison M. Douglas, *Contract Rights and Civil Rights*, 100 Mich. L. Rev.

1541 (2002); Kenneth W. Mack, *Rethinking Civil Rights Lawyering and Politics in the Era before* Brown, 115 Yale L.J. 256, 276–77 (2005).

97. Bracey, *supra* note 43; Roth, *supra* note 43.

98. Keller, *supra* note 36, at 268; *see also* Forbath, *supra* note 39, at 193.

99. *See* Powell v. Alabama, 287 U.S. 45, 71 (1932); Nixon v. Condon, 286 U.S. 73, 88–89 (1932); Nixon v. Herndon, 273 U.S. 536, 540 (1927).

100. *See* Kevin J. McMahon, Reconsidering Roosevelt on Race: How the Presidency Paved the Road to *Brown* 97–143 (2004).

101. Klarman, *supra* note 5, at 173–80.

102. *Id.*

103. Mary L. Dudziak, Cold War Civil Rights: Race and the Image of American Democracy (2000).

104. Memorandum from Earl Pollock to Chief Justice Earl Warren, May 3, 1954, Earl Warren Papers, Library of Congress, Box 397.

105. *See* chapter 6.

106. Indeed, the plaintiffs quoted this language from *Meyer* in their brief. Brief for Petitioners at 13, Bolling v. Sharpe, 347 U.S. 497 (1954).

107. Farrington v. Tokushige, 273 U.S. 284, 298 (1927). For background, see Noriko Asato, Teaching Mikadoism: The Attack on Japanese Language Schools in Hawaii, California, and Washington, 1919–1927 (2005).

108. This was, in fact, precisely the argument made in the plaintiffs' briefs and during oral argument. Brief for Petitioners at 13, Bolling v. Sharpe, 347 U.S. 497 (1954) (No. 4). Text of the oral argument can be found at http://www.lib.umich.edu/exhibits/ brownarchive/oral/Hayes&Nabrit.pdf (accessed May 31, 2009).

109. A hand-edited draft shows that Warren wrote next to the citations to *Meyer*, *Pierce*, *Bartels*, and *Farrington* and the accompanying text, "strikeout *Black*," "Black strikeout," and "*Out*"; next to a citation to *Meyer*, "Black *strike* out citation" and "Black out"; and next to expansive due process language and an accompanying footnote to *Wolf v. Colorado*, "Black says strike" and "Black-out." Undated draft of *Bolling v. Sharpe*, Earl Warren Papers, Library of Congress, Box 571.

110. *See* chapter 7.

111. 347 U.S. 497, 500 (1954).

112. Part of the problem, no doubt, was the extraordinary haste in which *Bolling* was drafted. The initial drafting was assigned to Warren clerks on May 4, 1954, the draft was distributed to the other justices on May 8, their comments were received the following week, and the opinion was released on May 17.

113. Griswold v. Connecticut, 381 U.S. 479, 517 n.10 (1965) (Black, J., dissenting).

114. Dennis J. Hutchinson, *Unanimity and Desegregation: Decisionmaking and the Supreme Court, 1948–1958*, 68 Geo. L.J. 1, 50 (1979).

115. *See, e.g.*, Ackerman, *supra* note 1, at 147. For an argument that the liberty of contract doctrine shielded African Americans from protectionist labor laws promoted by white interest groups, see David E. Bernstein, Only One Place of Redress: African Americans, Labor Regulations and the Courts from Reconstruction to the New Deal (2001).

116. *See* Berea College v. Kentucky, 211 U.S. 45 (1908) (Harlan, J., dissenting); Adair

v. United States, 208 U.S. 161 (1908); Plessy v. Ferguson, 163 U.S. 537 (1896) (Harlan, J., dissenting).

CHAPTER SIX

1. Samuel J. Konefsky, The Legacy of Holmes and Brandeis 261 (1956). In a similar vein, see David P. Currie, The Constitution in the Supreme Court 1888–1986, at 272 (1990); Beryl Harold Levy, Our Constitution: Tool or Testament 170 (1941); Melvin I. Urofsky, Louis D. Brandeis: A Life 619, 631–32 (2009).

2. E.g., James MacGregor Burns, Packing the Court: The Rise of Judicial Power and the Coming Crisis of the Supreme Court 132 (2009).

3. For example, Christopher Tiedeman's narrow view of the police power led him to advocate consistently libertarian positions on constitutional issues, including his claim that laws banning interracial marriage were unconstitutional. See chapter 1. After the Illinois Supreme Court issued a controversial opinion strongly endorsing liberty of contract for women in Ritchie v. People, it held that a statute prohibiting certain uses of the American flag was beyond the state's police power. Ruhstart v. People, 57 N.E. 41 (Ill. 1900); Ritchie v. People, 40 N.E. 454 (Ill. 1895). And, as we shall see, Supreme Court Justice James McReynolds, a strong advocate of liberty of contract, also wrote some of the most expansive opinions favoring individual liberty outside the economic sphere at the expense of state prerogatives.

4. See Eric Foner, The Story of American Freedom 178 (1999).

5. Quoted in Ken I. Kersch, Constructing Civil Liberties: Discontinuities in the Development of American Constitutional Law 151 (2004).

6. H. L. Mencken, Mr. Justice Holmes, American Mercury, May 1930.

7. See chapter 3.

8. Robert L. Hale, Coercion and Distribution in the Supposedly Non-Coercive State, 38 Pol. Sci. Q. 470 (1923); see Neil Duxbury, Patterns of American Jurisprudence 107–11 (1995).

9. See Ian Ayres, Discrediting the Free Market, 66 U. Chi. L. Rev. 273, 276 (1999); Barry Cushman, Some Varieties and Vicissitudes of Lochnerism, 85 B. U. L. Rev. 881, 999 (2005). Relatedly, Columbia professor Howard Lee McBain argued in 1927 that the Supreme Court's decision in Buchanan v. Warley, invalidating a residential segregation ordinance, "seemed to destroy rather than to protect private rights." McBain contrasted "the private rights [to be free from state-imposed segregation] . . . asserted under the Constitution" with the "private rights [to be free from integration resulting from private choices] that are asserted under the statute." Howard Lee McBain, The Living Constitution 78–79 (1927).

10. Justice Brandeis authored a famous dissent in the 5–4 decision in Olmstead v. United States, 277 U.S. 438 (1928), contending that the Fourth Amendment prohibits warrantless wiretapping. The issue of federal, as opposed to state, encroachment on civil liberties is beyond the scope of this chapter. However, it's worth noting that Brandeis was not a consistent advocate of a broad Fourth Amendment. See, e.g., Carroll v. United States, 267 U.S. 132 (1925). The most consistent advocates of Fourth Amendment and other constitutional protections against the excesses of Prohibition enforcement were "conservative" Justices Butler, McReynolds, and Sutherland, with Brandeis and Holmes

generally voting for the government. Lucas A. Powe, Jr., The Supreme Court and the American Elite, 1789–2008, at 193 (2009); Phillipa Strum, Louis D. Brandeis: Justice for the People 330 (1984).

11. *E.g.*, Twining v. New Jersey, 211 U.S. 78 (1908); Hurtado v. California, 110 U.S. 516 (1884). *See generally* Bryan H. Wildenthal, *The Road to* Twining: *Reassessing the Disincorporation of the Bill of Rights*, 61 Ohio St. L.J. 1457 (2000).

12. Allgeyer v. Louisiana, 165 U.S. 578, 589 (1897).

13. Twining v. New Jersey, 211 U.S. 78, 99 (1908).

14. Patterson v. Colorado, 205 U.S. 454 (1907).

15. *See* Foner, *supra* note 4, at 140.

16. Woodrow Wilson, Constitutional Government in the United States 14, 16 (1908).

17. Herbert David Croly, Progressive Democracy 135 (1914).

18. Morris R. Cohen, *The Bill of Rights Theory*, 2 New Republic 222, 222 (1915).

19. Eben Moglen, *The Transformation of Morton Horwitz*, 93 Colum. L. Rev. 1042, 1058 (1993).

20. Editorial, *An Unseen Reversal*, The New Republic, Jan. 9, 1915, at 7. Frankfurter maintained his hostility to enforcement of the Due Process Clause for many decades. *See* Morton J. Horwitz, The Transformation of American Law, 1870–1960: The Crisis of Legal Orthodoxy 340 n.83 (1992).

21. Melvin I. Urofsky, *The Brandeis-Frankfurter Conversations*, 1985 Sup. Ct. Rev. 299, 320.

22. *Id.*

23. *Id.* at 330.

24. *See* William G. Ross, A Muted Fury: Populists, Progressives and Labor Unions Confront the Courts, 1890–1937, at 65 (1994).

25. Michael Kammen, A Machine That Would Go of Itself 208–54 (1988).

26. *See, e.g.*, Thomas James Norton, *National Encroachments and State Aggressions*, in American Bar Association, Report of the Fifteenth Annual Meeting of the American Bar Association, 237, 237 (1926). *See generally* Howard Gillman, *The Collapse of Con-stitutional Originalism and the Rise of the Notion of the 'Living Constitution' in the Course of American State-Building*, 11 Studies in Am. Pol. Development 191 (1997).

27. William G. Ross, Forging New Freedoms: Nativism, Education, and the Constitu-tion (1994).

28. Kersch, *supra* note 5, at 257; *see also* Barbara Bennett Woodhouse, *Who Owns the Child?* Meyer *and* Pierce *and the Child as Property*, 33 Wm. & Mary L. Rev. 995, 1003–17 (1992).

29. 262 U.S. 390 (1923). There was also a companion case, Bartels v. Iowa, 262 U.S. 404 (1923).

30. *Meyer*, 262 U.S. at 401.

31. *Id.* at 403.

32. *See* James E. Bond, I Dissent: The Legacy of Chief [sic] Justice James Clark McReynolds (1992).

33. *Meyer*, 262 U.S. at 399–400.

34. *See* Robert C. Post, *Defending the Lifeworld: Substantive Due Process in the Taft Court Era*, 78 B.U. L. Rev. 1489, 1532–33 (1998).

35. For some speculation on Sutherland's motives, see Woodhouse, *supra* note 28, at 1092 n.529.

36. 262 U.S. 404, 412 (1923) (Holmes, J., dissenting).

37. Gerald Gunther, Learned Hand 377–78 (1994). *See generally* Note, *Validity of Foreign Language Statutes*, 22 Mich. L. Rev. 248, 251 (1923) (accusing the majority of reverting to an "individualism now rather generally discredited" and praising Justice Holmes's approach to the Fourteenth Amendment).

38. *See* Leonard Baker, Brandeis and Frankfurter: A Dual Biography 20–21 (1984).

39. Melvin I. Urofsky, *The Brandeis-Frankfurter Conversations*, 1985 Sup. Ct. Rev. 299, 320. Frankfurter's notes state that he agreed with Brandeis, contrary to his letter to Hand suggesting that he would have voted the other way in *Meyer*. Frankfurter is notorious for his attempts to curry favor with the powerful, so perhaps it's not surprising that he told both Brandeis and Hand that he agreed with their respective positions.

40. Editorial, *The Red Terror of Judicial Reform*, The New Republic, Oct. 1, 1924, at 113.

41. Felix Frankfurter, *Mr. Justice Holmes and the Constitution: A Review of His Twenty-Five Years on the Supreme Court*, 41 Harv. L. Rev. 121, 153 n.84 (1927).

42. Letter from Justice Frankfurter to Justice Rutledge, Jan. 22, 1944, *quoted in* Dennis J. Hutchinson, *Unanimity and Desegregation: Decisionmaking and the Supreme Court, 1948–1958*, 68 Geo. L.J. 1, 48 (1979).

43. Kersch, *supra* note 5, at 270.

44. William G. Hale, *Educational Regulations and the Constitution:* Meyer v. Nebraska, 3 Ore. L. Rev. 71 (1923); *see also* Carl Zollman, *The Fourteenth Amendment and the Part Time Religious Day Schools*, 10 Marq. L. Rev. 94 (1926).

45. 268 U.S. 510 (1925).

46. *See* Soc'y of the Sisters of the Holy Names of Jesus and Mary v. Pierce, 296 F. 928, 938 (D. Ore. 1924), *aff'd sub. nom.*, Pierce v. Soc'y of Sisters, 268 U.S. 510 (1925).

47. Felix Frankfurter, *Can the Supreme Court Guarantee Toleration?*, The New Republic, July 17, 1925, at 85, 86.

48. *Id.*

49. *See* Gerald T. Dunne, Hugo Black and the Judicial Revolution 266 (1976).

50. 273 U.S. 284 (1927).

51. Farrington v. Tokushige, 11 F.2d 710, 714 (9th Cir. 1926), *aff'd*, 273 U.S. 284 (1927).

52. *Tokushige*, 273 U.S. at 298, 299.

53. *E.g.*, William M. Wiecek, Liberty under Law: The Supreme Court in American Life 178 (1988).

54. Kersch, *supra* note 5, at 257; *see also* Powe, *supra* note 10, at 198.

55. Kersch, *supra* note 5, at 272.

56. Pierce v. Society of Sisters, 268 U.S. 510, 535 (1923).

57. *See generally* Edward J. Larson, Summer for the Gods: The Scopes Trial and America's Continuing Debate over Science and Religion (1997).

58. Gunther, *supra* note 37, at 582–83.

59. Donald K. Pickens, Eugenics and the Progressives 18–22 (1968); Thomas Leonard,

American Economic Reform in the Progressive Era: What Beliefs Inclined the Progressives to Eugenics?, 41 Hist. Pol. Econ. 109 (2009).

60. Sidney Webb, *Eugenics and the Poor Laws: The Minority Report*, 2 Eugenics Rev. 233, 237 (1910).

61. Michael Willrich, *The Two Percent Solution: Eugenic Jurisprudence and the Socialization of American Law, 1900–1930*, 16 L. & Hist. Rev. 63, 64 (1998).

62. Paul A. Lombardo, Three Generations, No Imbeciles: Eugenics, the Supreme Court, and *Buck v. Bell* 177 (2008). By contrast with the evangelicals, modernist religious leaders tended to embrace eugenics. *See* Christine Rosen, Preaching Eugenics: Religious Leaders and the American Eugenics Movement (2004).

63. *See* Stephen A. Siegel, *Justice Holmes,* Buck v. Bell, *and the History of Equal Protection*, 90 Minn. L. Rev. 106 (2005).

64. Mickle v. Henrichs, 262 F. 687 (D. Nev. 1918) (void as cruel and unusual punishment); Davis v. Berry, 216 F. 413 (S.D. Iowa 1914) (unconstitutional as cruel and unusual punishment); Williams v. Smith, 131 N.E. 2 (Ind. 1921) (procedural due process violated); Smith v. Board of Examiners, 88 A. 963 (N.J. 1913) (void as a violation of equal protection); *In re* Salloum, 210 N.W. 498 (Mich. 1926) (upheld); Smith v. Command, 204 N.W. 140 (Mich. 1925) (upheld); State v. Feilen, 126 P. 75 (Wash. 1912) (upheld).

65. Smith v. Command, 204 N.W. 140 (Mich. 1925) (White, J., dissenting).

66. Buck v. Bell, 274 U.S. 200 (1927).

67. *See* Lombardo, *supra* note 62.

68. *Quoted in* Phillip Thompson, *Silent Protest: A Catholic Justice Dissents in* Buck v. Bell, 43 Catholic Lawyer 126, 127 (2004).

69. Walter Berns, Buck v. Bell: *Due Process of Law?*, 6 W. Pol. Q. 762, 764 (1953).

70. Lombardo, *supra* note 62, at 172; Davis R. Stras, *Pierce Butler: A Supreme Technician*, 62 Vand. L. Rev. 695, 731 (2009); Thompson, *supra* note 68, at 138.

71. Frankfurter, *supra* note 41, at 153.

72. William E. Leuchtenburg, The Supreme Court Reborn: The Constitutional Revolution in the Age of Roosevelt 18–19 (1995).

73. Olmstead v. United States, 277 U.S. 438, 457 (1928) (Brandeis, J., dissenting).

74. Robert E. Cushman, *Constitutional Law in 1926–27*, 22 Am. Pol. Sci. Rev. 92 (1928).

75. Fowler V. Harper, *Scientific Method in the Application of Law*, 1 Dakota L. Rev. 110, 111 (1927).

76. Edwin Black, War Against the Weak 122 (2004).

77. *See* Mark Graber, Transforming Free Speech: The Ambiguous Legacy of Civil Libertarianism 11 (1991); David M. Rabban, Free Speech in its Forgotten Years 8 (1997); Gerald Gunther, *Learned Hand and the Origins of Modern First Amendment Doctrine: Some Fragments of History*, 27 Stan. L. Rev. 719 (1975).

78. Herbert F. Goodrich, *Does the Constitution Protect Free Speech?*, 19 Mich. L. Rev. 487 (1921); *see also* Edward S. Corwin, *Freedom of Speech and Press under the First Amendment*, 30 Yale L. J. 48, 51 (1920).

79. Graber, *supra* note 77; Mark Tushnet, The Rights Revolution in the Twentieth Century (2009).

80. Morton Keller, Regulating a New Society: Public Policy and Social Change in America, 1900–1933, at 99–102 (1994); *see also* Christopher Capozzola, Uncle Sam Wants You: World War I and the Making of the Modern American Citizen (2008); Donald Johnson, The Challenge to American Freedoms: World War I and the Rise of the American Civil Liberties Union (1963); Paul L. Murphy, World War I and the Origins of Civil Liberties in the United States (1979); Rabban, *supra* note 77, chs. 6–7; John Fabian Witt, Patriots and Cosmopolitans: Hidden Histories of American Law ch. 3 (2007).

81. Witt, *supra* note 80.

82. G. Edward White, The Constitution and the New Deal 135 (2000). This line of argument was not as novel as the standard narrative suggests. Charles L. Barzun, *Politics or Principle? Zechariah Chafee and the Social Interest in Free Speech*, 2007 BYU L. Rev. 259, 312–14 (2007).

83. *See* Rabban, *supra* note 77.

84. *Quoted in id.* at 293.

85. Abrams v. United States, 250 U.S. 616 (1919).

86. Indeed, Brandeis's famous 1890 article "The Right to Privacy" called for what amounted to "a form of press censorship." Kersch, *supra* note 5, at 57.

87. Bernard Siegan, Economic Liberties and the Constitution 122 (2d ed. 2006); *see also* White, *supra* note 82, at 139–40.

88. Graber, *supra* note 77, ch. 1; Rabban, *supra* note 77, at 182. For criticism of Graber and Rabban, see Barzun, *supra* note 82, at 302–10. Perhaps the most economically conservative president of the twentieth century, Warren Harding, abolished wartime speech restrictions and pardoned socialist leader Eugene V. Debs and other leftists whom the Wilson administration had prosecuted for their antiwar activism. *See* Robert K. Murray & Katherine Speirs, The Harding Era: Warren G. Harding and His Administration (2000); Eugene P. Trani & David L. Wilson, The Presidency of Warren G. Harding (1977). In 1924, Republican presidential candidate Calvin Coolidge, responding to Progressive Party candidate Robert La Follete's attacks on the Supreme Court, argued that in the absence of judicial review, "the freedom of religion, speech and the press, would have very little security." *Coolidge Sees Constitution or Despotism*, N.Y. Tribune, Sept. 26, 1924, at 1.

89. *See* Graber, *supra* note 77, at 33.

90. Gilbert v. Minnesota, 254 U.S. 325 (1920).

91. *Id.* (Brandeis, J., dissenting).

92. Gitlow v. New York, 268 U.S. 652, 666 (1925).

93. *See* Howard Gillman, *Preferred Freedoms: The Progressive Expansion of State Power and the Rise of Modern Civil Liberties Jurisprudence*, 47 Pol. Res. Q. 623, 639 (1994).

94. *Gitlow*, 268 U.S. 652 (Holmes, J., dissenting).

95. *Id.* at 672.

96. Charles Warren, *The New 'Liberty' under the Fourteenth Amendment*, 39 Harv. L. Rev. 431, 480 (1926). On Warren's Progressivism, see Michael Allan Wolf, Charles Warren, Progressive, Historian (unpublished PhD diss., Harvard Univ., 1991).

97. Fiske v. Kansas, 274 U.S. 380 (1927).

98. Whitney v. California, 274 U.S. 357 (1927); *see* Graber, *supra* note 77, at 78.

99. White, *supra* note 82, at 140.

100. Stromberg v. California, 283 U.S. 359 (1931).

101. Near v. Minnesota, 283 U.S. 697, 707 (1931).

102. New State Ice v. Liebmann, 285 U.S. 262, 280 (1932).

103. Grosjean v. American Press Co., 297 U.S. 233 (1936).

104. White, *supra* note 82, at 162–63.

105. *Id.* at 131.

106. Kurt T. Lash, *The Constitutional Convention of 1937: The Original Meaning of the New Jurisprudential Deal*, 70 Fordham L. Rev. 459, 475 (2001); *see also* David P. Currie, The Constitution in the Supreme Court 1888–1986, at 253 (1990).

107. *See generally* Arthur Ekirch, The Decline of American Liberalism (1960).

108. Taft wrote in 1920, "There is no greater domestic issue in the election than the maintenance of the Supreme Court as the bulwark to enforce the guaranty that no man shall be deprived of his property without due process of law." William Howard Taft, *Mr. Wilson and the Campaign*, 10 Yale Rev. 1, 19–20 (1921).

109. Nebbia v. New York, 291 U.S. 502, 533 (1934).

110. *See* W. Coast Hotel Co. v. Parrish, 300 U.S. 379 (1937).

111. For the latter position, see Barry Cushman, Rethinking the New Deal Court: The Structure of a Constitutional Revolution (1998); Richard D. Friedman, *Switching Time and Other Thought Experiments: The Hughes Courts and Constitutional Transformation*, 142 U. Pa. L. Rev. 1891 (1994). The controversy is reviewed in Laura Kalman, *The Constitution, the Supreme Court, and the New Deal*, Am. Hist. Rev., Oct. 2005, at 1052.

112. *See generally* Alan J. Meese, *Will, Judgment, and Economic Liberty: Mr. Justice Souter and the Mistranslation of the Due Process Clause*, 41 Wm. & Mary L. Rev. 3, 56 (1999) (noting that *West Coast Hotel* did not "overrule *Lochner* or any liberty of occupation case not involving an attempt to require [employers to pay] a subsistence wage").

113. Cushman, *supra* note 111, at 224–25; Jack M. Balkin & Sanford Levinson, *Understanding the Constitutional Revolution*, 87 Va. L. Rev. 1045, 1066–83 (2001).

114. This line of jurisprudence started in *United States v. Carolene Products Co.*, 304 U.S. 144 (1938).

115. United States v. Darby, 312 U. S. 100 (1941).

116. *See* Martin Shapiro, *Fathers and Sons: The Court, the Commentators and the Search for Values*, in The Burger Court: The Counterrevolution that Wasn't (Vincent Blasi ed., 1983).

117. 302 U.S. 319, 325 (1937).

118. United States v. Carolene Prods. Co., 304 U.S. 144, 152 n.4 (1938); *see* Tushnet, *supra* note 79, at 20; George Thomas, *Lochner's* Ghost in American Constitutional Development, 1937–1947 (unpublished).

119. *Carolene Prods. Co.*, 304 U.S. at 152 n.4.

120. *Id.* (citations omitted).

121. White, *supra* note 82, at 261.

122. *See* Powell v. Alabama, 287 U.S. 45 (1932); *see also* Moore v. Dempsey, 261 U.S. 86 (1923).

123. *See* Barry Friedman, The Will of the People: How Public Opinion Has Influenced the Supreme Court and Shaped the Meaning of the Constitution 221–22 (2009); M. B. Carrott, *The Supreme Court and Minority Rights in the Nineteen-Twenties*, 41 Nw. Ohio Q. 144 (1969).

124. Tushnet, *supra* note 79; Kersch, *supra* note 5, at 85–86.

125. For a very interesting look at the rise of modern legal liberalism in New York which emphasizes the role of non-WASPs, see William E. Nelson, The Legalist Reformation: Law, Politics and Ideology in New York, 1920–1980 (2001). The shift among reformers from a statist Progressivism to a more liberal egalitarianism has otherwise received much less attention than one might expect. *But see* Laura M. Weinrib, *Lawyers, Libertines, and the Reinvention of Free Speech, 1920–1933*, L. & Hist. Rev. (forthcoming).

126. William E. Nelson: The Fourteenth Amendment: From Political Principle to Judicial Doctrine 200 (1988).

127. Tushnet, *supra* note 79; John Wertheimer, *The "Switch in Time" Beyond the Nine: Civil Liberties and the Interwar Constitutional Retooling*, Studies in Law, Politics & Soc'y (forthcoming).

128. Wertheimer, *supra* note 127.

129. *Id.*

130. 316 U.S. 535 (1942); *see* Victoria F. Nourse, In Reckless Hands: *Skinner v. Oklahoma* and the Near-Triumph of American Eugenics (2008).

131. Interview of Justice Douglas by Prof. Walter Murphy, available at http://www.princeton.edu/~mudd/finding_aids/douglas/douglas7b.html.

132. Lombardo, *supra* note 62, at 232.

133. Paul Blanshard, American Freedom and Catholic Power 152, 269 (1949).

CHAPTER SEVEN

1. *See, e.g.,* Ferguson v. Skrupa, 372 U.S. 726 (1963); Kotch v. Board of River Port Pilot Commissioners, 330 U.S. 552 (1947).

2. *E.g.,* Lincoln Federal Labor Union No. 19129 v. Northwestern Metal & Iron Co., 335 U.S. 525 (1949).

3. Williamson v. Lee Optical, 348 U.S. 483, 488 (1955).

4. Pierce v. Soc'y of Sisters, 268 U.S. 510 (1925); Meyer v. Nebraska, 262 U.S. 390 (1923).

5. *See* Lucas A. Powe, Jr., The Supreme Court and the American Elite 227 (2009).

6. The debate between Black and Frankfurter has been analyzed in great detail elsewhere. *E.g.,* Jeffrey D. Hockett, New Deal Justice: The Constitutional Jurisprudence of Hugo L. Black, Felix Frankfurter, and Robert H. Jackson (1996); Mark Silverstein, Constitutional Faiths: Felix Frankfurter, Hugo Black and the Process of Judicial Decision Making (1984); James F. Simon, The Antagonists: Hugo Black, Felix Frankfurter and Civil Liberties in Modern America (1989). Frankfurter received academic support from Charles Fairman. *E.g.,* Charles Fairman, *Does the Fourteenth Amendment Incorporate the Bill of Rights?*, 2 Stan. L. Rev. 5 (1949); *cf.* William Winslow Crosskey, *Charles Fairman, "Legislative History," and the Constitutional Limitations on State Authority*, 22 U. Chi. L. Rev. 1 (1954) (criticizing Fairman).

7. As of 2009, the Supreme Court has not "incorporated" against the states the right to a jury trial in civil cases, the right of a criminal defendant to have a grand jury indictment, and the right to bear arms.

8. Conceptually, the liberty of contract line of cases involved an exercise of what historian G. Edward White calls "guardian review," policing the limits of state power, not

"substantive due process." Although critics complained for decades that the Due Process Clause should be limited to issues of procedure, the concept of substantive due process did not become firmly established in American jurisprudence until the 1950s. *See* James W. Ely, Jr., The Guardian of Every Other Right: A Constitutional History of Property Rights 103–4 (2d ed. 1998); Powe, *supra* note 5, at 169; G. Edward White, The Constitution and the New Deal 245 (2000); Kermit Roosevelt III, *Forget the Fundamentals: Fixing Substantive Due Process*, 8 U. Pa. J. Const. L. 883 (2006). Tom Grey argues that the very notion that law is divided into "substantive" and "procedural" spheres was a product of the positivist revolution, specifically the attack on common law pleading. Thomas C. Grey, *Judicial Review and Legal Pragmatism*, 38 Wake Forest L. Rev. 473 (2003).

9. *See* William E. Nelson: The Fourteenth Amendment: From Political Principle to Judicial Doctrine 200 (1988).

10. Consistent with the "rehabilitating *Lochner*" theme of this book, this formulation is meant to convey irony, not insult.

11. Stephen A. Siegel, *The Origin of the Compelling State Interest Test and Strict Scrutiny*, 48 Am. J. Leg. Hist. 355 (2006).

12. *See* Victoria F. Nourse, *A Tale of Two* Lochners: *The Untold History of Substantive Due Process and the Idea of Fundamental Rights*, 97 Cal. L. Rev. 751 (2009).

13. 347 U.S. 483 (1954).

14. *Cf.* V. F. Nourse & Sarah A. Maguire, *The Lost History of Governance and Equal Protection*, 58 Duke L.J. 955, 995–99 (2009).

15. *See* Gary Peller, *Neutral Principles in the 1950s*, 21 U. Mich. J.L. Reform 561 (1988).

16. Learned Hand, The Bill of Rights (1958).

17. *Id.* at 50–51, 56.

18. *Id.* at 56–73.

19. *Id.* at 54–55.

20. Herbert Wechsler, *Toward Neutral Principles of Constitutional Law*, 73 Harv. L. Rev. 1 (1959).

21. Norman Silber & Geoffrey Miller, *Toward "Neutral Principles" in the Law: Selections from the Oral History of Herbert Wechsler*, 93 Colum. L. Rev. 854, 864 (1993).

22. *See* chapter 6.

23. Howard Lee McBain, The Living Constitution 78 (1927). The articles critical of *Brown* generated a pro-*Brown* backlash among younger liberal law professors. *See, e.g.,* Charles L. Black, Jr., *The Lawfulness of the Segregation Decisions*, 69 Yale L.J. 421 (1960); Owen M. Fiss, *Racial Imbalance in the Public Schools: The Constitutional Concepts*, 78 Harv. L. Rev. 564 (1965); Louis H. Pollak, *Racial Discrimination and Judicial Integrity: A Reply to Professor Wechsler*, 108 U. Pa. L. Rev. 1 (1959).

24. For an exception, see Albert A. Mavrinac, *From* Lochner *to* Brown v. Topeka: *The Court and Conflicting Concepts of the Political Process*, 52 Am. Pol. Sci. Rev. 641 (1958). Mavrinac attacked the Court's ruling in *Brown* and defended *Lochner*.

25. Rehnquist later claimed that the memo, entitled "A Random Thought on the Segregation Cases," summarized Jackson's own tentative thoughts, a claim that has been met with justified skepticism. *See, e.g.,* Bernard Schwartz, *Chief Justice Rehnquist, Justice Jackson, and the "Brown" Case*, 1988 Sup. Ct. Rev. 245.

26. *See* Ferguson v. Skrupa, 372 U.S. 726, 729 (1963); Day-Brite Lighting, Inc. v. Missouri, 342 U.S. 421, 423 (1952); Lincoln Fed. Labor Union v. Nw. Iron & Metal Co., 335 U.S. 525, 535 (1949).The one exception was Fed. Hous. Admin. v. Darlington, Inc., 358 U.S. 84, 92 (1958) ("to protect the rights asserted here would make the ghost of *Lochner v. New York* walk again") (Douglas, J.).

27. Robert G. McCloskey, *Economic Due Process and the Supreme Court: An Exhumation and Reburial*, 1962 Sup. Ct. Rev. 34, 44 (quoting *Lincoln Fed. Labor Union*, 335 U.S. at 535, as decrying "the *Allgeyer-Lochner-Adair-Coppage*" doctrine).

28. 372 U.S. 726 (1963).

29. 381 U.S. 479 (1965).

30. Brief for Appellant at 14, 17, Griswold v. Connecticut, 381 U.S. 479 (1965).

31. *Id.* at 23.

32. Transcript of Oral Argument at 7–8, Griswold v. Connecticut, 381 U.S. 479 (1965).

33. Griswold v. Connecticut, 381 U.S. 479, 481–82 (1965) (citation omitted).

34. *Id.* at 484–85.

35. *Id.* at 488 (Goldberg, J., concurring).

36. *Id.* at 500 (citing Poe v. Ullman, 367 U.S. 497, 522 (1962) (Harlan, J., dissenting)).

37. *Id.* at 502 (White, J., concurring) (citations omitted).

38. *See* chapter 6.

39. *See* Jed Rubenfeld, *The Right of Privacy*, 102 Harv. L. Rev. 737, 743 (1989).

40. *Griswold*, 381 U.S. at 514–15 (Black, J., dissenting). The other cases he cited are *Coppage v. Kansas*, 236 U.S. 1, *Jay Burns Baking Co. v. Bryan*, 264 U.S. 504 , and *Adkins v. Children's Hospital*, 261 U.S. 525. *Id.* at 515.

41. *Id.* at 516 (citations omitted).

42. Lucas A. Powe, Jr., The Warren Court and American Politics 376 (2000).

43. Robert G. McCloskey, *Reflections on the Warren Court*, 51 Va. L. Rev. 1229, 1269 (1965).

44. *See, e.g.,* Alexander M. Bickel, The Supreme Court and the Idea of Progress 21 (1970).

45. Owen M. Fiss, Troubled Beginnings of the Modern State, 1888–1910, at 10 (1993).

46. Alfred H. Kelly, *Clio and the Court: An Illicit Love Affair*, 1965 Sup. Ct. Rev. 119, 155–58.

47. Gerald Gunther & Noel T. Dowling, Constitutional Law: Cases and Materials 982–84 (8th ed. 1970). An attorney used the phrase in a book published in 1969, suggesting that Gunther did not invent the phrase. Seymour I. Toll, Zoned America 17 (1969).

48. A Hein-on-Line search for "*Lochner* era" in the "most-cited law reviews" finds four uses between 1970 and 1972, and another six uses in 1973 and 1974, in the wake of *Roe. See* Gerald Gunther, *The Supreme Court, 1971 Term—Foreword: In Search of Evolving Doctrine on a Changing Court: A Model for a Newer Equal Protection*, 86 Harv. L. Rev. 1, 11 (1972); Laurence Tribe, *The Supreme Court, 1972 Term—Foreword: Toward a Model of Roles in the Due Process of Life and Law*, 87 Harv. L. Rev. 1, 7 n.35, 8 n.39, 12, 31, 45 & 52 (1973).

49. 410 U.S. 113 (1973).

50. *Id.* at 153.

51. *Id.* at 118.

52. *Id.* at 174 (Rehnquist, J., dissenting) (citations omitted).

53. John Hart Ely, *The Wages of Crying Wolf: A Comment on* Roe v. Wade, 82 Yale L.J. 920, 935–46 (1973); *see also* Harry H. Wellington, *Common Law Rules and Constitutional Double Standards: Some Notes on Adjudication,* 83 Yale. L. J. 221 (1973).

54. Gerald Gunther, Cases and Materials on Constitutional Law 564–70 (9th ed. 1975); Gunther & Dowling, *supra* note 47, at 963.

55. *See* Randy E. Barnett, *Justice Kennedy's Libertarian Revolution:* Lawrence v. Texas, 2003 Cato Sup. Ct. Rev. 21.

56. A search in the Hein-on-Line database for *"Lochner* era" in the "most-cited law reviews" finds thirteen uses of the phrase between 1975 and 1978.

57. Gunther, *supra* note 54, at 557.

58. Moore v. City of East Cleveland, 431 U.S. 494, 502 (1977) (citing Gunther, *supra* note 54, at 550–96). The first use of *"Lochner* era" in a Supreme Court brief was Petitioner's brief, *Dicks v. Naff,* 415 U.S. 958 (1974).

59. Just as Tribe's treatise was arriving in bookstores, an essay entitled "The Constitution and Economic Rights" was published that barely mentions *Lochner* and never uses the phrase *"Lochner* era." Martin Shapiro, *The Constitution and Economic Rights, in* Essays on the Constitution of the United States 74 (M. Judd Harmon ed., 1978). One would be hard pressed to find a similar neglect of *Lochner* after Tribe's treatise appeared. A Hein-on-Line search for *"Lochner* era" in the "most-cited law reviews" finds more than sixty uses of that phrase between 1979 and 1985. The growing prominence of *Lochner* in the 1970s is illustrated by concurrent editions of a book by Alpheus Thomas Mason. Mason's 1968 *The Supreme Court from Taft to Warren* contains only one reference to *Lochner.* Mason's 1979 *The Supreme Court from Taft to Burger* contains five references to *Lochner.* Alpheus Thomas Mason, The Supreme Court from Taft to Burger (1979); Alpheus Thomas Mason, The Supreme Court from Taft to Warren (1968). Professor Randy Barnett, a student in Professor Tribe's constitutional law class in the fall of 1975, informs me that Tribe taught from Gunther's casebook. One can therefore plausibly infer that Gunther's use of the phrase *"Lochner* era" influenced Tribe.

60. Laurence H. Tribe, American Constitutional Law 434–35 (1978).

61. Tribe, *supra* note 60, at 455, 564.

62. John Hart Ely, Democracy and Distrust: A Theory of Judicial Review (1980); *see* chapter 6.

63. There were a few libertarian dissenters. The most significant work signaling a revival in sympathetic attention to *Lochner*ian jurisprudence was Bernard Siegan, Economic Liberties and the Constitution (1980); *see also* William Letwin, *Economic Due Process in the American Constitution and the Rule of Law, in* Liberty and the Rule of Law (Robert L. Cunningham ed., 1979); Eric Mack, *In Defense of 'Unbridled' Freedom of Contract, Am. J. Econ. & Sociology, Jan. 1980, at 1.*

64. *See* Gillman, *De-Lochnerizing* Lochner, 85 B.U. L. Rev. 859, 861 (2005). For examples, see Robert H. Bork, The Tempting of America 44 (1990); William H. Rehnquist, The Supreme Court: How It Was, How It Is 205 (1987).

65. Robert H. Bork, *Neutral Principles and Some First Amendment Problems,* 47 Ind. L. J. 1, 11 (1971).

66. *See* Daniel O. Conkle, *Three Theories of Substantive Due Process*, 85 N.C. L. Rev. 63, 79 (2006).

67. Jonathan O'Neill, Originalism in American Law and Politics 26 (2005).

68. West Coast Hotel v. Parrish, 300 U.S. 379, 453 (1937) (Sutherland, J., dissenting); *see also* Muller v. Oregon, 208 U.S. 412, 420 (1908) ("constitutional questions are not settled by even a consensus of present public opinion, for it is the peculiar value of a written constitution that it places in unchanging form limitations upon legislative action, and thus gives a permanence and stability to popular government which otherwise would be lacking").

69. Political scientist Edward Corwin was a prominent exception, but his own substantive views were antioriginalist. *See* chapter 3.

70. Jamal Greene, *Selling Originalism*, 97 Geo. L.J. 657, 676–77 (2009).

71. *See* Howard Gillman, *The Collapse of Constitutional Originalism and the Rise of the Notion of the "Living Constitution" in the Course of American State-Building*, 11 Stud. Am. Pol. Dev. 191, 192–94 (1997). For further discussion of this point, see chapter 3.

72. *See* Charles Fried, Saying What the Law Is: The Constitution in the Supreme Court (2004); Steven G. Calabresi, *Text vs. Precedent in Constitutional Law*, in Originalism: A Quarter Century of Debate 199, 204 (Steven G. Calabresi ed., 2007). While the justices who supported liberty of contract were originalists, it's also true, as Calabresi suggests, that they were not necessarily textualists. *See* Nourse, *supra* note 12, at 763.

73. *See, e.g.*, Robert H. Bork, The Tempting of America: The Political Seduction of the Law 31–32 (1990).

74. Barbara H. Fried, The Progressive Assault on Laissez Faire: Robert Hale and the First Law and Economics Movement 207 (1998).

75. *See* Bruce Ackerman, We the People: Transformations 255–78 (1998); Fiss, *supra* note 46, at 9–21.

76. Cass R. Sunstein, Lochner's *Legacy*, 87 Colum. L. Rev. 873 (1987).

77. White, *supra* note 8, at 24, 25; *see also* David E. Bernstein, Lochner's *Legacy's Legacy*, 82 Tex. L. Rev. 1 (2003). Sunstein graciously responded that "Bernstein examines the Court's performance with far more care than I did; he greatly illuminates the era, and he offers reasons to question my basic claims." Cass R. Sunstein, *"Lochnering,"* 82 Tex. L. Rev. 65, 65 (2003). Sunstein brilliantly played a recurring role for liberal constitutional law professors after the New Deal period, as described by political scientist Ken Kersch: "to provide a succession of ingeniously serviceable legitimating rhetorics for whatever progressive spirited reform imperative is imagined to be at the moment." Ken I. Kersch, Constructing Civil Liberties: Discontinuities in the Development of American Constitutional Law 339 (2004).

78. For overviews of the revisionist literature, see David E. Bernstein, Lochner *Era Revisionism, Revised*: Lochner *and the Origins of Fundamental Rights Constitutionalism*, 82 Geo. L.J. 1 (2003); Barry Cushman, *Some Varieties and Vicissitudes of Lochnerism*, 85 B.U. L. Rev. 881 (2005); Gary D. Rowe, Lochner *Revisionism Revisited*, 24 L. & Soc. Inquiry 221, 242 (1999); Stephen A. Siegel, *The Revisionism Thickens*, 20 L. & Hist. Rev. 631 (2002); *see also* David E. Bernstein, Only One Place of Redress: African Americans, Labor Regulations and the Courts from Reconstruction to the New Deal (2001); Bruce Ackerman,

We the People: Transformations 269 (1998); Barry Cushman, Rethinking the New Deal
Court: The Structure of a Constitutional Revolution (1998); Siegan, *supra* note 63.

79. *E.g.*, Fried, *supra* note 74; William E. Leuchtenburg, The Supreme Court Reborn:
Constitutional Revolution in the Age of Roosevelt (1995); Manuel Cachán, *Justice
Stephen Field and "Free Soil, Free Labor Constitutionalism": Reconsidering Revision-
ism*, 20 L. & Hist. Rev. 541, 549-50 (2002); Barry Friedman, *The History of the Counter-
Majoritarian Difficulty, Part Three: The Lesson of* Lochner, 76 N.Y.U. L. Rev. 1383
(2001); Paul Kens, Lochner v. New York: *Rehabilitated and Revised, But Still Reviled*,
1997 J. Sup. Ct. Hist. 31; Ronald F. Wright, & Paul Huck, *Counting Cases About Milk,
Our "Most Nearly Perfect Food,"* 36 L. & Soc'y Rev. 51 (2002).

80. Old myths die hard, however, and, as noted in chapter 1, many scholars still care-
lessly attribute the rise of liberty of contract to Social Darwinist ideology.

81. *See, e.g.*, Daniel R. Ernst, *Free Labor, the Consumer Interest, and the Law of In-
dustrial Disputes, 1885–1900*, 36 Am. J. Legal Hist. 19, 19 (1992); William E. Forbath, *The
Ambiguities of Free Labor: Labor and the Law in the Gilded Age*, 1985 Wis. L. Rev. 767,
792-96; Charles W. McCurdy, *The "Liberty of Contract'" Regime in American Law*, in
The State and Freedom of Contract (Harry N. Scheiber ed. 1998); William E. Nelson, *The
Impact of the Antislavery Movement upon Styles of Judicial Reasoning in Nineteenth
Century America*, 87 Harv. L. Rev. 513, 558-60 (1974); G. Edward White, *Revisiting Sub-
stantive Due Process and Holmes's* Lochner *Dissent*, 63 Brook. L. Rev. 87, 105-6 (1997).

82. Fiss, *supra* note 46 (social contract); Herbert Hovenkamp, Enterprise and American Law, 1836-1937, at 99-101 (1991) (classical economics); Robert C. Post, *Defending
the Lifeworld: Substantive Due Process in the Taft Court Era*, 78 B.U. L. Rev. 1489
(1998) (personal autonomy); Aviam Soifer, *The Paradox of Paternalism and Laissez-Faire
Constitutionalism: United States Supreme Court 1888–1921*, 5 L. & Hist. Rev. 249 (1987)
(anti-paternalism).

83. *See* chapter 1.

84. 505 U.S. 833, 861-62 (1992). For a devastating critique, see Alan J. Meese, *Will,
Judgment, and Economic Liberty: Mr. Justice Souter and the Mistranslation of the Due
Process Clause*, 41 Wm. & Mary L. Rev. 3, 62-64 (1999).

85. *Casey*, 505 U.S. at 861-62.

86. Washington v. Glucksberg, 521 U.S. 702, 761 (1997) (Souter, J., concurring); Dred
Scott v. Sandford, 60 U.S. (19 How.) 393 (1856).

87. *Glucksberg*, 521 U.S. at 761-62. *See generally* David D. Meyer, Lochner *Re-
deemed: Family Privacy after* Troxel *and* Carhart, 48 U.C.L.A. L. Rev. 1125 (2001).

88. Alden v. Maine, 527 U.S. 706, 814 (1999) (Souter, J., dissenting); Seminole Tribe v.
Florida, 517 U.S. 44, 166 (1996) (Souter, J., dissenting); United States v. Lopez, 514 U.S.
549, 604 (1995) (Souter, J., dissenting); C & A Carbone, Inc., v. Town of Clarkstown, 511
U.S. 383, 423-24 (1994) (Souter, J., dissenting); *see also* Dolan v. City of Tigard, 512 U.S.
374, 406-9 (1994) (Stevens, J., dissenting).

89. 539 U.S. 558, 564 (2003).

90. State Farm v. Campbell, 538 U.S. 408 (2003); *see also* E. Enter. v. Apfel, 524 U.S.
498, 539 (1998) (Kennedy, J., concurring).

91. *See, e.g.*, Steven G. Calabresi, introduction to Originalism: A Quarter Century of

Debate 13 (Steven G. Calabresi ed., 2007); A. Raymond Randolph, Barbara K. Olson Memorial Lecture, Federalist Society, Nov. 11, 2005, http://www.fed-soc.org/Publications/Transcripts/randolphBKO.pdf.

92. Michael H. v. Gerald D., 491 U. S. 110, 122 (1989), quoting Snyder v. Massachusetts, 291 U. S. 97, 105 (1934).

93. *See, e.g.*, Richard A. Epstein, *Liberty, Equality, and Privacy: Choosing a Legal Foundation for Gay Rights*, 2002 U. Chi. Legal F. 73, 84–93 ("The traditional *Lochner* framework supports *Griswold*'s outcome without its messy resort to penumbras in the desperate effort to distance itself from *Lochner*"); *see also* Barnett, *supra* note 55 (defending *Lochner* and praising Justice Kennedy's extension of *Griswold* in *Lawrence*).

94. *E.g.*, Ellen Frankel Paul, *Freedom of Contract and the "Political Economy" of Lochner v. New York*, 1 NYU J.L. & Lib. 515 (2005).

95. *See, e.g.*, Laurence Tribe, American Constitutional Law 1378 (2d ed. 1988); Walter Dellinger, *The Indivisibility of Economic Rights and Personal Liberty*, 2003–4 Cato Sup. Ct. Rev. 9; Leonard W. Levy, *Property as a Human Right*, 5 Const. Commentary 169, 169 (1988); David A. Strauss, *Why Was* Lochner *Wrong?*, 70 U. Chi. L. Rev. 373, 375 (2003).

96. *E.g.*, Craigmiles v. Giles, 312 F.3d 220 (6th Cir. 2002).

97. 539 U.S. 558 (2003).

98. *Id.* at 592 (Scalia, J., dissenting).

99. United States v. United Foods, Inc., 533 U.S. 405, 429 (2001) (Breyer, J., dissenting).

100. *Id.*

101. Charles W. McCurdy, *The Roots of "Liberty of Contract" Reconsidered: Major Premises in the Law of Employment, 1867–1937*, 1984 Sup. Ct. Hist. Soc'y Y.B. 20.

102. James Y. Stern, Note, *Choice of Law, the Constitution, and* Lochner, 94 Va. L. Rev. 1509, 1558 (2008).

103. Arguably, this process started before the New Deal in cases like *Buchanan* and *Meyer*, where the Court rejected proffered police power rationales for the laws in question, rationales that struck many observers at the time as eminently reasonable.

104. The Court's treatment of *Adkins v. Children's Hospital* is an exception. In *West Coast Hotel v. Parrish*, 300 U.S. 379 (1937), the Supreme Court rejected *Adkins*'s defense of both liberty of contract and women's right to legal equality in the workplace. *Adkins*'s perspective on women's rights, at least, has been amply vindicated by modern Supreme Court precedents, though the Court has never given Justice Sutherland's opinion credit for its prescience.

105. Christopher Tomlins, *Necessities of State: Police, Sovereignty, and the Constitution*, 20 J. Pol'y Hist. 47, 59 (2007).

106. Even Justice Holmes was not fully consistent in his determination to defer to legislative enactments. *See, e.g.*, Pennsylvania Coal Co. v. Mahon, 260 U.S. 393 (1922).

107. As Larry Yackle notes, "The analysis in *Lochner* is dead only in the sense that the Court's *application* of substantive due process in that case is now uniformly disclaimed. But the *Lochner* analysis is very much alive in the sense that substantive due process remains intact." Larry Yackle, Regulatory Rights: Supreme Court Activism, the Public Interest, and the Making of Constitutional Law 98 (2007).

108. Donald Drakeman, *The Substance of Process*: Lochner v. New York, in Great Cases in Constitutional Law 130, 131 (Robert P. George ed., 2000).

CONCLUSION

1. For a recent elaboration of the traditional, unnuanced liberal view, see James MacGregor Burns, Packing the Court: The Rise of Judicial Power and the Coming Crisis of the Supreme Court (2009).

2. This perspective also retains vestigial support among s few scholars with more liberal leanings. *See, e.g.,* Jeffrey Rosen, The Most Democratic Branch: How the Courts Serve America xiii (2006) (defending the tradition "famously associated with judges like Oliver Wendell Holmes, Felix Frankfurter, and Learned Hand . . . that courts should play an extremely modest role in American democracy").

3. For example, while standard histories from both left and right characterize Justice Holmes as a hero and Justice McReynolds as a villain, the vast majority of constitutional scholars would agree that McReynolds's important due process opinions in *Meyer v. Nebraska* and *Pierce v. Society of Sisters* have held up far better than Holmes's dissents in *Bailey v. Alabama* and *Bartels v. Iowa* (the companion case to *Meyer*), or his opinion in *Buck v. Bell*.

4. Howard Gillman, *De-Lochnerizing* Lochner, 85 B.U. L. Rev. 859, 861–62 (2005).

5. For a related discussion of how scholars have constructed a false history of American civil liberties to serve the cause of liberal state building, see Ken I. Kersch, Constructing Civil Liberties: Discontinuities in the Development of American Constitutional Law (2004).

6. *See* Barry Friedman, The Will of the People: How Public Opinion Has Influenced the Supreme Court and Shaped the Meaning of the Constitution (2009); Gerald Rosenberg, The Hollow Hope: Can Courts Bring about Progressive Legal Change? (2d ed. 2008).

INDEX

abolitionists, 10

Ackerman, Bruce, 73

Adair v. United States, 45, 50, 51–52, 77

Adkins v. Children's Hospital, 50, 53, 67–69, 94, 95, 103, 116, 118, 123, 184n104

African Americans, 52, 111, 123, 157n108, 171n115

   eugenics and, 96

   interwar period, 86–87

   See also civil rights; segregation

Albany Law Journal, 38

Allgeyer v. Louisiana, 19–20, 41, 77, 91, 102, 118

American Association for Labor Legislation, 62

American Bar Association, 92

American Citizens' Equal Rights Association of Louisiana, 74

American Civil Liberties Union, 99

American Constitutional Law (Tribe), 117–18

American Federation of Labor, 52

   protective labor laws for women, 65–66

Anti-Coolie League of California, 25

antigambling laws, 21

antimiscegenation laws, 21, 74

arms, right to bear, 110

Bailey v. Alabama, 45–46, 80, 82

Baker's Journal, 24, 28, 37

Bakers Review, 28

Bakery and Confectionery Workers' International Union, 23–28, 147–48n146

Bakeshop Act, 26–29, 32–34, 37–38

baking industry, 1, 23

   ethnic considerations, 24

   improvements after *Lochner*, 37–38

   small v. large bakeries, 23–25

Baltimore News, 39

Baltimore Sun, 39

Barnett, Randy, 147n131, 181n59

Bartels v. Iowa, 87, 94

bartenders, 72

Beard, Charles, 45

Bell, Derrick, 73

Benedict, Michael Les, 134n6

Berea College v. Kentucky, 76–77

big business, 8

Bill of Rights, 92, 101, 104, 109

   applied to states, 109

Binghamton Press, 39

Black, Hugo, 87, 109, 116

Blackmun, Harry, 117

Blakely, Clayton, 80–81

Blanshard, Paul, 107

Bolling v. Sharpe, 87–88, 171n112

Bork, Robert, 10, 119

Bradley, Joseph, 14–15, 17–18

Brandeis, Louis, 3, 41, 44, 50, 51, 59–60, 63, 69, 90, 91, 92, 94, 100, 101, 103, 124, 151n36

"Brandeis Brief," 59–60, 66, 81

Braun, Emil, 28

Brennan, William, 85

Brewer, David, 20, 21, 33, 61, 62, 167n34

Breyer, Stephen, 122

Brooklyn Citizen, 39

Brooklyn Eagle, 25–26, 39

Brooklyn Standard Union, 38

Brooklyn Times, 39

Brown, Henry, 19, 33, 48, 51, 60, 74

Brown v. Board of Education, 87, 111, 112

Bryan, William Jennings, 139n105